SHAKESPEARE PERFORMANCE STUDIES

Taking a "performance studies" perspective on Shakespearean theatre, W. B. Worthen argues that the theatrical event represents less an inquiry into the presumed meanings of the text than an effort to frame performance as a vehicle of cultural critique. Using contemporary performances as test cases, Worthen explores the interfaces between the origins of Shakespeare's writing as literature and as theatre, the modes of engagement with Shakespeare's plays for readers and spectators, and the function of changing performance technologies on our knowledge of Shakespeare. This book not only provides the material for performance analysis, but places important contemporary Shakespeare productions in dialogue with three influential areas of critical discourse: texts and authorship, the function of character in cognitive theatre studies, and the representation of theatre and performing in the digital humanities. This book will be vital reading for scholars and advanced students of Shakespeare and of Performance Studies.

W. B. WORTHEN is the author of many books on drama, performance theory, and Shakespeare, including *The Idea of the Actor* (1984), *Modern Drama and the Rhetoric of Theater* (1992), *Shakespeare and the Authority of Performance* (Cambridge, 1997), *Shakespeare and the Force of Modern Performance* (Cambridge, 2003), *Print and the Poetics of Modern Drama* (Cambridge, 2005), and *Drama: Between Poetry and Performance* (2010). He has edited and co-edited several volumes of drama and theatre scholarship, and has served as an editor of *Theatre Journal* and *Modern Drama*, guest editor of *Renaissance Drama*, and is the editor of *The Wadsworth Anthology of Drama*.

SHAKESPEARE PERFORMANCE STUDIES

W. B. WORTHEN

CAMBRIDGE
UNIVERSITY PRESS

University Printing House, Cambridge CB2 8BS, United Kingdom

Cambridge University Press is part of the University of Cambridge.

It furthers the University's mission by disseminating knowledge in the pursuit of education, learning and research at the highest international levels of excellence.

www.cambridge.org
Information on this title: www.cambridge.org/9781107055957

First published 2014

Printed in the United Kingdom by Clays, St Ives plc

A catalogue record for this publication is available from the British Library

Library of Congress Cataloguing in Publication data
Worthen, W. B.
Shakespeare performance studies / W. B. Worthen.
pages cm
ISBN 978-1-107-05595-7 (Hardback)
1. Shakespeare, William, 1564–1616–Dramatic production–Handbooks, manuals, etc. I. Title.
PR3091.W67 2014
822.3′3–dc23 2013047344

ISBN 978-1-107-05595-7 Hardback

For Hana

Contents

List of figures

Acknowledgments

It is a pleasure to acknowledge the many people and institutions who have helped me in writing this book. My sincere thanks to Erika Fischer-Lichte, Gabrielle Brandstetter, and Christel Weiler of the "Interweaving Performance Cultures" International Research Institute of the Freie Universität, Berlin for the fellowship – which extended over several years – during which this book was written; allowing me summers in Berlin to engage with the work of the other fellows provided the support without which this book simply could not have been undertaken. I would also like to thank the artists and companies who provided me with information and access to their work, especially Kelly Copper and Pavol Liska for answering a multitude of questions and providing me with a DVD of the Nature Theater of Oklahoma *Romeo and Juliet*, and Peter Nigrini and Alick Crossley for permission to use their photographs, and to PDNYC, LLC for permission to use photographs of *Sleep No More*. I'm also grateful to Todd Barnes, and to Emily Buttner, Alex Shaw, and Emily Wallen for sharing their experiences as "immersed" performers in *Sleep No More*; and especially to my colleagues Helene Foley – for her advice and especially for stepping into the breach and allowing me a semester away from service as department chair – and Peter Platt, for conversation about Shakespeare, baseball, and other critical matters. It will be clear that much of my work has developed here – as it has done for some time – in dialogue with Robert Weimann and with Barbara Hodgdon; I'm grateful for their conversation and their many shrewd insights into my oversights and overstatements, too. I'm particularly pleased to thank Nico Foley both for his instruction in the practical performance of cognitive neuroscience research, and for the many lively conversations in which he entertained, corrected, and enlarged my understanding of the field. My thanks to audiences at the Dahlem Humanities Center, Notre Dame University, "Interweaving Performance Cultures," the Shakespeare Association of America, and the American Society for Theatre Research where many of these ideas were tried out; to the anonymous readers for Cambridge University Press, whose comments suggested many ways to sharpen and improve the argument; and especially to Sarah Stanton, for her patience, encouragement, and advice. Finally, my sincere thanks to Hana Worthen, for her inspiration as a scholar, for introducing me to Berlin, and for putting up so graciously with all that Shakespeare.

Some of the arguments developed here have been previously explored in articles; while all of these texts have undergone substantial reconsideration, expansion, and revision, I am grateful to the publishers for the opportunity to have presented this work, and for the opportunity to use it in altered form here: "Fond Records: Remembering Theatre in the Digital Age," *Shakespeare, Memory, and Performance*, ed. Peter Holland (Cambridge University Press, 2007); "Intoxicating Rhythms; Or, Shakespeare, Literary Drama, and Performance (Studies)," *Shakespeare Quarterly* 62 (2010): 309–39; "Shakespeare Performance Studies," *Shakespearean International Yearbook* 10 (2010):77–92; "'The written troubles of the brain': *Sleep No More* and the Space of Character," *Theatre Journal* 64 (2012): 79–97; "'What light through yonder window speaks?' The Nature Theater of Oklahoma *Romeo and Juliet* and the Cult(ure) of Shakespeare," *Shakespeare and the Urgency of Now*, ed. Cary diPietro and Hugh Grady (Houndmills: Palgrave Macmillan, 2013); "Stanislavsky and Cognitive Theatre Studies," *The Cambridge Companion to Stanislavsky*, ed. Andrew White (Cambridge University Press, 2013).

CHAPTER I

Shakespeare Performance Studies

Shakespeare Performance Studies: the words themselves summon a host of questions, though nothing should seem more straightforward. Surely Shakespeare – that consummate poet, playwright, actor, and sharer in the dominant theatrical enterprise of his era – has always had to do with performance? Today, though, the two terms – and, more important, what they represent to various audiences and agents of scholarship – often point to alternative ways of understanding the common ground between them, dramatic performance. Shakespeare's contemporaries saw him as a maker both of poetry and of theatre, a recognition that has gained greater, though not uncontroversial, traction in the past half-century or so. And yet *performance* perhaps implies something more unstable than *theatre*, at least in the context of contemporary scholarly and disciplinary debate, leveraging a sense of the stage resistant to notions of authorial, literary, textual determination.

For this reason, though, Shakespearean drama remains a rich site of inquiry into the work of writing in performance: as foundational documents in western print culture, Shakespeare's plays have a distinctive status in literary, cultural, and theatrical history. Performances of Shakespeare's plays number among the defining landmarks of the development of western theatre from the early modern period to the present, and mark the expansion of new technologies of performance from the rise of the professional stage to the dissemination of digital production. They also sustain a (constantly changing) definition of theatre – if "definition" is the right word for the rangy cohort of events taking place in your local high school or college, on Broadway and the West End, in the Schaubühne and the Cartoucherie, in workshops and experimental venues from Stratford to Singapore, nearly everywhere "theatre" is encountered.

To be sure, Shakespeare performance cannot be definitive of performance per se; but Shakespeare performance provides a powerful instrument for examining the intersection of dramatic writing, the institutions of theatre, and evolving ideologies of performance. Yet, Shakespeare performance sometimes seems to evoke a specific and relatively narrow sense of genre: performance that depends on, exists to reproduce, is defined by the determining algorithm of Shakespeare's writing. Is Shakespeare performance a sub-subset of performance, a subset even of dramatic theatre, where special rules about the proper role of the text – a principle of the conservation of textual meaning – should prevail? Perhaps. Yet, at the same time, the uses of Shakespeare's writing by an ever expanding range of stage practice, from the *Lear*, *Desdemona*, and *Search: Hamlet* of Ong Keng Sen's TheatreWorks to Ivo van Hove's *Roman Tragedies* with Toneelgroep Amsterdam, dramatize a more mobile, decentered, yet not quite deauthorized understanding of the ways writing can be made to function in performance. Is the accent on *Shakespeare* or on *performance*?

Shakespeare Performance Studies considers how stage Shakespeare articulates a vision – a critical vision – not of Shakespeare but of its medium: contemporary dramatic performance. My title intentionally joins two sometimes antagonistic disciplines: Shakespeare Studies, constructed through centuries of textual scholarship and interpretation and so perhaps constitutively dismissive of the work of Shakespeare onstage, and Performance Studies, engrained with a disciplinary suspicion of the regulatory work attributed to writing, textuality, and the archive in performance, and so perhaps constitutively dismissive of dramatic theatre. The Shakespeare in/as/through performance question arises at the intersection of the shifting ideological paradigms that govern, license, and institutionalize both performance and the disciplines of performance studies. It is also a function of the technologies of cultural creation and transmission, the means of "knowledge representation" within which Shakespeare is understood – in manuscript and print; through dramatic, nondramatic, and critical adaptation; on the stage, and on film, television, and digital media (Kirschenbaum, "Digital Humanities" 419). As writing, acting, and the entire practice and material structure of theatre constantly change, so their purchase on one another and on the Shakespeare they evoke change as well. To seize Shakespeare performance today is to ask how Shakespeare has become an instrument for exploring the continually contested parameters of performance, the boundaries between writing and doing, between onstage and offstage acting, between literature, theatre, and other technologies of mediated performance. In this book I use contemporary Shakespeare performances to explore some of these frontiers, marking the interface between the imputed origins of Shakespeare's writing (as literature, as theatre), the modeling of licensed modes of engagement with

Shakespeare's plays (by readers and by spectators), and the function of changing performance technologies on our knowledge of Shakespeare. Shakespeare is also a prominent object and instrument of critical practice, a particularly important site for the performance of contemporary inquiry into the practice of the humanities. Rather than taking Shakespeare Performance Studies as a linear declension – *studying*, in other words, how *performance* reproduces *Shakespeare* – I ask instead how contemporary theatre practice might provide the means for seizing alternative conceptions of the work of writing in the event of performance, and so provide a means to locate performance in dialogue with more formal critical discourse. What makes Shakespeare a productive vehicle for thinking through the means of performance is also the largest obstacle to this line of thinking: the massive cultural and literary authority of Shakespeare's writing, which tends to inflect "Shakespeare performance" as a genre finally *about* the Shakespearean text, as merely another interlocutor with Shakespeare's literary designs. So we might step back for a moment, to consider the question from a slightly different angle. What is the changing role of writing in our imagination of dramatic performance? And how might Shakespeare Performance Studies imagine a more productive encounter, a more productive *study* of *performance* through *Shakespeare?*

Postdramatic Shakespeare

To think about a conception of dramatic performance unmoored from determination by the literary text, using writing but not restricted to its "interpretation," is indeed to move sharply away from a conventional view of the dramatic theatre toward what Hans-Thies Lehmann has attempted to capture with the term *postdramatic theatre*. Despite being degraded to a catchphrase, *postdramatic theatre* describes a tectonic shift both in theatrical practice and – perhaps more accurately – in the ways the event of performance is valued. For Lehmann, both as a mode of performance and as a critical perspective, *postdramatic theatre* exerts a decisive pressure on the conventional paradigm of dramatic performance. At the same time, a postdramatic Shakespeare might well seem a contradiction in terms, pointing to the need for a significant clarification of Lehmann's informing dichotomy between dramatic and postdramatic performance.

Shakespearean drama is – and has been largely since its creation, despite its theatrical origins – the invention of print. Indeed, given the degree to which dramatic performance has been influenced by the paradigms of print reproducibility, Lehmann's useful insight into the practice of contemporary postdramatic theatre opens out from a moment of epochal technological change: "With the end of the 'Gutenberg galaxy' and the advent of new technologies the written text and the book are being called into question," and with them a print-inflected understanding of dramatic performance, the theatre of the book. Though the specific question remains elusive, Lehmann's model of technological and cultural succession is clear enough, and sustains an implied paradigm for fashioning the "dramatic" and the capacities of the "human" as well: "The mode of perception is shifting: a simultaneous and multi-perspectival form of perceiving is replacing the linear-successive" mode, the sequentiality of reading (*Postdramatic Theatre* 16). Lehmann's influential *Postdramatic Theatre* is surely right to draw our attention to the practices of the "new theatre," and to the range of ways written documents are (and are not) both used *in* performance and conceptualized within a justifying rhetoric *of* performance. Yet as Robert Weimann implies, noting that "on the Continent the preoccupation with performance-oriented productions of Shakespeare is most prominent and most virulent" ("Performance in Shakespeare's Theatre" 15), the tension between a productive and a reproductive vision of dramatic theatre is neither new nor definitive of recent theatre. Since "the Gutenberg paradigm does not go unchallenged by other modes and channels of information, among them such vastly different forms as oral, pictorial, and digital means," we have long been able to conceive a "theatre that is not necessarily and not entirely dominated by one (scriptural) mode of utterance and expression" ("Performance" 16). Rather than prolonging the subordinate place of dramatic performance in the rhetoric of print culture, we might take a "postdramatic" perspective as a means to review and revise the logic it seems to displace, an ideology of dramatic performance that has perhaps held critical practice captive for too long.

The critical value, then, of *postdramatic theatre* has less to do with historical description than with an altered theoretical paradigm: at its most suggestive, the term models a sense of performance that sidesteps a print-inflected view of theatre troped to the text to open a perspective in which the practices, conventions, and technologies of performance are understood to shape the function of the writings they use. Admittedly, conceiving postdramatic theatre in this way demands a recalibration of Lehmann's more tendentious reasoning. To Lehmann, dramatic theatre is a specific genre of performance in which written texts are assigned a perdurable function, and sustain a specific ideology of performance: the reproduction of textual *mimesis*. Lehmann's dramatic theatre is fundamentally a theatre of *speech* (*Postdramatic Theatre* 53), a logocentric theatre (93) whose appropriate purpose is to represent existing literary works: "Dramatic theatre is subordinated to the primacy of the text. In the theatre of modern times, the staging largely consisted of the declamation and illustration of written drama" (21). Insofar as the literary work encodes a "*fictive* cosmos" (31), the purpose of dramatic theatre is to deliver this "world" to its audiences. This cosmos is a closed totality: the dramatic theatre (as conceived by Aristotle and developed for over two millennia) stages the "'whole' of the plot, a theoretical fiction," which governs "a flow of time, controlled and surveyable" (40); "Wholeness, illusion and world representation are inherent in the model 'drama'; conversely, through its very form, dramatic theatre proclaims wholeness as the *model* of the real" (22). This emphasis on "world representation" (54) finally demands – despite the material presence of actors, clothing, objects – "the internally necessary *exclusion of the real*" (43) from the determining form of performance. In Lehmann's account, dramatic theatre absorbs and subordinates its material vehicle to textual representation, to the fiction it conveys. Despite astonishing differences in theatre architecture and technology, dramatic style, political orientation, audience disposition, practices of performance, and habits of participation, dramatic theatre from the Greeks to Ibsen and Strindberg to the theatre of the absurd "could thus be experienced as variants of one and the same discursive form" (48). This structural dependence on the text defines dramatic performance as a parasite of literature, where the focus "on the questions whether and how the theatre 'corresponds to' the text [...] eclipses everything else" (56).

Lehmann tactically limits dramatic performance to a rigidly literary model of performance-as-reproduction. Nonetheless, postdramatic theatre marks an important conceptual shift in both the making and the understanding of performance, posing a "fundamental *shift from work to event*" (61). This *shift* is nonetheless considerably less a shift in practice than a shift in values and emphasis, one long marked in the disciplinary self-definition of Performance Studies and increasingly visible in dramatic performance critique as well. For as Erika Fischer-Lichte points out, the notion that the "performance's status as a piece of art, its aestheticity, is not due to a 'work', an artifact which it creates, but to its particular eventness" has a long lineage in theatre studies, which is traceable to Max Hermann's foundational work in the 1930s (*Theatre, Sacrifice, Ritual* 24). The "*withdrawal of representation*" (Lehmann, *Postdramatic Theatre* 172) in the postdramatic theatre undoes the critical sequestration of the presentational *means* from the represented *work*, an "unsettling that occurs through the *indecidability* whether one is dealing with reality or fiction" (101). Yet the intransigent materiality of performance, its tendency to remain fully visible alongside the *mimesis* of the text's represented narrative, is an intrinsic part of dramatic theatre. In this sense, while distinctively "postdramatic" productions actively work to shed the "deceptively comforting duality of here and there, inside and outside" by "the *mutual implication of actors and spectators in the theatrical production of images*" (185–186), the conception of a postdramatic theatre is important not merely for demarcating an emerging performance aesthetic but more for revealing, perhaps backhandedly, the evident failure of dramatic theatre to circumscribe the undeterminable, material eventness of performance. Postdramatic performance alerts us to the mutual agency of all the theatre's participants in framing the significance of theatrical events, even those undertaken with the most fixedly "dramatic" intentions.

Theatre changes. For Lehmann, this shift from reproduction to production, "*from work to event*," marks both a conceptual and a historical opposition in the framing of performance. Yet the perception of change is often marked by imagining the past as simple in relation to the complexity of the present. Characterized as a discrete genre of textual reproduction, the "dramatic theatre" that emerges for Lehmann is thoroughly conditioned by print; or, more accurately, conditioned by values ascribed to print as a mode of cultural production. Lehmann is surely correct to point out the influence of print on the modern understanding of theatre, yet his straightforward representation of a "theatre of the book" is often at odds with the actual, material uses of written documents in the making of dramatic performance.[1] Actors in Shakespeare's company, after all, learned their parts from sides, hardly vehicles of the "'whole' of the plot." Today, a variety of iPhone and iPad apps (admittedly, only available some time after the publication of *Postdramatic Theatre*) rapidly digest a play into sides, and provide the actor with an audio track of his or her part, cues and all. That is, while postdramatic theatre – like postmodernity, posthumanism – may include "the presence or resumption or continued working of older aesthetics" (27), the textual practices alleged to drive theatrical production are richly, ideologically, differentiated. Even the most conventional "dramatic" performance today uses writing across a range of platforms (manuscript, print, electronic), cutting, rewriting, translating, and multiplying texts, all as part of leaving them *as texts* largely behind. Much more visible is an insistent rhetoric of textual fidelity, of scriptural determination alleged – by actors and directors, audiences, scholars, and theorists – to structure the dramatic theatre, a rhetoric that Lehmann, like others, mistakes for how theatre actually uses writing in practice.[2]

After all, most of what happens even in a conventional performance has no specification in the text at all. "Who's there?" Barnardo asks, the opening line of *Hamlet* (well, the opening line of two of the three early versions, more or less – Q2: "VVHose there?"; F: "Who's there?"; Q1: "Stand: who is that?").[3] Although these may be its first words, any production of *Hamlet* is already under way, asserting a significant space variably continuous with and distinct from the space inhabited by the audience. The audience is rhetorically positioned by the actor's performance, and by how the words s/he engages as acting are given performative force within the circumstance of their utterance, an act that transforms them from words into deeds. What does s/he use these words to do? Challenge? Question? Where is the actor facing? Toward the actor playing Francisco? Does s/he see him/her? How tall/short/thin/heavy is s/he? It's dark in Denmark: is it dark on the stage? Is it dark in the theatre? When does Barnardo recognize Francisco? Is the actor speaking English? Is Barnardo? This framework of performative signification clearly extends well beyond the text, having more to do with the ideological structuring of an event in which the text plays a part. Much as digital textuality has helped to dramatize the difference between the ideological and material structure of print – are two differently published editions of the "same" text the "same" thing? – the "postdramatic" resituation of writing among the signifying practices of performance perhaps helps us to reconsider what was there all along: that the text was never "suitable material for the realization of a theatrical project" (Lehmann, *Postdramatic Theatre* 56), if what we mean by that project is the direct, uncomplicated representation of distinct fictions, the reduction of performance to the *presentation* of *the play*. The "text-based" dramatic theatre has always been a mirage, used to model a specific vision of the appropriate hierarchy of artistic relations.

Lehmann's notion of postdramatic theatre has considerable descriptive and analytic power, but much less utility as a historicizing or a periodizing term. Its value instead arises in locating two ideologies competing to define the work of contemporary theatre: an *interpretive* rhetoric, in which performance is valued for its capacity to repeat, realize, and communicate the dramatic work to an audience; and a *productive* rhetoric, in which the theatre frames performance as an event, speaking not merely *to* the spectator but also *through* the spectator's agency in the performance. Taking dramatic theatre as "the declamation and illustration of written drama" (21), Lehmann foregrounds a view of dramatic performance as a form of textual mimesis, embodied on the stage and transmitted to a body of spectators, who perform as readers-by-other-means, so to speak. To draw dramatic performance, Shakespeare performance, into a sense of the *performance event* requires a different conception of the spectator's share, a spectator "emancipated," as Jacques Rancière might say, from the passivity sometimes imagined as the spectator's only agency in the spectacle. Surely "interpretation" of various kinds sustains the production process, and transpires during the performance, too. But dramatic *performance* cannot be valued *as performance* if it is framed in critical practice primarily as a vehicle for a readerly audience passively to absorb the stage's "interpretations" toward a fuller, richer, more dynamic understanding of the Shakespeare play. In Chapter 2 I consider how the distinction between reading and spectating is articulated in Shakespeare studies, but the notion of performance-as-textual-interpretation – Lehmann's "dramatic theatre" – has broader consequences for an understanding of dramatic performance and of the spectator's share in the performance event.

Peter Kivy has undertaken a critique of reading as a mode of performance that is useful here, precisely because it underwrites the consequences of equating performance with "interpretation." Kivy's account deploys several familiar metaphors – the text as score, the text as recipe – often used to express the determining role ascribed to writing in dramatic theatre. For Kivy, musical and dramatic works are similar in that their textual transmission provides the means for creating performances. In this regard, we might say that Kivy takes an algorithmic view of dramatic writing, framing it as – like a musical score – instructions for making the performance event in which the work of art actually emerges. (Kivy tactically – though perhaps unwisely – must, then, set reading plays apart from reading narrative fiction or poetry, despite the institutional absorption of dramatic writing to the canons of literature and the attitudes of "literary dramatists" like Ibsen and Shaw, even Shakespeare perhaps, who imagined an audience of printform readers as well as a theatrical public.)

For Kivy, what performers of any kind – actors, pianists, readers – do when they perform is to "interpret," and what they produce is an "interpretation":

> A performance is a *version* of the work performed. And in order for a performer to produce a credible performance, a credible version or "reading" of the work, she must have an *interpretation* of it. She must have her own idea of how the music goes: what makes it tick. She bases her performance on that idea; on that interpretation. Her performance, then, literally displays forth her interpretation. If she had a facility with words she

> could tell us what her interpretation of the work is, as an analyst or theorist might. But in any event, one can show an interpretation as well as tell it, as we have seen. And what the musical performer does is to show her interpretation through her performance. (*Performance of Reading* 61)

Although for Kivy the score and the script have no other purpose than being interpreted in performance, as an interpretation, the performance is not a work-in-itself, an event. The identity of the performance derives from the script it interprets and transmits; based on "that idea," it can be experienced only in relation to that absent authority.[4] Discounting Kivy's purely technical limitation of "interpretation" merely to discerning what "makes it tick," "interpretation" requires a sense of performance-as-communication: the proper operation of the medium would guarantee the appropriate transfer of the text's signifieds to the audience without too much distracting noise. There is considerable "interpretation" behind both musical and theatrical performance, assessing technical features of pace, tempo, dynamics, and phrasing toward an overall sense of the purposes of the performance, and the significantly different technical and semantic interpretation of various elements of a play, line-readings, blocking and movement, function of the *mise en scène*, thematics, character psychology and motive (if there are characters, psychology, motive), and so on. But although interpreting is essential to making the performance, should we restrict the significance of performance to the adequate communication of an "interpretation," a kind of commentary, to a receiving public?

Revealingly, for Kivy, the significant analogy between music and theatre is less between playing a sonata and the *mise en scène* of a Shakespeare play than between playing a sonata and writing a critical study of Shakespeare.

> We call what critics say about the meaning and significance of art works interpretations of them, and we call performances interpretations of them. Thus, we contrast A. C. Bradley's Hegelian interpretation of *Hamlet* with Ernest Jones' Freudian interpretation; and we contrast Schnabel's Romantic interpretations of the Beethoven piano sonatas with Brendel's rather more precise and laid back ones.
>
> But, of course, these two uses of the term "interpretation" are closely related. To begin with, contrary to what some believe, it is my view that the term is applied univocally to, for example, A. C. Bradley's written interpretations of Shakespeare's plays and Schnabel's performances of Beethoven's piano sonatas. They are all literally, and in the same sense, interpretations, the difference being that Bradley's book on Shakespeare's plays *tells* you his interpretations, whereas Schnabel's performances of Beethoven *show* you his interpretations. (38)

Kivy's framing here conveniently displays the problems engrained in regarding theatrical performance as delivering a textual interpretation, a "reading." First, unlike Schnabel's Beethoven, Bradley's performance hardly claims identity with *Hamlet*. And even if Bradley chose to perform/interpret this material, his rereading of his essay on *Hamlet* would be a different performance, a different essay, lecture, commentary, conversation. If Artur Schnabel could *tell* us what his interpretation *shows* completely and fully, it would necessarily differ from his performance, and not only because words are not notes of music. Interpretation – Bradley's essay, Bradley's commentary on his essay, Schnabel's verbal account of Beethoven – makes propositions about the performance, and so cannot be understood as the performance itself.

With the possible exception of the 2007 Wooster Group *Hamlet*, in which actors visibly mimicked the "text" of the Richard Burton *Hamlet* film running on a large screen upstage, most performances absorb, work *on*, and work *with* the text rather than making "propositions *about* the text" as an interpretive essay would do (Saltz, "What" 301). Of course, interpretation happens all the time, we can't help it: a Wooster Group spectator might well be thinking – as some reviewers clearly were – that next to Burton's, Scott Shepherd's performance was less powerful, less moving, a lesser Hamlet. As Benjamin Bennett has suggested, performance might even be understood to frame a kind of "interpretivity," an ongoing effort not to grasp what the performance is proposing about the text, but to seize where the event of performance is going, what it is doing, what it might mean to participate in this act here and now, happening in this way (*All Theater* 185). Bennett locates spectators rigorously within the event of theatre; spectators engage with the processual forms, moods, and shapes of the performance, rather than merely decanting an embodied commentary on the play offered from the stage. A performance can only be *re*constructed as propositional, and "the text" or "the play" is only one of the things a performance might be conceived to make propositions about. When Lars Eidinger, playing Hamlet in Thomas Ostermeier's brilliant production at the Schaubühne in Berlin (it opened in 2008), stuffs his mouth full of dirt it's difficult to feel that textual mimesis is predominant: the corporeal materiality of this act interferes with the represented action, emphasizing the actor's opacity to the fiction. Eidinger's act gives rise to a number of interpretive possibilities: Hamlet is as penetrated by corruption as everything else in Elsinore; Eidinger is a remarkable showman; the director's authority is unchallenged at the Schaubühne. Richard Burton's or Kenneth Branagh's or Lars Eidinger's performance as Hamlet are akin to Schnabel's; they are not making propositions about *Hamlet* communicated to the audience, nor are they merely re-presenting Shakespeare's words. The performance may be based on a prior interpretation, and certainly on interpretations that develop over the course of the rehearsals and run. But here and now, during the performance, the audience participates in making something for which the text is only one mediating instrument – the performance.[5]

The significance of the event can't be reduced to mere communication, the transmission of an "interpretation" of Shakespeare's play, in part because so little of the event is actually involved in representing the *text* at all. Insofar as the event involves activities that while representational are also presentational, at once discursive and behavioral, and insofar as most performance conventions (architecture, design, acting) have a temporal *durée* independent of the interpretive conventions applied to different forms of textuality, it's misleading to characterize the full experience of dramatic performance merely as the communication of an "interpretation" of the text. Nor does it seem adequate – or historically accurate – to reduce the spectator's proper function to "reading" an "interpretation" of Shakespeare's play delivered in the form of a performance. A tendentious production may well offer an "interpretation" of the play. In his film, Olivier intoned (from beyond the playing) that his *Hamlet* was about a man who could not make up his mind; spectators may well wonder what Shakespeare, or Beckett, or Churchill would make of a given performance, whether it would align in any way with their intentions for the play. As the next several chapters will illustrate, the work of Performance Studies is in part to "interpret" the performance, to suggest its discursive interaction with other forms of action, other histories of behavior, even with other forms of writing than those used to make the performance. Yet, as an event, the significance of dramatic performance cannot be reduced to an "interpretation" of the text communicated to an "interpreting" audience: there are too many agents, too many of them are neither interpreting the text nor offering an "interpretation," nor can the text alone govern the work that performers – all of them, including the spectators, who have no text – undertake during the performance.[6]

Dramatic theatre can be a vehicle for textual transmission, but it's a poor one: there's too much noise in the system. Stage performance uses writing not to communicate with words to an audience, but to create those problematic performatives of the stage, the entwining of the fictive in the actual, the drama in its *doing*, that animates (our appetite for) dramatic performance.[7] Postdramatic critique alerts us to the eventness of any dramatic performance, an event that the notion of performance-as-textual-interpretation is simply not robust enough to grasp, in part because it regards the practices of performance as transparent, ministerial means for reproducing meanings fashioned elsewhere. Noise and information are, of course, mutually constitutive; so, too, the meanings of performance emerge not as parasites of textual-delivery-by-other-means, but through a genre of experience specific to the theatre, and an awareness that the highly conventionalized practices of theatre are marked, represent actions *in* the world precisely because they are not *of* the world, only of the stage. What we practice in the theatre is theatrical performance, acting and spectating. Performance operates in the mode of behavior – the actors', the audience's – intrinsic to the theatre. And the behaviors distinctive to theatre have proven challenging to assimilate to critique in the humanities, other than by reading them back into a foundational text, taking them as transparent means of transmission rather than as themselves the objects and vehicles, the media, of our attention and participation. One of the challenges, then, of *Shakespeare Performance Studies* is to model a way of engaging with performance that attends to its practices, to the use it makes of Shakespeare in fashioning the precise differential between the theatrical and the worldly where the meanings of performance are born.

Western dramatic writing has frequently, and arrestingly, foregrounded the independent work of the theatrical process, everything it works to do that is in excess of the mere transmission of scripted words. The dithyrambic chorus and the dramatic role as instruments of internecine competition in Athens, Herod raging in the village street, Queen Anne dancing among the masquers descending from the House of Fame, the Officer praising Louis's magnanimity in pardoning Orgon, nineteenth-century popular melodrama, to say nothing of the plays of Brecht, Beckett, Churchill; defining dramatic performance as limited to the representation of the dramatic fiction seems to ignore the specificity of performance, and the ways theatre, *dramatic theatre*, shapes a specific structure of experience for its audiences. Rather than a purely formalist metatheatre (the world is like the stage), this vision of the *event* of theatre depends on its identity *as theatre*, a mode of performance distinct *to* theatre, however much it may also represent a larger, even a theatricalized, world. Although the postdramatic theatre can be seen as an alternative to dramatic theatre, what Lehmann more effectively locates is a tension within dramatic performance itself, arising from where and how it locates mimesis (if it locates it at all), and whether that mimesis is conceived in fundamentally literary terms, as "subordinated to the primacy of the text." While one form of theatrical pleasure (the kind of pleasure usually associated with Shakespeare performance) seems to arise from calibrating how closely a given performance hews to the conceptual design attributed to a play at any moment in history, even that pleasure depends on the material and conceptual particularity of the event, an event that is "postdramatic" to the extent that its determining forms of action and behavior arise outside and beyond the text, however deeply a given production – and its participants – may regard them as serving the text's priorities. And, of course, much of the sensual, affective, intellectual, critical pleasure animating any performance arises from, is sustained within and tempered by the ineluctably material, nonetheless ideological, thoroughly spectacular disposition of performance itself.

Emancipating Shakespeare performance

To consider drama in this way is to propose a theory of textual impropriety, one perhaps essential to the theatre, marking the dramatic stage as a genre of production distinct from the "reproductive" activity assigned to an "interpretive" theatre in literary culture. Some contemporary theatre is already far removed from the "text-based" aesthetic, though even in New York (where I live) most theatre asserts a conventionally mimetic reproduction of the "world of the play," an attitude that I would say is also true of much Shakespeare performance. But writing has a dialectical relation to performance, serving at once as one of the materials the performance works on and as one of the instruments it works with. The most extreme cases – the various furors surrounding the violation of Beckett's stage directions, for instance – demonstrate that writing cannot control its use, cannot calibrate the analog continuity of performance to the digital distinction of the word. Justifying theatre according to the adequacy of its performed mimesis to the dramatic fiction is one important strain of western theatre's self-understanding. Yet locating theatrical mimesis as merely reproductive tends to repress the behavioral rhetoric distinctive to performance, how even the assertion of mimesis is sustained by a network of practices operating within the symbolic, social, and material geography of a given theatre, practices that construe the appearance, violation, or irrelevance of such mimetic fidelity. After all, though Aristotle distinguishes drama from lyric and epic through its mode of performance – "with all the people engaged in the *mimesis* actually doing things" (*Poetics* 53) – the *Poetics* attends largely to the composition of the literary mimesis (plot, character, thought, diction), instigating a long tradition of conceptualizing the purpose of dramatic performance as the delivery of an already composed work rather than the composition, here and now, of an event in which the drama's mimesis is a part, refashioned by the means of theatre, *opsis*. Given the manifest tribal, civic, and competitive function of the classical Athenian theatre (in which many in the audience were, or had been, themselves performers), perhaps we should also include the audience among "all the people engaged in the *mimesis* actually doing things."

The critical tradition has largely spoken otherwise, typically conceiving dramatic performance as communication: the author's message is transmitted – with more or less static – through theatrical means to a recipient receiver, who processes and reconstitutes the message from the actor's noisy signal. I will return to the increasingly familiar critique of an "information" model of theatre-as-communication in Chapter 4. For now, though, it's perhaps enough to remark that one of the problems of this understanding of dramatic-performance-as-textual-communication is that the performance itself is paradoxically conceived as "noise," as a regrettable distraction to sending/receiving the dramatic signal, rather than as the purpose of playing, in which "the noise *is* the art" (Clarke, "Information" 164). Performance as "interpretation" is consistent with this model of theatre as a vehicle for the transmission of Shakespeare's script, repressing the materiality of theatrical practice in ways consistent with the modern ideology of print, as contaminating noise corrupting the Shakespearean signal. Nonetheless, Bruce Clarke's sense that "the noise *is* the art" calls attention to the challenge of analyzing the multiphasic event of performance without privileging the verbal as its principal channel, without, that is, finally valuing performance – particularly Shakespeare performance – merely for the adequacy of its communication of a mimesis inscribed in the written text.

Perhaps we shouldn't value dramatic performance as a medium of textual *communication* at all. If a critical vision of Shakespeare performance depends in part on the "*shift from work to event*" (Lehmann, *Postdramatic Theatre* 61), it also depends on a shifting view of the politics, agents, and activities of performance, an emancipation opened with particular force in Jacques Rancière's work. For Rancière, the assertion that dramatic performance depends on the essential passivity of the spectator as recipient of performance-as-interpretation encodes a comprehensive, and oppressive, vision of social life.

> These oppositions – viewing/knowing, appearance/reality, activity/passivity – are quite different from logical oppositions between clearly defined terms. They specifically define a distribution of the sensible, an *a*

> *priori* distribution of the positions and capacities and incapacities attached to these positions. They are embodied allegories of inequality. (*Emancipated Spectator* 12)

Here, Rancière alerts us to the symmetry between theatre and politics as spatial distributions of the sensible, a symmetry he has richly explored across the wide range of his writing. For him, politics is the "configuration of a specific space, the framing of a particular sphere of experience"; indeed, "politics is the very conflict over the existence of that space" (24). Similarly, the history of the aesthetic depends on a complex genealogy, naming a "specific regime for the identification of art" as social and cultural practice, locating its doers and makers, positioning the objects of their creation, and identifying their proper modes of effect and engagement (*Aesthetics and its Discontents* 8). In other words, much as "Politics revolves around what is seen and what can be said about it, around who has the ability to see and the talent to speak, around the properties of spaces and the possibilities of time" (*Politics of Aesthetics* 13), so, too, "Aesthetics refers to a specific regime for identifying and reflecting on the arts: a mode of articulation between ways of doing and making, their corresponding forms of visibility, and possible ways of thinking about their relationships" (10).[8]

In Rancière's "emancipatory" critique, the attribution of passivity to the theatrical spectator figures the pervasive imagination of unequal social relations: in "the past, property owners who lived off their private income were referred to as *active* citizens, capable of electing and being elected, while those who worked for a living were *passive* citizens" (*Emancipated Spectator* 12–13), the spectators of the naturally inscribed structure of social relations enacted in the theatre of social life. In any field of action, "Emancipation begins when we challenge the opposition between viewing and acting" as itself a structure of "domination and subjection," emancipation that can begin "when we understand that viewing is also an action that confirms or transforms this distribution of positions" (13). Like Lehmann's sense of the postdramatic event, the theatrical implications of Rancière's critique are analytic rather than periodizing. Even in the most anti-Brechtian, narcotic theatre of commodified illusion, the spectators *act*, even if that action is only to confirm the distribution of power and privilege encoded by taking a seat, and watching from the dark while others – actors and characters – act before them. And that acting takes place at the pivot point between the manifestly conventional forms of *acting* in the theatre and the apparently – and only apparently – unconstructed modes of worldly behavior they represent and necessarily distanciate.

The widespread notion that the spectator passively consumes "interpretations" of Shakespeare while the reader actively creates them – common both in academic and nonacademic accounts of Shakespeare performance (see Chapter 2) – confirms the purchase of Rancière's argument. Even in the modern commodity theatre, where the spectator's agency appears to be limited to the rental of a small piece of real estate from which to observe the play, this position of silent and occluded economic and epistemological privilege locates a significant site of *action*, as the subtle metatheatricality of box-set, fourth-wall dramas from Ibsen and Strindberg and Chekhov to Beckett and Churchill and Stoppard and Mamet amply witnesses. "I see . . . a multitude . . . in transports . . . of joy" (*Endgame* 106). Insisting that the spectator actively performs as part of the theatre's significant distribution of the sensible, Rancière frames the meaning and purpose of the dramatic event as relational, neither limited to the originating inscription of the text, the actor's expression, nor to the spectator's cognition. Performance is "owned by no one, whose meaning is owned by no one, but which subsists between them, excluding any uniform transmission, any identity of cause and effect" (*Emancipated Spectator* 15).

Rancière's scene of the social spectator amplifies the participatory dimension of the eventness of theatre. Perhaps not surprisingly, Rancière recalls Brecht's central topos of dramatic performance, the street scene:

> in a theatre, in front of a performance, just as in a museum, school or street, there are only ever individuals plotting their own paths in the forest of things, acts and signs that confront or surround them. The collective power shared by spectators does not stem from the fact that they are members of a collective body or from some specific form of interactivity. It is the power each of them has to translate what she perceives in her own way, to link it to the unique intellectual adventure that makes her similar to all the rest in as much as this adventure is not like any other. (*Emancipated Spectator* 16–17)

Like Brecht, Rancière articulates the spectator at the critical interface of production and reception, the conjunction of the rhetorical, the affective, and the critical. The spectator's activity engages "the distribution of the sensible" (19) in the specific – and now specifically *aesthetic* – terms of the event, a uniquely intellectual and affective adventure undertaken through the elaborately conventional means of theatre.

Athenian theatre (masks, male actors, *kothurnoi*) and drama (complex verse and formal structures, the dancing Chorus) are manifestly conventional, but Rancière rightly understands Aristotle to frame theatrical mimesis in his theatre as transparent: since the processes of performance are identified with "the language of nature," these practices – the transformation of "nature" into an "exhibition of signs," to say nothing of the construction of the "language of nature itself" – are neutralized within the appropriate field of the spectator's seizure of mimesis, that unambiguous *reading* of nature enabled by dramatic performance.

> This is what *mimesis* means: the concordance between the complex of sensory signs through which the process of *poiesis* is displayed and the complex of the forms of perception and emotion through which it is felt and understood – two processes which are united by the single Greek word *aisthesis*. In the first instance, *mimesis* means correspondence between *poiesis* and *aesthesis*. (*Emancipated Spectator* 60–61)

In contrast to Plato's suspicion both of the degrading character of mimesis and the coarsening of the state introduced by professional "mimetizers," so to speak, Aristotelian mimesis depends not only on the sense that the "stage, the audience and the world were comprised in one and the same continuum" (61), but that the rhetorical structure of mimetizing – the practices of stage performance, the symbolic and civic geography and temporality of the theatre, even the palpable axes of justice and ethics of the dramatic action – vanishes into the object of mimesis itself.[9]

Rancière in one sense explains the absence of performance, the direct treatment of the elaborate conventionality of Athenian theatre, from the *Poetics*: the signifying means of theatre (*aesthesis*) are, for Aristotle, regarded only as a means of display, and so are fully naturalized to the creative, mimetic work of *poesis*, literary *making*. For Rancière this understanding of theatrical mimesis is particular to the classical stage, and is in a sense undone by the art of the modern *mise en scène* emerging with Craig, Appia, Jacques-Dalcroze and others, in which performance symbolized "the collective potential of bodies that have discovered their capabilities, by abandoning the passive attitude of those who watch shows in a theatre" (*Aisthesis* chapter 10), and so "carried the logic of renovation to the extreme point where it signalled the death of spectacle performed on stage by actors for spectators."[10] For while in Rancière's view the rise of the *aesthetic* as a category tends to denaturalize the instruments of art, forcing the theatre's material and semiotic objects and practices to stand apart (spatially, culturally, socially) from the "language of nature," Aristotelian mimesis nevertheless continues to be brought forward to legitimate the function and purpose of dramatic performance, particularly when a "realist" rhetoric – shared notably by the dominant, Stanislavsky-inspired lineage of modern actor training and widely invoked by contemporary "cognitive" theatre studies – insists on the transparency of performance conventions to human nature, and so to Shakespeare, admittedly much the same thing to many readers and audiences (see Chapter 3).

While critique of Shakespeare performance has often concentrated on a specific production's adequacy to "the text," or the ways the text's incipient meanings can be framed to address a contemporary audience, the most salient work in Shakespeare Performance Studies has already begun to chart an alternate course, one more responsive to the "noise" of performance ("noise" that is "noise," of course, only so long as we take Shakespeare to be "the information"), the interplay between performing agents using Shakespeare as an instrument of inquiry into the significance of stage performance. Robert Weimann, for instance, reviews contemporary anxieties about the relationship between writing and performing, both in the sphere of Shakespeare and in the sometimes vexed field of Performance Studies, arguing that an understanding of the dual identity of drama – arising first in the "largely untested encounter of literature and theatre as two different institutions, two different modes of cultural production" ("Performance in Shakespeare's Theatre" 3) – in the early modern period should more urgently drive contemporary efforts to displace performance from a merely ministerial role, the apparent performance of textual reproduction. Taking up the connection between the pacification of the spectator and the modern notion of theatre as a site of textual mimesis, Weimann seizes more directly on the emergence – on the stage and in scholarship – of a "non-representational concept of performance" generally "at odds with the theatre as an institutionalized site of rendering dramatic images of characters in worldly circumstances" (8) prescribed by the text. Deftly declining merely to engage in the "rash reversal of hierarchies" (13) characteristic of some more polemical writing (including my own), Weimann instead proposes to resist the vision of a strictly "ministerial" or "magisterial" conception of the relationship of performance to writing (13). Refusing to "sanction any absolute resistance of performance to textual modes of signification" (13), while at the same time refusing to sanction the inherent dominion of textual to theatrical modes of signification in the sphere of dramatic performance, he suggests that the Shakespeare theatre, evincing "an unprecedented degree of interpenetration between writing and playing" (15), provides a paradigm of performance, at least a paradigm for those forms of performance using writing as one instrument of performing. Shakespeare, our (Performance Studies) contemporary.

Weimann proposes to rethink the Shakespearean text/performance problematic in ways that – emulating the open field of early modern theatricality – sidestep a simple binarism; after all, in the early modern theatre, the possibility that deliquescent dramatic texts could be reproducible by means other than the stage was just beginning to be explored. Taking neither the "magisterial" nor the "ministerial" position, Weimann considers how performance, neither liberated from nor inscribed within the text, deploys writing within the changing disposition – social, aesthetic, practical, technological – of theatre. Placing Shakespeare on the horizon of contemporary performance, he asks not what performance has to say about Shakespeare's writing (a question only writing can answer), but what kind of work we understand Shakespearean writing to afford in those forms of theatre most attentive to the critical work of performance today. Tracking Benno Besson, Heiner Müller, and Peter Handke through the light of Brecht, Artaud, and Grotowski, Weimann locates the contemporary use of *Hamlet* as part of a wider critique of "ministerial" theatre, a theatre in which the actor's task is taken to be already prescribed by the writing, a genre surely cognate with Shakespeare performance for some audiences. More to the point, he raises the question of the extent to which contemporary communication technologies, in their ideological work, retrain and reprivilege the senses, notably affecting an apparent (d)evolution "from letters to pictures, from reading to viewing, from verbal to pictorial perception. In this momentous move the two media in the theatre are vitally involved," once again redefining the frontier between them. And yet, "If on contemporary stages, language and show, text and performance, experience a reversal in the order of which is magisterial and which is ministerial it appears only appropriate for Shakespeare's plays in *mise-en-scène* to put up some resistance," at least insofar as the "pre-representational heritage" of Shakespeare's plays encodes a dialectical encounter with performance that should prevent the "Shakespearean text" from being entirely reduced to "a ministerial element in the production" ("Performance in Shakespeare's Theatre" 25).

While digital technologies have massively reordered the practices of visual, verbal, and inscribed communications, they have also alerted us to the latent ideological landscape of the theatre of manuscript and print. Rather than resolving whether dramatic performance should be understood as the ministerial servant to textual protocols or the magisterial overlord remaking the author's written creation, Weimann (perhaps rather anxiously) suggests a third alternative. Actors' bodies, the weather in outdoor theatres, the fraying rope and the ill-mannered dog: like all materials of performance, writing resists the *mise en scène*, generates friction, creates resistance in the work we do with it, and so enables us to *do* work, to make a performance. The resistance that texts create is sometimes material – in some texts of Beckett's *Footfalls*, the number of steps May recites as she walks is different than the number marked in Beckett's scrupulous diagram of her wheeling – and always semantic, a resistance that arises, like the friction offered by an actor's body or the weight of canvas or the amperage of a fuse, at the intersection between the capacity of the thing and what we want to use it to accomplish. Or almost like: as objects made of words, Shakespeare's texts are both tools and technologies, already inscribed in a dense and constantly changing social understanding of their proper meaning and use, and in a constantly changing theatrical understanding of the emerging affordances they may provide for making legible theatre. Shakespeare's texts generated this resistance in their original theatre – the boy actor's ridicule of squeaking Cleopatras is one sign of it; Hamlet's advice is another – but the kind of friction writing provides is a function of the work we ask it to do, an affordance arising in our understanding of the mutual interplay between writing, the *mise en scène*, and the distribution of the sensible in the theatre. Although the "text" never appears "on contemporary stages," the *mise en scène* is always altering its instruments and how it disposes them, instruments that include acting and actors, habits of direction and design, but also the leverage provided by print, by literature, and now by electronic digital technologies, which pervade every aspect of dramatic performance today.

Although Weimann points to the ineluctably nonrepresentational dimension of theatre (everything happening onstage is happening, *doing* something as well as sometimes *representing* something, too), a mimetic or representational vision of Shakespeare performance is still very much with us: so many outdoor *Dreams* among the pines and mosquitoes. But theatre is no longer on the cusp of traditional modes of nontheatrical performance, and the question Weimann proposes has to do with the longevity of Shakespeare, the sense that transformations in the technology of performance necessarily transform our understanding of its tools, its instruments and purposes. Keeping alive to what Weimann terms "nonderivative and non-ministerial performance practice" nonetheless calls for a "stubborn resolve" to account for the ways performance practice claims and disclaims, embraces and disdains the warrant of authorial writing ("Performance in Shakespeare's Theatre" 14–15). To keep this dialectic open, though, I'm reluctant to distinguish between "performance-oriented productions of Shakespeare" (however "virulent") and, well, whatever the alternative to that might be: text-oriented productions? theatre-oriented productions? the real deal? (15). We can be certain that Shakespeare's theatre produced nothing akin to Ostermeier's or Besson's *Hamlet*, or Olivier's for that matter; we can also be certain – as the rapid evolution of digital performance technologies demonstrates – that we will fail to anticipate how emergent modes of production will locate new affordances in Shakespearean drama, enable Shakespeare performance to do new work as performance. I don't think we have to be concerned about "the fate of Shakespeare's text on stages exposed to these unsettled relations of language and performance" (23): as Weimann (more richly than Lehmann) has shown, the interinvolvement of writing and performance has always been unsettled, even in the narrow-bore notion of "dramatic theatre."

If Performance Studies underlines the constitutive work of performance practice in the signification of events, so Shakespeare Performance Studies nonetheless combines this heuristic with a desire to account for the specific density of Shakespearean textuality in performance, however that "text" has been multiplied, modified, and transformed in its necessary instrumentalization in performance. Finding ways to enable Shakespeare's plays to speak to contemporary issues and contemporary politics (along the lines of feminist *Shrews*, multicultural *Romeo and Juliets*) only suggests the rather limited reach of an "interpretive" theatre: the themes attributed to the play can be usefully directed toward unanticipated situations. But a broader and more urgent Shakespeare Performance Studies undertakes a different kind of inquiry, asking not how performance can interpret the text in light of its ways, means, and concerns, but how performance – in its ineluctably contemporary ways of using text, space, acting, audience, the entire "distribution of the sensible" – represents a genre of Shakespearean knowledge, framed in the distinctive idioms of the stage.

Performing Shakespeare Studies

And yet, what can that knowledge be knowledge *of* if not knowledge *of* Shakespeare? The chapters that follow provide one kind of answer to that question, an effort to read some of the ways Shakespeare performance today uses the idioms of contemporary theatre to speak through Shakespeare about the distinctive interplay between the working of aesthetic performance and the world it at once inhabits, represents, dissimulates, and displaces. The possibility of Shakespeare Performance Studies faces the slippery configurations of contemporary academic, popular, and performance cultures, where the relationship between literature and theatre, the proper functioning of bodies in and as texts, the appropriate purposes of theatre as a cultural form, the succession of performance technologies, and even these keywords – *Shakespeare*, *performance*, *studies* – are understood, practiced, and valued in very different ways. As they are in performance, in Shakespeare Performance Studies the normative practices of *meaning* and *making* Shakespeare are at once confirmed and contested. Since both textuality and performance are institutional, we might well expect the functionality attributed to texts to alter with the changing locations and institutions of theatre. How texts function in different theatres identifies what texts *are* and what *work they can do* in and for those theatres. In this regard, Shakespeare Performance Studies is perhaps not directly assimilable to the familiar practices of "performance-oriented criticism," which, assuming that the values attributed to Shakespeare's writing are to be transmitted by the stage, tends to read the materiality of performance as the appropriately redundant expression of transcendent canons of prescribed textual meanings, of a form of Shakespearean knowledge prior to its decanting in performance.

If, with David Schalkwyk, we imagine the full "reach of performance criticism" ("Text and Performance, Reiterated" 72) merely to be the documentation of performance as a kind of embodied commentary on the plays, then the game is surely lost. A consequential Shakespeare Performance Studies must be shaped neither by the determinants of performance alone (as though the regulatory regime of the contemporary distribution of the sensible evoked in the theatre were a kind of second nature), nor by the figural license of "the text," itself neither the origin nor the object of performance. The animating purpose of Shakespeare Performance Studies is not merely to explain the opposition or redundancy between "critical" and "theatrical" perspectives on the plays in a given era. Rather, its purpose is to ask what Shakespeare performance is and is for *as performance* historically, how the material practices of performance media speak with and through Shakespearean drama by remaking it as performance, speak as acting on stage and on large, small, and pixellated screens, speak with and through its audiences. How does Shakespeare performance speak about performance? And how does it place Shakespeare performance – so local, so internal to its media of production – in dialogue with other, nontheatrical ways of understanding performance, other ways of using performance as a means of experiential inquiry, even of "knowledge representation"?

Shakespeare Performance Studies emphasizes the work of performance in "Shakespeare performance," a challenging prospect given the overwhelming influence of a sense of textual determination in the understanding of western dramatic theatre, especially Shakespeare theatre. To throw the emphasis on performance requires a mutiplex shift in attention. Perhaps the most significant alteration is a rethinking of the functioning of writing in performance, not as a cultural constraint, an object to be preserved, a message to be communicated, or a mimetic vision to be achieved – all visions of dramatic performance associated with a print-inflected understanding of theatre as "text-based" – but as one instrument among many in making performance. The postdramatic – taking "postdramatic" not as a genre but as a perspective on performance – movement from "*work to event*" has several consequences here. First, it implies a critical reconception of dramatic performance away from a notion of performance as *communicating* an *interpretation* of the text toward a notion of *affordance*: the text is one part of an ensemble of agents, objects, and practices, whose perceived properties mutually interact in the process of producing the signifying work, the *poiesis* of performance. Second, this shift entails the inscription of the spectator as one of the agents of theatre, not the receiver of interpretations but a performer sustaining the signifying structure of the performance event, whose acts – however mute and motionless – frame, like the actor's, the event's significance. Finally, it means engaging the technologies of performance, the work they are understood as capable of performing, and the ways they are seen to afford new forms of making performance, Shakespeare performance.

Each of the following chapters centers on a contemporary performance; in part by standing apart from (some) of the (overt) conventions of contemporary dramatic performance, each enables a specific interrogation of the uses of Shakespeare to conceptualize performance today. My argument here is hardly exhaustive in the materials or questions it trains on these works, and I'm well aware that the three productions I consider here fall short of representing the global range of Shakespeare today. Yet, by raising several contemporary contestations of Shakespeare/Performance – the question of Shakespeare as literary dramatist or man of the theatre; the function attributed to "character" in an emerging "cognitive" model of theatrical participation; the place of performance technologies in the genres of "knowledge representation" modeled by the digital humanities – I hope to evoke the contribution of Shakespeare performance to these debates, an understanding in which *performance* is conceived as a collective means of knowledge *making*, not merely a site where knowledge gained through other means is retailed, retold, replayed. A prominent leitmotif of my argument concerns the status of performance as it is represented in the discourses of the humanities today, especially in emerging critical formations in which theatrical performance provides surprisingly constitutive, if negative, leverage: textual materialism and authorship, the promotion of neurochemical and adaptive models of cognition as instruments for analyzing human function in the arts, and the address of digital culture to the performance of the humanities. For this reason, each of the chapters that follow asks how a specific performance "of" Shakespeare ramifies a specific understanding of the purposes of drama, theatre, and performance.

I stand back from that "of" with a purpose. Some of the performances I take up here will not be universally recognized as closely enough motivated by the Shakespearean script to be legitimately performances "of" Shakespearean drama at all. Precisely for that reason, though, these productions interrogate our unstated assumptions about the proprieties of Shakespeare performance: "virulent" though they may be, these productions often depend on virulently conventional ways of modeling stage performance. And while they're not quite "mainstream" Shakespeare, they're hardly eccentric to the main currents of contemporary performance work: one is by a leading experimental theatre company, widely toured in Europe; one centers on a *Macbeth* sold out in New York for (at the time this book is published) more than three years; and one tracks the representation of performance in a well-known – if sometimes vilified – film. More to the point, though, rather than attempting merely to phrase an "interpretive" dialogue between critique and performance, a practice that typically maintains performance as a subordinate means of reframing the insights and attitudes digested in formal criticism (the approach both of J. L. Styan's *The Shakespeare Revolution* and Gary Taylor's *Reinventing Shakespeare*, for instance), I hope here to suggest what a mutually constitutive dialogue between the discourse of performance and the discourse of critique might look like, a way of conceiving Shakespeare performance as framing an inquiry, not into Shakespeare but through Shakespeare into the medium of performance, and how it represents the work of performance in relation to other forms of representation. Performance is never identical with itself, and never synchronous with its interpretation. Performance is never identical with its nontheatrical simulacra. Performance is local and transient, too. While one performance I consider here – Michael Almereyda's *Hamlet* – dramatizes the conceptual challenges of imagining the "same" performance produced across different digital media temporalities (film, DVD, online) in the apparently "fixed" form of film, the Nature Theater of Oklahoma *Romeo and Juliet* and Punchdrunk Theatre's *Sleep No More* have continued to evolve in large and small ways. And while they have been accessible only to those fortunate enough willingly to occupy their spatiotemporal coordinates, they will eventually close, a liability – if it is a liability – that goes with the territory. Performance, after all, represents both the materials of knowledge and the act of knowing as arising fleetingly, in the temporal experience of an intermedial event. This, too, is one of the ways performance represents Shakespeare: as an unpredictable practice, an experience of invention, a doomed instigation to remember, an inquiry vanishing as the question is posed.

In the next chapter I examine one of the most deservedly influential books in recent Shakespeare studies, Lukas Erne's *Shakespeare as Literary Dramatist* and the "return of the author" it has motivated, in order to consider the pressure the dual identities of Shakespearean writing exert on Shakespeare Performance Studies: as "literature" and as an instrument of performance. Erne argues that the notion that Shakespeare was primarily a "man of the theatre" rather than a "poet" fails to take into account the variety of ways in which early modern plays could be understood as designed for an audience of readers as well as for a cadre of actors and an audience of theatrical spectators. In this regard, Erne is part of a wider resistance to what is perceived as an overtheatricalization of Shakespeare in post-1960s scholarship and pedagogy. Here, then, I provide both an overview and a critique of some aspects of this important work. At the same time, I also consider the consequences of conceiving the theatre as an "authorized" mode of literary, theatrical, and pedagogical performance. To do so, I turn to a striking production which directly situates Shakespearean drama in the history of literary and theatrical transmission, and in the figuration of Shakespeare across the horizon of contemporary popular culture: the Nature Theater of Oklahoma *Romeo and Juliet* (2009). In this disarmingly complex production, the Nature Theater uses *Romeo and Juliet* to trace the history of acting, the performance of pedagogy, and the role of the spectator in the cultural reproduction of "Shakespeare," all in a production in which the dynamics of performing are visibly, even anxiously, at stake. I set this populist, modern-language production of *Romeo and Juliet* astride several contexts in which "literary authorship" openly sustains the significance attributed to Shakespearean writing in performance: the history of Shakespearean populism in the United States, its invocation by the National Endowment for the Arts "Shakespeare in American Communities" project as the rationale for public funding of the arts, and the popularity of "modernized" editions of Shakespeare for school use. Taking a populist and historical perspective on the theatrical and cultural performance of Shakespeare, the Nature

Theater of Oklahoma *Romeo and Juliet* also illustrates the surprising crudeness of the terms with which Shakespeare performance continues to be conceptualized, a blunt distinction between "progressive" and "nostalgic" elements that are, in performance, deeply intertwined.

The third chapter takes up another contemporary critical "return," the "comeback" of character as an analytic category in Shakespeare studies. The study of "character" has long ridden the tides of Shakespeare scholarship. Naturalized as the transparent representation of human nature in both academic and popular writing in the late nineteenth and early twentieth centuries, under the influence of a formalist New Criticism "character" was to a considerable degree displaced as a realistic signifier of personhood, and absorbed into the rhetoric of poetry. The characters were, like imagery and metaphor, the figures in the carpet that sustained the poetic design of the drama. Regarding character with the same suspicion it regarded the assertively depoliticized aesthetics of the New Criticism, much theoretical and critical work of the 1970s and 1980s displaced character as a transparent signifier of real people, seeing it less as a distillation of human nature or as a merely functional element in the poetic design of the literary work than as a zone where the ideological containment of personhood and agency – in terms of gender, race, sexuality, class, power – could be realized and/or contested.

Recently, however, a number of critics, some motivated by an understanding of human cognition drawn from neuroscience and theories of evolutionary adaptation, have claimed the engagement with character as a defining dimension of human nature, and so as definitive of the purpose of drama and theatrical performance as well. Chapter 3 considers the function attributed to character as an organizing dimension of the spectator's experience in recent Shakespeare scholarship, a discussion inflected by the rhetoric of contemporary "cognitive" theatre studies, where a realistic understanding theatrical mimesis sustains a sense of proper performance, and legitimate performance commentary. What are we looking at, and how are we looking at it, when we are watching an actor performing, say, Macbeth? Here, I turn to a signal performance, Punchdrunk Theatre's scenically rich, brilliantly choreographed, wordless *Macbeth, Sleep No More* (2011). In many respects, this production depends both on a conventional understanding of psychologically invested character and on a deep commitment to the verbal imagery of the play: indeed, the landscape of the performance seems almost literally to externalize and concretize New Critical readings of *Macbeth* from the 1940s and 1950s. At the same time, though, this "immersive" performance depends on a postdramatic insertion of the spectator into the event, one that seems to test the assertion of an essentially *realist* understanding of theatrical performance – and of the spectator's proper role in it – urged in cognitive theatre studies. Richly imagined as a performance "of" *Macbeth*, a largely wordless event engrained in the visual imagery of Shakespeare's poetic composition, *Sleep No More* surprisingly hews to the spectatorial dynamics of realist theatre, yet does so – at least in part – in ways that complicate and contest the reciprocal, ideologically inflected play of "character" and "spectator" naturalized by realist theatricality. Performance uses the means of performance to locate a critique of the cognitive proprieties of (Shakespearean) performance.

In the final chapter I address a nontheatrical performance, Michael Almereyda's 2000 film, *Hamlet*. Setting his *Hamlet* in contemporary New York, and more to the point in a densely mediatized setting – full of televisions, VCRs, laptops, and cameras – Almereyda established what has become one of the performance conventions of *Hamlet* in the third millennium: the prince as digital *maker*. Almereyda's prince, devoted to obsolescent technologies, marks a decisive moment of historical change: the invention of the practice (and of the term) of the digital humanities. Rapidly theorized and institutionalized as an academic discipline, the digital humanities stakes a contradictory relation to theatrical performance. On the one hand, the field prizes a Hamlet-like commitment to *making* things: digital humanists write software, develop archives and databases, devise applications that are changing our understanding of the objects and instruments of the humanities and the kind of "knowledge" that humanistic scholarship can engage and represent. On the other hand, in the digital humanities, theatre is sometimes articulated as conceptually redundant, its "dramatic" elements represented via digital textuality and its "performance" dimension cognate with recorded media. In a sense, *theatre* appears in the disciplinary discourse of digital humanities, when it appears at all, as a mode of obsolescence.

In contemporary performance, too, *Hamlet* is about technological succession. Thomas Ostermeier's brilliant 2008 production at the Schaubühne in Berlin, and the Wooster Group's 2007 *Hamlet* both imagine the play as an instrument for exploring the interface between what Diana Taylor calls the *archive* and the *repertoire*, between recorded and enacted performance, and between residual and emergent technologies of drama. Almereyda's Hamlet is a filmmaker, reviewing the history of recorded Shakespeare (Gielgud as Hamlet, Mikhoels as Lear) in a *Hamlet* with no troupe of wandering players: this *Hamlet* conspicuously frames the question of the interpenetration of old and new media in the ongoing exploration of Shakespeare performance. Yet, for all its effort to appear technologically *au courant*, even in the moment of its origin Almereyda's *Hamlet* was marked by pastness, as though *Hamlet*'s central meditation was not on the emergence of new media, but on the historical interplay, the archaeological succession of the instruments of performance. Recorded performance is what Hamlet makes, and in his making offers an allegory of the interplay between the media of performance, the corporate environment of making and seeing, and, finally, the "lossy" anonymizing of theatre in an emerging culture of digital humanities.

Engaging the question of technological obsolescence at the interface between writing, theatre, media, and digital reproduction, this chapter also provides a fitting retrospective to the moment of Shakespeare Performance Studies, less a summary of where we have been than an opportunity to reflect on the ways an emerging paradigm of theatrical performance, and a changing paradigm of Shakespeare performance, reciprocates with changing technologies – social and aesthetic – of performance. Both digital media and their use in the digital humanities reflect the wider issues of *Shakespeare Performance Studies*: the uses of Shakespeare performance as interpretive pedagogy and cultural politics; the understanding of performance as a practice of evolutionarily determined cognition; and the sustaining sense that Shakespeare performance – as a means of "knowledge representation," perhaps – does its deepest work through the means of its medium, *performance*.

Books, *bodies*, and *bits*: *Shakespeare Performance Studies* points to a cultural anxiety about the persistent incommensurability of writing and theatre that haunts, and perhaps constitutes western drama, an anxiety configured in different ways at the early modern emergence of professional publishing and playmaking, in the contemporary theatre, and perhaps in contemporary humanities as well. Rancière's account of the spectator helps us to define the spectrum along which dramatic performance is conceived today. At one end, dramatic performance is modeled as a means for delivering the author to the spectator, providing a stable – manipulative, fashionable, outrageous, edifying, merely boring, what you will – "interpretation" for the passive spectator to consume. At the other end, the spectator is dis-identified from the role of passive observation, positioned as an active agent of a spectacle which not only refuses an "interpretive" status, but seems to dispense with the familiar generic expectations of "dramatic performance" altogether. The framing of contemporary Shakespeare underlines the difficulty of conceptualizing dramatic performance without predicating it on literary mimesis, while simultaneously underlining the inadequacy of that paradigm, staging the productive incommensurability of writing and performance. As Erika Fischer-Lichte observes, "Performance does not consist of fixed, transferable, and material artifacts"; fashioning a Shakespeare Performance Studies requires the recognition that the signification of performance will be decided "in the continuous becoming and passing" of performance, and cannot be calibrated to the measure of the "artifact" it may appear to communicate (*Transformative Power* 75). Perhaps this is a defining lesson of an emerging Shakespeare Performance Studies: that the author is always returning, and invariably fails to appear, as the priorities we attribute to writing are necessarily deployed, displaced, disidentified – even "de-dramatized" – in the purposeful, aleatory fashioning of dramatic performance.

CHAPTER 2

Intoxicating rhythms: Shakespeare, literature, and performance *Nature Theater of Oklahoma,* Romeo and Juliet

I've never heard it in American before.
(A spectator, Nature Theater of Oklahoma, *Romeo and Juliet,* Hebbel am Ufer, Berlin, 30 June 2013)

As Patrick Cheney notes, there has been a remarkably uncontroversial "'return of the author' in Shakespeare studies" ("Introduction" 19). Stimulated in large part by Lukas Erne's fresh engagement with the evidence for *Shakespeare as Literary Dramatist* in 2003, Shakespeare studies has taken up the case for Shakespeare not only as an entrepreneurial writer for the stage, churning out actable material, but "as a self-conscious, literary author" (Erne, "Reconsidering Shakespearean Authorship" 26), who used print publishing to shape a career as a "literary dramatist" parallel to his career as a working playwright in the theatre. Erne's important study attempts to both redress "an increasingly dated view that threatens to reduce Shakespeare to 'a man of the theatre'" (32) and to restore a sense of Shakespeare fashioning works as dramatic poems and as performable plays, intended for a reading as well as a spectatorial audience. He marshals a variety of evidence, ranging from the frequency with which Shakespeare's plays were published and republished during the first decade of his career in the 1590s (noting the increasing prominence of his name on those quarto volumes), to an ingenious argument for the essentially "literary," print- and reader-directed address of many of Shakespeare's longer plays: too long for performance, he argues, the length of these plays – mainly the tragedies – may witness Shakespeare's intended appeal to a reading public, understanding as he did that the plays would necessarily be cut for the stage. As Charlotte Scott puts it, Erne's "Shakespeare wrote differently for the stage and the page, including in the text to be read things that would normally be performed (mannerisms, entrances, exits, physical behaviour, expressions)" (*Idea of the Book* 192).

Taking issue with Erne, David Scott Kastan observes that these claims about Shakespeare's authorship have nonetheless "remarkably changed our sense of Shakespeare almost overnight," galvanizing a latent scholarly "eagerness" to confirm the distinctive inscription of a "literary dramatist" ("'To think these trifles'" 46) and the image of Shakespeare, and of dramatic performance, it appears to summon.

> The excitement the book has generated is itself evidence of how important Shakespeare is to us, and how much authorship itself matters. We want to believe in a Shakespeare who is an author, to rescue him from the necessary collaborations of the stage, even from the agency of the printing house, which, it seems to me, largely invented Shakespeare the Literary Dramatist for its own purposes rather than for those of the author it created, or for those of the playwright and writer he unquestionably was. (47)

However created, "Shakespeare" bestrides the book and the stage. Robert Weimann and Douglas Bruster locate their reading of *Shakespeare and the Power of Performance* by noting the "swing of the critical pendulum" toward a "renewed stress on the page" (*Power of Performance* 13), and Richard Dutton groups Kastan's *Shakespeare and the Book* alongside *Shakespeare as Literary Dramatist* and Patrick Cheney's *Shakespeare, National Poet-Playwright* as part of "a concerted backlash against the long-standing certainty that Shakespeare is primarily defined by his role in the theater" (Review 374).

The "return of the author" requires a sustaining understanding of the appropriate function of writing in the theatre. Were the plays motivated by an individual conceptualizing himself as an "author" or did they emerge collaboratively from the busy hive of the early modern playhouse? Was the "literary dramatist" a cause or a consequence of the fashioning of plays in print? These important questions also index a tangential problem: how conceptualizing the documents and their creator discipline a conception of theatrical propriety. Rescuing Shakespeare from the stage enacts a vision of literature and theatre, and of their conjunction, dramatic performance. The "return of the author" (was he ever really gone?) in *Shakespeare* studies, whatever it may say about Shakespeare's responses to and manipulation of the emergent institutions in which he worked, surely says something about us: it points to the ongoing challenges of fashioning *performance* as an object and perspective of inquiry in Shakespeare *studies* today, and, perhaps more urgently, to an animating cultural dialectic *between* Shakespeare and performance. How does the "return of the author" represent Shakespeare at the intersection of drama's (early) modern means of production, and furthermore imply a paradigm of Shakespeare performance?

Although conceptualizing performance may not be essential to the project of excavating the "literary dramatist," the vision of performance that emerges here is an important register of how writing and performance are imagined, related, and regulated in Shakespeare studies, where making the case for a "self-conscious, literary" Shakespeare apparently requires the derogation of "performance criticism" of Shakespearean drama and a surprisingly narrow view of the warrant of dramatic performance itself. Moreover, while this "return" might seem to be confined to the purely scholarly or "academic" precinct of formal Shakespeare studies, "Shakespeare" is one of the (relatively few) sites of scholarly inquiry in the humanities where academic contestation has purchase outside the academy – in the more popular address of scholars like Jonathan Bate, Harold Bloom, Marjorie Garber, or Stephen Greenblatt; in the host of guides addressing Shakespeare performance by well-known directors and instructors, such as Kristin Linklater, Adrian Noble, and others; in the perennial media fascination with the authorship "controversy"; in Shakespeare as an inevitable touchstone in cultural politics; and in two places where the literature–theatre interface provides an essential ground of purpose and value: stage performance and general education. In positioning dramatic performance as "interpretation," the mimesis of a textually coherent fiction, the "return of the author" legitimates a specific understanding of Shakespeare performance, stabilizing what we might call, following Rancière, a specific "distribution of the sensible" in the theatre (*Emancipated Spectator* 12).

This chapter opens by framing the "return of the author" as an index of the ways writing is understood to configure the terms of Shakespeare performance. To frame a dialogue between the "return of the author" and contemporary performance, I then turn to a recent production of *Romeo and Juliet* by an inventive theatre company, the Nature Theater of Oklahoma. Like the "return of the author," this lively and provocative stage work can be seen to address an asymmetry between a literary and a theatrical Shakespeare, and to locate it in the context of contemporary education and artistic politics, to evoke, so to speak, an inquiry into the implications of our valuation of the media in which Shakespearean knowledge is represented and performed.

Intoxications

In a sense, the "return of the author" dramatizes less the etiolation of Shakespeare as literary dramatist than the challenges of framing an authentic Shakespeare Performance Studies. Since the seventeenth century at least, the plays have been recognized as part of the formation of both "literature" and of "theatre," though these institutions have not often shared a common perspective on the plays' value, utility, or aesthetic identity. The notion that the plays, and perhaps dramatic writing in general, were beginning to have a print identity as "literature" in the 1590s, one more acknowledged than invented by Ben Jonson's 1616 *Works*, surely has important implications for our understanding of the careers of playwrights in that period, as well as of the cultural impact of playwriting.[1] Early modern dramatic writing flourished as an essential element of an expanding commercial theatre system, a system, as Tiffany Stern has shown, that produced the dramatic "text" as an assemblage of "patchily" written documents, derived from an initial scenario and often written and organized by different hands: "The dialogue and all that happens within that dialogue exchange was in performance made up of separate manuscripts: learnt actors' parts, backstage-plots, and songs, scrolls, prologues and epilogues all of which might be read onstage, and all of which have their own histories" (*Documents in Performance* 253). And yet, whatever the provenance of their printed texts, playbooks were a visible segment of the book trade, and among them Shakespeare's plays formed a very significant part.[2] They were also slowly assimilated to nascent canons of vernacular "literature" emerging through the expansion of commercial print publishing and its often contested relation to more settled modes of communication and models of authorship, and to the uneven spread of literacy.[3] Whether Shakespeare was self-consciously part of a systematic publishing program or not (and regardless of whether supervising the publication of the quartos was even a realistic possibility, which Erne thinks unlikely [*Literary Dramatist* 96]), as house playwright and sharer in his company, Shakespeare could not have been unaware of efforts to publish the company's plays, of the general trade in printed drama, or of a potential readership for plays, including his own.[4] He was likely a reader of printed drama, and his plays frequently meditate on the varied uses of writing in performance, even on the specificity of writing for performance in print culture.[5]

No one disputes that the theatre was the engine for the writing of stage plays: without the market incentive of the entertainment industry's voracious need for new and appealing work, would Marlowe, Jonson, Shakespeare, and many others have turned such energetic attention to plays, let alone to the invention, refinement, and proliferation of the distinctive new genres of vernacular drama?[6] After all, as Scott McMillin notes, theatrical companies paid as much for a single play as the "run-of-the-mill writer of 'fine' literature might earn" in a year ("Professional Playwrighting" 227). Shakespeare published poems during his lifetime, laden with the identifying apparatus of patronage: he was, and was known as, a poet, whose work was worth reading, copying, remembering. He was also known and praised as a playwright whose plays were popular onstage, and whose published texts were marked for commonplacing (see Lesser and Stallybrass, "First Literary *Hamlet*"), a sign of the perceived – or at least marketable – value of the "fine filed phrase" of his dramatic verse, as Francis Meres noted in 1598 (*Palladis Tamia* 282). The writing of new plays in late sixteenth-century London was driven by the demand of the theatre for new material; despite their emphasis on verbal dexterity (clearly part of the drama's stage appeal), the plays had to be palpably performable – with whatever cuts, additions, revisions – to be purchased by an acting company. Though not in great demand, individual volumes of printed contemporary plays were bought and read; Shakespeare's plays were popular in both print and theatrical arenas. Identifying the playwright on the title page (also used as a poster) became more – though not universally – common, and in his lifetime, Shakespeare assumed a recognizable and familiar position, "amphibiously occupying the worlds of printed books and of the theater" (Burrow, Review 325).[7] By 1623, it was possible to assert the extratheatrical identity of contemporary *Comedies, Histories, & Tragedies* materially, in an impressive, modestly expensive, folio-size book.[8]

Willy-nilly, Shakespeare contributed to the success of professional theatre, to the rise of printed drama, and to something else: the conceptualization of printed play texts as "dramatic literature." What is surprising about the contemporary "return of the author" is the leverage it seeks from the assertion of Shakespeare's *intentional* framing of the plays as "literature," and from the apparently consequent necessity to disable "performance" as a critical context for conceiving Shakespearean dramatic writing. "Literary" and "theatrical" drama are here taken to be mutually exclusive, however much the use of writing in western dramatic performance sustains their variable consubstantiality, and however much Shakespeare's plays were affected by the playwright's business: acting and investing in, and writing for the most influential theatre company of the era. The "return of the author" urges us not only to discriminate the "literary" from the "theatrical" modes of production framing Shakespeare's plays, but to distinguish the "literary" from the "theatrical" elements within Shakespeare's dramatic writing, however "porous" the relation between them may have been (Erne, "Preface" 4).[9]

This dichotomy both reflects and reciprocates the defining gesture of "performance criticism" in the 1970s, nicely epitomized in J. L. Styan's *The Shakespeare Revolution*: "When performance critics claim, for instance, that 'the stage expanding before an audience is the source of all valid discovery' and that 'Shakespeare speaks, if anywhere, through his medium' they are simply ignoring one of the two media in which Shakespeare's plays exist and existed" (*Literary Dramatist* 22, quoting Styan, *Revolution* 235). Fair enough. "Performance criticism" has often taken a relatively untheorized and unjustifiably dualistic view of its foundational terms – text, performance – and of the aims and methods of the critical heuristic they seem to support. Even so, Erne characterizes *Shakespeare as Literary Dramatist* as a "timely intervention" (20) in the wider field, in which performance has not only "become a central component of Shakespeare studies" (20), but is indeed "omnipresent" there (14). He is rightly irritated by the exclusionary cant behind the "claim that his plays were written in order to be performed" (14), as though their theatrical instigation should or could govern the kinds of attention appropriately directed to dramatic writing as an instrument of critical performance, whether in scholarly writing or on the stage. It could also be observed – *pace* Styan – that authorial intention falls aslant the practice of theatre, which consists of using writing to make an event that reframes verbal signification in the spatial, embodied, gestural, kinesthetic means of nonverbal action; it also falls aslant the practices of Shakespeare's theatre, where the "text" of the performed play was typically comprised of a host of documents (often by various authors) that may or may not have followed the dialogue-script into print (see Stern, *Documents in Performance*). Nonetheless, the "dogmatic" claim that plays were written for the stage, however inept as a prescriptive instrument of critical practice (and however symmetrical with claims that the literary intentions of plays *written for* readers should determine their cultural use and signification), has apparently had huge and troubling consequences, even leading multi-volume editions of the plays to give "ample space to the theatrical dimension as evidenced not only in copious stage histories but, increasingly, throughout the introduction and the annotations" (20). While we may wonder what *the* theatrical dimension is (do plays have a single literary dimension?), it seems that "If we have erred in the last thirty years or so, we have erred on the side of performance and at the expense of the text" (23).

Even though "the return of the author" is typically framed as an historical corrective to the misapprehension of the institutional – publishing, professional theatre – landscape of Shakespeare's career, it rapidly opens out toward the assertion of more essential critical and disciplinary principles. In what sense does attending to Shakespeare's plays as instruments of "performance" (not the same thing as a flawed "performance criticism") have as its constitutive critical liability the sacrifice of "the text" of those plays? The most rebarbative, experimental Shakespeare production stands in some relation to a "Shakespearean" text, even when, as is the case in the Nature Theater of Oklahoma's *Romeo and Juliet*, which ran in New York in the 2009/2010 season and has toured internationally since, the production is both about the failure to remember the play's language and narrative and consequently about the challenges of materializing Shakespeare as a property of human being. An errant interest in performance "at the expense of the text" of Shakespeare has, so far, hardly cost us much. Though Erne rightly questions the pretensions of the Oxford edition to have produced a more authentically "theatrical" version of Shakespeare's scripts, editions nonetheless multiply, as does the fundamentally text-centered critique of Shakespearean plays as "literature," critical practice that sustains much "performance criticism," too. Moreover, setting aside the large literature using performance to make Shakespeare appealing as a school subject (a literature fully imbued with a sense of the literary value of the writing, to be more palatably seized through the "interpretive" instrument of performance), "performance criticism" of Shakespeare is not only a significantly subordinate part of Shakespeare scholarship, but is often – in terms of the critical priority it assigns to the texts, and its general valuation of "Shakespeare" – cognate with the values and practices of literary critique. Understanding performance as an "interpretation" of the "text," Shakespeare "performance criticism," far from sacrificing the text as some familiar forms of literary critique (new historicist, feminist, psychoanalytic, name your poison) are sometimes also alleged to do, often stabilizes performance on the (apparently) firm foundations of a dramatic script fully imbued with literary value.

While some "performance criticism" claims to eschew a purely "literary" approach to Shakespeare's plays, it rarely challenges the centrality of "the text" and its meanings to appropriate Shakespearean performance. The determining role of the text in "performance criticism" is, in fact, precisely captured in Styan's presiding metaphors: "the plays as blueprints for performance" and "the text-as-score" (Styan, *Revolution* 235). As a metaphor, the "score" evinces a powerfully text-governed, algorithmic conception of performance. Rightly noting that the "text-as-score" advocated by Styan and others to regulate "interpretation" to an essentialized notion of stagecraft is a false analogy, Erne suggests, "while musical scores are usually intended for performers, a printed play generally is not, but is (and was) meant for readers instead" (*Literary Dramatist* 22). Early modern printed texts – something like trade editions today – addressed readers, not actors, yet the function Styan attributes to the score as a licensed image of the appropriate authority of writing in performance remains standing. That is, the image of writing ideally determining the order, pacing, incarnation of performance remains a sustaining metaphor of "performance criticism," despite the fact that the preponderance of dramatic performance evades location in the script, whether in manuscript or in print.

However misaligned with stage performance, this appropriation of the score metaphor reflects a pervasive aesthetic ideology. As Lydia Goehr has shown, by the late nineteenth century the growing, post-Romantic conception of the musical "work" demanded a critical parallel between fidelity to the "work" (*Werktreue*) and to the score or text (*Texttreue*): "To certify that their performances be of specific works, [performers] had to comply as perfectly as possible with the scores composers provided. Thus, the effective synonymity in the musical world of *Werktreue* and *Texttreue*: to be true to a work is to be true to its score" (*Imaginary Museum* 231). A "performance met the *Werktreue* ideal most satisfactorily, it was finally decided, when it achieved complete transparency. For transparency allowed the work to 'shine' through and be heard in and for itself" (232). For Styan, the text-as-score is a similar invocation of *Werktreue* via *Texttreue*, a metaphor that is misplaced for Erne only because Styan misjudges the cultural function of print in Shakespeare's era, not because he misstates the proper relation between writing and performance.

So, given the relatively low profile of "performance criticism" in Shakespeare studies, its nearly complete lack of purchase outside academic critique of Shakespeare (in Performance Studies, for instance), its literary assimilation of *Werktreue* to *Texttreue*, and its constitutive reciprocality with the values of literary drama, we might well wonder whether "so-called performance criticism," now well past its "heyday" in the "1970s to the 1990s," poses much of a threat to Shakespeare's "return" (Erne, *Book Trade* 7). Indeed, by the second, 2013, edition of *Shakespeare as Literary Dramatist*, performance criticism is emphatically past-tense: "Appearing at a time when performance criticism had acquired importance in Shakespeare studies and when the view of Shakespeare as a 'man of the theater' was prominent, *Shakespeare as Literary Dramatist* offered a reconsideration of Shakespeare's authorial status" ("Preface" 1). The "return of the author" is finally animated by something considerably more important than rescuing the plays from the isolated preserve of "performance criticism": the "far-reaching emancipation of Shakespeare's text from the stage" altogether (Erne, *Literary Dramatist* 77). While Erne suggests that the "New Critical obsession with close readings that turned plays into poems needed a corrective, this corrective may have led some to consider Shakespeare's plays exclusively as scripts to be performed, a view that is not justified by the double existence these plays had in the late sixteenth and early seventeenth centuries" (23), or that they have enjoyed much more massively ever since, given Shakespeare's foundational role in the conception of literature and culture sustaining the predominant position of his plays in the world's classrooms, libraries, bookstores, and theatres and on its television, cinema, and computer screens (sites that Shakespeare's plays were never "written for," however much some may resemble early modern avatars). Although the "literary dramatist" appears to restore equilibrium between literary and theatrical senses of the *work* in the changing ecology of early modern writing and performing, in practice this argument urges the priority of Shakespeare's literary intention and imagination to a proper estimation of the works themselves, to the appropriate means of their critique, and implicitly to a proper sense of the genre of "Shakespeare performance" as well.

The reconstruction of early modern text-and-performance is inflected by a revealing panoply of early and late modern labels: *author, poet, dramatist, man of the theatre* serve as shorthand to license critical practice, justify the attribution of value, and prioritize the means of creation. Ben Jonson was a "poet." Like Shakespeare, he wrote plays "for" performance within the highly disseminated system of generating "text" – what we might call "content" today – for the stage, all the while irritably announcing their essentially literary status. No danger, then, that Jonson would fall foul of the "increasingly dated view that threatens to reduce Shakespeare to 'a man of the theatre'" (Erne, "Reconsidering Shakespearean Authorship" 32).[10] The "poet" or "dramatist" and the "man of the theatre" hardly carry comparable cultural freight. John Heminges, David Garrick, Constantin Stanislavsky, David Belasco, Harley Granville Barker, Harold Clurman, and Sir Peter Hall are "men of the theatre," though several were playwrights, too; Sophocles, Shakespeare, Goethe, Ibsen, and Beckett are "dramatists," though all had considerable experience in practical theatre-making. *Henslowe in Love*? Qualifying several of Erne's specific interpretations, Kastan also shares the hesitation that Shakespeare was "simply [!] a practical man of the theater, as many have held" ("'To think these trifles'" 46), raising the question of whether, as Richard Dutton puts it (arguing against the "'theatre-centric' approach to Shakespearean authorship, which in many ways is the modern orthodoxy"), the "nature of the Shakespearean 'author' need not, therefore, be confined to the traditional extremes of 'reader-focus' and 'performance-focus'" ("'Not one clear item'" 120).[11] Is the stage-and-page, playwright-and-dramatist double perspective apparently sought by the "return of the author" really possible – or desirable – in contemporary Shakespeare studies?[12]

Even accounts accommodating the man of the theatre to the dramatist find this dichotomy inescapable. Resisting Erne's claim that the "creation of the dramatic author in early printed playbooks preceded the creation of the dramatic author in the playhouse," Jeffrey Knapp takes a surprisingly protheatrical position from within the "critical movement [. . .] titled 'The Return of the Author'" (*Shakespeare Only* ix). His Shakespeare is an onlie begetter, a singular creator whose "authorial self-consciousness" is nevertheless "fundamentally shaped by his immersion in the theater business" (122–123). Countering the widespread "historicist" argument that the "collaborative" and even "collective" working environment of the early modern theatre, at least before some time in the early seventeenth century, obviates the application of a purposeful sense of "authorship" to the practice of writing plays, this Shakespeare intervened in "the standard, received model for understanding how scripts got written," an "essentially literary" notion of authorship that "was not equipped to treat the playwright's engagement with other artistic forces in the theater as anything but a struggle for authority." Yet while Shakespeare "did help theatricalize the concept by acknowledging the formative power of actors and audience on his playwriting," the figure of the "author" preserves an intrinsically literary conception of the work of drama, at least as a fact of early modern institutional history: "so dominant was the literary model of authorship that Shakespeare could not or would not entirely dispel its bias against collaborative mass entertainment," embracing instead "the thought that an author writing plays for the commercial stage must suffer a loss of sovereign authority as well as respectability" (102). Shakespeare's sympathies may not be "wholly on one side or the other of the battle-line Hamlet draws between scripting and clowning," the figure of the "player-author" perhaps implying a more fluid sense of the "complexity of his means, aims, and methods as a theatrical professional." At the same time, it seems as though Shakespeare the author finally absorbs "the decisive effect of his audience and fellow actors" into "*his* dramaturgy" (my emphasis) as a means of resisting the theatre's innate remaking of the fiction of the sovereign authority of the script (90, 123).[13] Knapp's Shakespeare absorbs the lessons of performance into texts that will, it seems, always fail to exert their properly sovereign authority over theatre and theatre practice. Perhaps the exception proves the rule: Shakespeare the theatrically aware author, reluctantly subduing his scripts to the multifarious purposes of the stage, still had an out – "Shakespeare expected his plays to be read as well as performed" (166 note 78).

Like the farmer and the cowman, the literary dramatist and the man of the theatre should be friends, but the landscape, and how we want to use it, keeps getting in the way. The "return of the author" has a visibly redressive purpose, expressed in Alan H. Nelson's relief (cited approvingly by Erne) that Shakespeare's plays and poems can once again be approached "as verbal and dramatic art, as – dare I think it? – English Literature" (Nelson, "Bibliophiles" 70; see Erne, "Reconsidering Shakespearean Authorship" 30), as well as in John Jowett's measured sense of the benefits of Erne's impact on editorial theory, "a new emphasis at the beginning of the twenty-first century, one that pares back the theatrical dimension and asserts on new grounds the presence of Shakespeare the author in the field of textual study" ("Editing Shakespeare's Plays" 18). Patrick Cheney imagines "a collaborative man of the theatre who wrote plays for both page and stage" (*Authorship* xii), but – unlike Weimann and Bruster in this regard – his adjectives sharply belie the bland conjunctions (the "working dramatist or jobbing playwright" xi), enforcing a critical hierarchy at precisely the moment when book and theatre, print and performance, page and stage are supposed to be equitably recalibrated: "During the past five years, a sobering piece of news has awakened some from the pleasures of performance intoxication: if we seek historical accuracy, no longer can we separate theatre from book, performance from print, in criticism on William Shakespeare" (9–10).

Performance intoxicates, dulls the senses, dizzies the mind, lowers inhibitions and whatever the man of the theatre may have been, Shakespeare the poet was no mere sensualist: "To simplify matters, performance tends to speak to the senses, while a printed text activates the intellect. As I will attempt to demonstrate in the second part of this study, some of the Shakespearean playbooks bear signs of *the* medium for which they were designed" (Erne, *Literary Dramatist* 23, my emphasis), the mentally activating medium of print literature.[14] While it does address us through what Stephen Gosson memorably called the "privie entries" of the senses (*Schoole* B7r), the theatre is hardly incapable of activitating the intellect (though we would be wrong to identify its forms of thinking merely with the words it uses), nor is reading essentially an unmixed intellectual activity: think of all the writing, from romance fiction through propaganda and advertising, designed to speak to the senses, to say nothing of the sensual appeal of imagery, meter and rhythm, let alone paper, typography, illustration, binding. Attributing intellectual activity to Shakespeare's readers, and conceiving a reciprocal sense of Shakespeare's spectators as passive consumers of affective spectacle, the "return of the author" foregrounds the deeper and more complicated function of "performance" at work here, where "Shakespeare in performance yields too easily to our desires" (Kastan, *Shakespeare and the Book* 7; see also Knowles, Review 546). "Why identify gaze and passivity, unless on the presupposition that to view means to take pleasure in images and appearances while ignoring the truth behind the image and the reality outside the theatre" (Rancière, *Emancipated Spectator* 12), or in this case, the truth of the critical encounter between the intellect and the text? Despite the claims to integrate performance and print, the "return of the author" tends to emancipate the text from the stage, the poet from the man of the theatre, writing from the body, intellectual judgment from the intoxicating seduction of the senses, and so appears to restore the practices of theatre to their proper place *in* history: subordinate *to* writing in the work of dramatic performance.[15] To know Shakespeare performance is not to know Shakespeare.

The recourse to "performance" is less revealing than the belief in its enabling necessity as the grounding opposition to Shakespeare's "literary drama." This is a familiar gesture in Shakespeare studies, where even "performance criticism" often locates the authority of performance in the script-as-score. And while for many readers of Shakespeare – many of *us*, that is – the performance *of* a *Shakespeare play* tends to be conceived in terms of its representation of the fiction encoded in the dramatic text, the calibration and valuation of these terms has been quite differently conceived in disciplines attending more directly to the process, structure, and effect of performance. The most significant work in Performance Studies has challenged an essential subordination of performance to writing, of what Diana Taylor terms the *repertoire* to the *archive*. While I think this work requires important qualifications – to my mind, Taylor's searching study tends to reiterate a literary sense of the function of writing in theatrical performance, which she associates with the *archive* – it does invite us to take a different perspective on the construction of writing and performance than has been imagined either in "performance criticism" or in the current excitement about the "return of the author," inviting a sense of the unscripted *repertoire* of performance practice constantly reshaping the potentialities of the *archive*, the capabilities of the text as an imagined instrument of performance.[16] Theatrical experience cannot enable an adequate, let alone authentic, encounter with dramatic writing as long as performance is conceived as an impoverished interpretive iteration of one dimension of the text. Despite the overanxious concern that performance "is currently replacing the author as the holy grail of Shakespeare studies" (Dillon, "Is there a Performance" 85; approvingly cited by Erne, *Literary Dramatist* 181), the "return of the author" nonetheless depends on a specific, literary orientation to the proprieties of performance. It may not be fair to hold Erne, Cheney, and others to a more plausible grasp of performance; this meticulous encounter with the material life of printed texts is immensely provocative and rewarding, and it should be clear that I am taking issue with its rhetorical framing of "performance," not with the revisionist account of the process and cultural impact of dramatic publishing. But insofar as the "literary dramatist" gains traction from an implied model of performance, it is fair to consider how it models performance in relation to writing, and what the consequences of this implicit paradigm might be for a Shakespeare Performance Studies.

Performance takes a specific shape here, described as a means for the enunciation of writing: the "plays as presented on stage" (Erne, *Literary Dramatist* 175). This choice of words is revealing; Cleanth Brooks and Robert Heilman's influential 1945 New Critical textbook, *Understanding Drama*, also prefers the phrase "stage presentation" (3), rarely using the word *theatre*, and reserving *theatrical* as a purely derogatory term for "artificially contrived effects," the "melodramatic" and "'sensational,'" the "highfalutin instead of the truly poetic" (504).[17] "Presenting" the play implies a kind of transference, as though the "literary drama" could be preserved from the contrived contamination of merely "theatrical" sensations. This sense of theatre as properly "presenting" a work – rather than making new work, using writing as one element in a performance – sustains Erne's argument that the long plays in particular contain considerable writing that was never to be "presented," and so was not addressed to the stage at all. In this view, Shakespeare didn't just provide his company with too much material; he encoded elements of his text as "for" print, dramatic literature. He "must have written with an awareness that much of it would not survive the text's preparation for the stage but that he and his company made available to a readership" (*Literary Dramatist* 196). Since this writing was not intended for "presentation," its identity was never predicated on the theatrical work it might enable. The conception of a theatre of textual "presentation" is critical to the discrimination of "literary" from "theatrical" writing: a theatre understood to "present" its texts provides a warrant for defining writing as literary that exceeds the stage's presentational practices or capacity. A theatre "presenting" writing can be brought to bear as an instrument for deciding which elements of texts are essentially irrelevant to theatrical "presentation," "literary."

I am less concerned here with the historical plausibility of the "too-long-for-performance" argument – assessed in detail by Michael J. Hirrel – than with the ways it models an appropriate relation between text and performance, literary drama and theatre.[18] For whether dramatic texts were or were not too long for performance is for my purposes less crucial than the critical practice this notion appears to provide for discriminating the "literary" from the "theatrical" factors of dramatic writing: the encoding of distinctive representational and presentational elements. Understanding performance as presentation-of-text sustains the notion that certain aspects of writing – both elements of the dialogue, and (more arresting) some paratextual elements such as stage directions – can be seen as essentially literary in intention because they seem to provide "information" either irrelevant or redundant to stage "presentation." "Literariness" is, of course, "a matter of canonicity; it describes the cultural use to which certain texts are put for those periods (often short, sometimes widely separated, rarely continuous) during which they satisfy hermeneutic needs" (Robert S. Knapp, *Shakespeare* 37–38). Perhaps surprisingly, then, the bits of writing that emerge as decisively distinguishing the literary ontogeny of several Shakespearean texts are not only the "poetic highlights" copied into commonplace books (Erne, *Literary Dramatist* 228). Instead, the essentially literary dimension of Shakespeare's writing is signified by words and phrases that seem to narrate dramatic action and behavior, words, that is, that confirm a sense that dramatic writing represents a coherent fiction for readers rather than providing an instrument for actors to create an event in the here and now shared with an audience. (The "too long for performance" claim is, perhaps, not really essential to Erne's case for a literary Shakespeare after all; even if the long plays could be performed in the allocated time, these elements could nonetheless be seen to distinguish between an appeal to stage presentation and an appeal to a literary audience of readers.)

The conservation of narrative "information" required to "present" the dramatic fiction provides the principle for discriminating the "literary" from the "theatrical" elements of the printed drama: text that conveys "information" that could be duplicated in stage "presentation" (does performance ever duplicate textual "information"?) indicates the literary orientation of the text at hand. Various stage directions in *Antony and Cleopatra*, for instance – "Enter Pompey, Menecrates, and Menas, in warlike manner," "Enter Ventidius as it were in triumph," "Enter Caesar . . . with his Counsell of Warre," "Enter the Guard rustling in" – strike Erne as "descriptive stage directions that seem directed at readers rather than at the bookkeeper" (*Literary Dramatist* 113), because in the theatre the conspirators' warlike manner would be evident from their appearance, Caesar's council would be identified by the dialogue, and the guard would enter with the usual rustling hustle and bustle of officious underlings. The pictoriality of such directions is inconsistent with the pure instrumentality of most early modern stage directions, suggesting to Erne that they're principally intended to provide readers with "information" essential to assembling a dramatic fiction in the mind's eye. Granted, actors rehearsed from sides or parts, which tended to contain a very modest number of action-oriented directions (*Enter*, *Exit*); all the same, in the absence of a clear sense of the provenance of these "literary" directions, we should also be wary of denying them the theatrical purpose they might otherwise plainly seem to have.[19] Here and elsewhere, the "literary dramatist" argument depends on being able to isolate the representational from the presentational, the mimetic from the instrumental elements of dramatic writing. Yet history is rife with examples of how the text apparently once provided "presentational" opportunities that seem – now – un-Shakespearean: the bevy of dancing witches in *Macbeth*; Garrick's bobbing wig; Cleopatra's barge.[20] More to the point, perhaps, performance history also shows how actors and directors have found means to *use* elements of a written script that were initially seen as baffling or merely irrelevant to performance: Kate's *exit* – or lack thereof – at the close of *The Taming of the Shrew*; the ellipses, *Pause*s, and white space in the texts of Pinter's plays; the entire action of *Waiting for Godot*.[21] As the many controversies surrounding Beckett's stage directions remind us, discriminating the literary from the theatrical elements of the page remains far from straightforward.

For this reason, we should also be wary of assuming that the protocols of reading in the emergent discourse of printed drama observe our own, post-Shavian sense of the readerly utility of narrative stage directions (Shaw used his "novelistic" directions to position the spectator before an imagined proscenium, not in the fictive action). Erne suggests that Shakespeare's early modern readers "showed little interest in inferring stage action from the play text" ("Reconsidering Shakespearean Authorship" 33), implying that the only proper function of narrative directions was to appeal directly to early modern readers' imagining of the fictive rather than the theatrical action. This distinction may or may not be convincing as a hypothesis about Shakespeare's intentions toward different audiences;

what we might well wonder, though, is whether it is plausible to segment the potential functionality of dramatic writing along these lines.

Dialogue, too, sometimes appears to serve a more properly "literary" than "theatrical" function. In the Folio version of *Henry V*, Gloucester's description of Mountjoy after the slaughter of the English boys provides a key piece of evidence: "His eyes are humbler than they vs'd to be" (Erne, *Literary Dramatist* 221). Noting that this line and its prompting line appear only in the "readerly" F text and not in the "theatrical" Q1, Erne argues:

> If we understand the Folio text and the script behind Q1 as designed for two different media, what seems significant about the two missing lines [. . .] is that they can be *acted* and therefore do not need to be *spoken*. In performance, the words would unnecessarily reiterate what the actor conveys through body language. [. . .] The two lines present in the readerly but absent from the theatrical text are thus crucial for what Harry Berger calls "imaginary audition." They allow a reader to imagine a point of stage business that could otherwise only be conveyed in performance. (222)

Erne is alert to the tautology of assigning readerly values to F and then deriving a literary origin from them; more recently, Tiffany Stern has argued that the inclusion of the prologue and chorus in the play imply the Folio text's proximity to performance.[22] For my purposes, what's more important here is how this argument understands performance as a means of "presenting" – but not violating, enlarging, remaking – apparently textual meanings. In what sense is the performance of these lines redundant, reiterative? In any performance the line hardly describes what we can unambiguously see for ourselves. Like all language onstage, it works in an active dialectical counterpoint to behavior, and gains its sense from the scene in which, and the purposes with which, it is performed as action. How does the actor make his eyes "humbler"? Or does he? Must *we* see what Gloucester says *he* sees? Even a slavishly "faithful" performance of humbled eyes will necessarily signify well beyond what Gloucester says of them – defeat, abjection, anger, contempt, all the indescribable meaning of a single glance – and so both specify and qualify Gloucester's description. Similarly, when Juliet beseeches her father "on my knees," as she does in Q2 *Romeo and Juliet*, Erne takes this phrase as redundant stage information (pointing to the "literary" designs of this text) because – as the stage direction in Q1 "*She kneeles downe*" informs us – Juliet is already kneeling: only readers need Juliet to say she is kneeling (*Literary Dramatist* 223). And yet, pointing out that one is kneeling makes "beseeching" a different act; insofar as performance transforms the language it uses into action, even descriptive words must be made to do something beyond what they say. For this reason, assigning a "literary" origin to language describing action seems to depend on a limiting misconception of the work of words in performance.

Perhaps *Antony and Cleopatra* is larded with narrative stage directions intended for a principal audience of readers. Yet in the context of that play, it is unusually difficult to know how to segregate descriptive directions and descriptive dialogue from the kind of writing proper to theatrical performance. Taking Gloucester's lines about Mountjoy's "humbler" eyes as a paradigm, is Philo's opening speech, mourning Antony's transformation into the "bellows and the fan / To cool a gipsy's lust" (1.1.9–10), also expendable in the theatre? It's immediately illustrated in action, of course – or is it? A stage production of *Antony and Cleopatra* without Philo's lines opening and closing the first scene, without Caesar's description of Antony's physical decline from his exploits at Modena, without Enobarbus's description of Cleopatra, and of course without Cleopatra's theatrically redundant "boy my greatness" (a speech which perhaps also conveys theatrical "information") would omit the play's determined oscillation between "textualized," even literary accents of "information," and information-in-the-making, performance. One element of *Antony and Cleopatra* is its remarkable use of stage narration to invoke, replace, displace, challenge the live performers and their audiences, as though the scripted "abstract" of character and its embodied action constitute two distinctive, competing, finally incommensurable performances, expectations the play strategically magnifies when the principals leave the stage, are described by others, and then return. The play's great narrative set piece, Enobarbus's "the barge she sat in," focuses a challenge essential to the play, and essential to the use of writing in performance: how can a boyish Cleopatra – who enters almost immediately thereafter, and of course later reenacts this scene in the climactic suicide – or *any* Cleopatra hope to compete with our narrative expectations, expectations exposed to the materialities of performance? Shakespeare's blatant theft of North's Plutarch, prose widely celebrated for stylistic brilliance in its day, seems to assert a specific text-and-performance problem. Here, and throughout the play, narrative and histrionic "information" are shown not to be redundant but at once complementary and incommensurable. Erne may well be right about the print orientation of *Antony and Cleopatra*: perhaps the play that made it into print was imagined by its author as a literary document addressed to readers. But I don't think this understanding of how writing functions in performance provides much evidence either way.

The understanding of performance sustaining the "return of the author" is also visible in the qualified assault on the Oxford edition of Shakespeare's plays, the "edition which has most fully embraced the shift to performance-centered criticism" (Erne, *Literary Dramatist* 175). Erne takes issue with the "as they were acted" claims of the edition, claims no more plausible coming from Oxford University Press than from the title pages of the many sixteenth-century quartos, or indeed from any book. Whether in Folio or quarto versions, Erne argues, all of Shakespeare's long plays would have required additional cutting, so it is simply impossible to know which parts would have been eliminated for performance. Moreover, printed plays had little agency in the theatre: print was for reading, while the manuscript approved by the Master of the Revels, providing – at least in part – the basis for rehearsal parts, was for acting.[23] Erne quite properly observes that a "theatrical" edition encodes an anachronistic paradigm: edition-as-performance. From Erne's perspective the Oxford editors' decision to add "theatrical" stage directions, describing possible stage business to make "the staging intelligible" (Stanley Wells, quoted in Erne, "Reconsidering Shakespearean Authorship" 32), both violates the structure of the early texts and fabricates "a more theatrical and less literary play text than Shakespeare ever intended," since Shakespeare's readers apparently "showed little interest in inferring stage action from the play text" ("Reconsidering Shakespearean Authorship" 33).[24] Yet while the Oxford editors err in supplying "theatrical" directions that mar the integrity of an intrinsically literary conception of drama, what Erne shares with them is the notion that the representational and the instrumental dimensions of dramatic writing can be readily and permanently identified and differentiated. Erne calls for an editorial practice that adds "literary" instead of "theatrical" stage directions, directions describing the "dramatic fiction":

> An editorial practice that encourages readerly engagement with the fictionally represented seems all the more appropriate as Shakespeare's early modern play texts contain not only theatrical but also fictional stage directions: in *Coriolanus*, characters "*enter the City*" (TLN 568); in *Timon of Athens*, the protagonist enters "*out of his Caue*" (TLN 2360); in *Julius Caesar*, Brutus enters "*in his Orchard*" (TLN 615); and a stage direction in *2 Henry VI* records a "*Fight at Sea*" (TLN 2168)" ("Reconsidering Shakespearean Authorship" 33)

The "return of the author" tends to polarize these apparently presentational and representational elements, even when, as Weimann and Bruster have argued, the early modern theatre is taken as the site of "varieties of representation that tended to defy closure and plenitude," and so would tend to frustrate "unyielding critical contest" between literary and theatrical perspectives on Shakespeare's plays (*Power of Performance* 11, 226 note 32).[25] Understanding Shakespeare to write at a moment of extraordinary "liquidity in relations between text and performance" (15), Weimann and Bruster see "early modern performances as a miscellaneous assemblage of contingent, formally and culturally variegated practices" in which "relations between the practice of performance and the authority of writing were as yet rather unsettled": Shakespeare's plays were written to exploit this interactive milieu (3). Although *Shakespeare and the Power of Performance* interrogates the specific ideological encounter of differently authorized elements in Shakespeare's theatre, it necessarily makes more general claims about dramatic performance: "The act of performance is primarily, though not exclusively, anchored in bodily practice. Representation, in particular its world-picturing function, is primarily, though again not exclusively, indebted to scriptural uses of language. It is in and through written discourses that a remote, absent, complex world can be represented" (3). Weimann and Bruster are engaged in a searching problem: how to locate the function of the language we value in performance without assigning it a determining value over performance. As the warrant for their extraordinarily rich and provocative account of Shakespeare's writing, though, they suggest that performance combines bodies and words in discernible ways. In performance, the body can be seen as the vehicle of the presentational, the poet's language heard as the vehicle of the represented; Shakespeare's text can be conceived to document this relationship. For while the "boundaries between the verbal signs of language and the visible signs of the body became as porous as they were contingent," nonetheless, the signal capacity of Shakespeare's writing has to do with the fact that "the dramatist's language itself has already assimilated the player's *gestus*, speech rhythm, and kinetic thrust prior to any subsequent embodiment." In this account, "Verbal and visible signs come together in the literary as well as the material production, but also in the audiovisual response of auditors-spectators," so that all three are "conjoined in a dramatic discourse that is an object of, as well as an agency in, the staging of the play" (9). While this sense of performance perhaps resonates with Hans-Thies Lehmann's sense of the "fundamental *shift from work to event*" characteristic of some contemporary performance (*Postdramatic Theatre* 61), it also gestures toward a familiar image of writing in performance: "language in the composition of a stage play proceeds by itself to assist in rendering, even directing the 'swelling scene'" (Weimann and Bruster, *Power of Performance* 9). The documented variety of performance in Shakespeare's theatre gave rise to a uniquely interactive but not unfamiliar image of dramatic performance: "In our convenient phrase, rather than having the author's pen inspired by player's voices [*sic*], we should expect to find the author's pen guiding, inspiring, disciplining, and fashioning an excellent actor's voice and body into character" (19).[26] Shakespearean drama may have emerged in a decisive moment of autopoetic interplay with performance, but Shakespeare's plays, in this view, provide the instrument for asserting a decidable hierarchy of writing to the playing it delivers in the theatre.

Erne stands "With Robert Weimann" not only in taking Shakespeare to participate "'in a residually oral culture that affected certain variant playtexts,'" but also in modeling how difficult it is to keep the moment of text/performance, literary/oral interplay open (*Literary Dramatist* 220, discussing Weimann, *Author's Pen* 43). Imagining Shakespeare performance here seems to demand the discovery of a critical practice – however refined – that enables the inscription of the presentational in the text's representational work. The question is "to what extent Shakespearean drama constitutes 'an almost oral art' or, conversely, 'is already a fully literary art'" ("Reconsidering Shakespearean Authorship" 31). If it inclines toward the oral, then performance is its essential medium; as "a fully literary art," though, Shakespearean drama can only be reduced, traduced, or corrupted by performance, at least by performance other than reading. And yet, as we should be well aware, technological change is difficult to capture in a strictly dualistic paradigm, perhaps especially where the interfacing genres of orality and literacy, performance and writing are concerned. Much as theatre in the West has been decisively shaped by print and the values – stability, identity, reproducibility – attributed to printed documents, it seems nonetheless difficult to characterize western theatre, with its multiform ways of using writing, as predominantly oral or literary in formation. The tension between writing and performance, the letter and the body, the virtual and the immediate pulses across the textual interface of dramatic performance, from the era of manuscript to those of print and digital media. The "return of the author" witnesses perhaps the largest obstacle to imagining Shakespeare Performance Studies: engaging a sense of Shakespeare performance that is not conceived as a sensually appealing means of merely *presenting* the text. And, if Shakespeare performance is something other than textual *presentation*, then what is it?

Seductive interpretations

Performance in the theatre asserts a richly materialized semiosis, one that enforces an intellectual, sensory, affective encounter with an estranged worldliness, representation balanced within the process of its presenting. The "return of the author" poses "literary drama" as an alternative to "theatrical drama," in part by legitimating theatre as merely a vehicle sustaining the playwright's scripted representation, presenting it to a passive viewing audience. Emancipating plays from the stage into the liberty of writ is, then, an arresting move insofar as an "interpretive" sense of theatre defines both the properties of literary drama and the proprieties of performance, the performance of both actors and spectators. This vision of theatre as the vehicle of a fundamentally literary representation also locates the "return of the author" on the horizon of contemporary performance and Performance Studies, more or less epitomizing the "anti-textual" manner in which dramatic performance (in this sphere often called "text-based performance") has been positioned as a conservative, ideologically captive mode of performance (Puchner, "Entanglements" 24). The "return of the author" – much like "performance criticism" – invokes a series of rigid dichotomies: dramatists (not *men* of the theatre), whose texts are traced by the signs of their intentions to write *for* one medium or the other, which appeal to different capacities, understood as active and passive, intellectual and affectual, in their audiences. Although the "return of the author" appears merely to rebalance Shakespearean dramatic writing on the pivot between literature and theatre, in imagining the proper work of writing in performance it programmatically displaces the warrant of Shakespeare Performance Studies.

To relate texts to performance, Erne and others rely chiefly on Harry Berger, who had the "courage to 'state the case against the stage-centered approach,'" defining an apparently performance-sensitive critical practice in his 1989 *Imaginary Audition* (Erne, *Literary Dramatist* 25).[27] Berger's utility here stems from the assertion that Shakespeare's texts are "overwritten from the standpoint of performance and the playgoer's limited perceptual capacities" (*Literary Dramatist* 25; Berger, *Imaginary Audition* 29–30), a sense of the inherent complexity of Shakespeare's texts unseizable by the stage sustaining Erne's claims for the literary orientation of Shakespeare's too-long plays as well (in this model, even a *Texttreue* performance can never, finally, be *Werktreue*).[28] Back in 1989, Berger quite effectively kneecapped the critical assumptions of much "performance criticism": "first, that the criterial status of actual performance conditions is self-evident; second, that any interpretation that does not conform to those conditions must be non- or antitheatrical and violate the Shakespeare text (by treating it as a text rather than a script); third, that a valid interpretation must match or reproduce the experience of actual playgoers" (*Imaginary Audition* 32). Nonetheless, Berger's revival as a critical touchstone sustaining the "return of the author" arrestingly dramatizes the ways "interpretation" models a literary valuation of both the process and the product of performance.

Berger brilliantly seizes on the dialogic structure of dramatic writing as the basis for a specific reader-oriented critical practice, *imaginary audition*, which figures reading as a more complex (ambiguous, multiplex, simultaneous) version of what he takes to be the spectator's (unambiguous, singular, sequential) activity in the theatre: *audition*, a distinctive mode of listening to characters.

> We practice imaginary audition when, in a dialogue between A and B, we imagine the effect of A's speech on B; listening to A with B's ears, we inscribe the results of this audit in the accounts we render of B's language. But we can also do something else, something persistently encouraged by Shakespearean writing, and this something is central to the practice, distinguishing it from more casual forms of auditory attention: we listen to B's language with B's ears. We premise that every interlocutory act is partly a soliloquy in which the speaker constitutes himself as the theater audience he shares confidences with or tries to persuade, affect, deceive. As readers we join B, or B joins us, in monitoring his speech acts. This perspective converts B's speech to continuous self-interpretation or -interrogation so that if at one level we posit B as a speech effect, a character constituted by (our interpretation of) his speech, at another level B reproduces this posit by continuously representing and responding to himself as a speech effect. (*Imaginary Audition* 45–46)

The sense that Shakespeare's plays are "overwritten" arises from the belief that as intrinsically literary documents they require a specific mode of production: "decelerated reading," the slow, back-and-forth, thoughtfully imaginative "imaginary audition" that enables a reader to multiply the potential signification of lines, generating the simultaneous proliferation of several plays – or playings – at once, performances constrained not by the materiality of the theatre, the practices of acting, or the passing of stage time, but only by the reader's skill and power to conceive the audition of Shakespeare's dialogue by occupying and projecting, *audition*ing, the positions of several simultaneous subjects-in-the-making.[29] But while Berger's reader actively recreates this "mighty world / *Of eye*, and ear – both what they half create / And what perceive," his theatrical spectator is dumbly in his being pent, allowed only a wide-eyed, alienated consumption of a single "interpretation" (the actor's decision to render a given line this way rather than that), a one-dimensional act of passively *realized* audition. Reading enables a conceptually multiplex performance of the text, notably imagined as principally auditory, the hearing of words, rather than in the visual, kinesthetic spatial terms of the stage. Attending a performance is at best a streamlined hermeneutic activity, or much worse, merely the consumption of someone else's hermeneusis – and a man of the theatre's, at that. As Harold Bloom put it, praising *Imaginary Audition*: "In the theater, much of the interpreting is done for you, and you are victimized by the politic fashions of the moment" (*Shakespeare* 720). Reading a Shakespeare play demands our presence, our active performance, a commitment to creative *jouissance*. Seeing a play is a secondary pleasure, watching someone else doing it.

Berger's challenging conception of reading and spectating, like much of the "text and performance" discussion in Shakespeare "performance criticism" and elsewhere, uses the notion of "interpretation" to bridge the gulf between literary and theatrical drama: performance is framed as offering its audiences an "interpretation" of the text, which they duly consume, much as they might consume an "interpretation" advanced in an article by Harry Berger or J. L. Styan, recognizing all the time that this "reading" is not the thing itself, the play. *Imaginary Audition* – like those followers excited about the "return of the author" – liberates Shakespeare from the stage by understanding performance to present a single "interpretation" of the script delivered to the wide-eyed spectator, taking reading to demand a multilayered performance more fully adequate to the essential nature of the Shakespearean artwork. While it is not surprising that we – all of us who richly encounter Shakespeare in books – might be drawn to model performance as a version of textual "interpretation," this metaphor ultimately distracts at least as much as it delivers.[30]

Defining the legitimate "capacities and incapacities attached" to its performers (Rancière, *Emancipated Spectator* 12), "interpretive" theatre locates one strain in the cultural politics of the spectacle. Yet while Berger and others celebrate the reader's activity, spectators are hardly passive. In Rancière's terms, "in a theatre, in front of a performance, just as in a museum, school or street, there are only ever individuals plotting their own paths in the forest of things, acts and signs that confront or surround them" (16). The "collective power shared by spectators does not stem from the fact that they are members of a collective body or from some specific form of interactivity" (16), but from an active, "unpredictable interplay of associations and dissociations" (17).[31] If dramatic writing is "overwritten" for the theatre, the stage also realizes an "overtheatrical" utility relative to the text, the sense that performance always does more with the text, makes more of it than what its mere words seem (to us, now, here) to say, even more than we may be able effectively to account for with words.

A reader can imagine the richly ambiguous interplay of materialized assertion and nuance, the complex armature of embodiment, posture, and gesture, certainty and uncertainty, the dialectic of opportunity and agency enlarging and implementing Shakespeare's writing onstage. To the extent that writing becomes part of an event, it is part of something that is hardly limited to what the words say, or to what we might imagine they should or could do, or to how they are actually used. An actor uses a line in a specific way: that specificity resonates with and against the thousand other specificities of that moment, gaining its force in relation to them. "Imaginary audition" is facilitated by the temporal extension of the reader's decelerated play with potential speech acts; performance facilitates the spatial extension of the spectator's co-present play with potential social acts, acts including those that transform words into deeds, that special class of theatrical performatives. Dramatic performance takes place on the stage, in a densely signifying space, the compacted "heterotopia" of Foucault's "Of Other Spaces." Yet as Samuel Weber suggests, theatre "entails not just *space* but, more precisely, its disruption and rearrangement. In other words, *theatricality emerges where space and place can no longer be taken for granted or regarded as self-contained*" (*Theatricality as Medium* 300), or, I would say, regarded as already prefigured by the representational work of the dramatic text. Our play is conducted not merely as the processing of performed language, but through the deep resonance of the theatre's material means, the embodied actions and gestures that position us as agents – *witnesses* in Freddie Rokem's terms (*Philosophers and Thespians* 155–160) – within a complex event, between the interinvolvement of present acting and represented action onstage and its reciprocal incorporation and reflection of the behavioral world beyond the stage, both the world of the theatrical audience and the larger social world it extends toward.[32]

To refine "literary drama" away from theatre, the "return of the author" understands performance as an act of textual presentation, offering an "interpretation." As I have argued in the previous chapter, though, I don't think performance directly performs "interpretation" for us, nor is our activity in the theatre principally "interpreting" the players' interpretation of "the text." The case for a "literary dramatist" seems to require understanding performance as an entrancing, even intoxicating, yet finally impoverished mode of textual reiteration. It's easy to feel that contemporary stages and screens have abandoned the literary dramatist, as productions (of *King Lear* by Young Jean Lee, Mabou Mines; *Hamlet* by Thomas Ostermeier, Heiner Müller, Michael Almereyda, the Wooster Group) seem to dispense with the (always illusory) warrant of the text. And yet such productions also imply that insofar as dramatic performance is not the practice of interpretation, it does not work to distinguish writing from doing, the poetic from the performed, the represented from the means of presentation. Dramatic performance depends on the de-dramatizing principle Lehmann unduly limits only to the "postdramatic": the "peculiar *temporality* and *spatiality of the scenic process*" instrumentalizes writing, and, as a "scenic *écriture*," exerts a richly dialectical pressure on an understanding of writing, text, drama (*Postdramatic Theatre* 74).

Much as the idea of the idea of the "literary dramatist" appears to require "performance" as its artificially enabling foil, so modern theatre is deeply implicated in the notion of a "literary drama," sometimes at just those moments when Shakespeare seems most distant, unspoken. The "return of the author" constitutes "literary drama" in an essential dichotomy with performance, the intellectual versus the intoxicating. Yet if, as Kastan puts it, performance "yields too easily to our desires" to avoid Shakespeare's essential "historicity," enabling Shakespeare to become "for every age a contemporary playwright" (*Shakespeare and the Book* 7), on the contemporary stage, much Shakespeare performance seems to yield to a desire for the "relative canonical stability" of the book (Kidnie, "Where is *Hamlet*?" 115), the desire for an authentically reembodied literary Shakespeare as the signifier of the theatre's ongoing seriousness, purpose, and value. As Margaret Jane Kidnie remarks, "every time a reviewer comments that 'the director is imposing a private agenda on the play rather than exploring and resolving its difficulties – which is much harder work,' or a critic seeks to 'free Shakespeare' by restricting the limits within which the plays are legitimately performed," a "conception of 'Shakespeare's play' is being brought into existence, performatively, in language" (116), a conception viewing Shakespeare's ineffable literary value through a suspicious regard for its means of embodied transmission: the culturally ambiguous, potentially (de)legitimating practices of theatre. In a variety of ways, the Nature Theater of Oklahoma *Romeo and Juliet* addresses the complex concatenation of issues surrounding the understanding of text and performance in the construction of contemporary Shakespeare through a salient meditation on the history, social experience, and culture of literary drama. Perhaps more surprising, *Romeo and Juliet* not only positions the text-and-performance question in broadly cultural terms, but also directly envisions the consequences of reducing the significance of performance to an anxiously authorized replaying of the text.

"What light through yonder window speaks?": Nature Theater of Oklahoma *Romeo and Juliet*

> So he went to marching up and down, thinking – and frowning, horrible, every now and then; then he would hoist up his eyebrows; next he would squeeze his hand on his forehead and stagger back and kind of moan; next he would sigh, and next he'd let on to drop a tear. It was beautiful to see him. By and by he got it. He told us to give attention. Then he strikes a most noble attitude, with one leg shoved forwards, and his arms stretched away up, and his head tilted back, looking up at the sky – and then he begins to rip and rave and grit his teeth – and after that, all through his speech, he howled, and spread around, and swelled up his chest, and just knocked the spots out of any acting ever *I* see before. (Huck Finn on the Duke of Bilgewater; Mark Twain, *Huckleberry Finn* 178–179)

For all its power in articulating the notion of a "literary dramatist," the "return of the author" extends what Michael Bristol calls "the incessant border disputes, skirmishes, and raids carried out between advocates of performance-oriented interpretation and the practitioners of more strictly and textually-based hermeneutic procedures." For Bristol, the "largely trivial character of this debate" has largely to do with its focus on "precedence and the allocation of authority" in an economy in which "precedence" has long been guaranteed: the assertion of the literary character of Shakespeare's writing as motivating the force of "interpretive" performance is a nearly frictionless position both in contemporary Shakespeare scholarship and throughout the popular understanding of Shakespeare performance (*Shakespeare's America* 97). The notion that performance has to be displaced for the author to "return" to literary studies should be paired with a pendant question: has the author ever really left the apparently unruly precincts of the stage?

The Nature Theater of Oklahoma *Romeo and Juliet* may not seem to address the question of Shakespeare Performance Studies at all. Shakespeare's play figures largely in the performance, but very few lines of *Romeo and Juliet* are actually spoken, and when they are, they're routinely spoken as quotations, usually misremembered quotations at that. Rather than undertaking a merely fashionable "deconstruction" of "the presence of

Shakespeare's most famous love tragedy in the contemporary Western cultural unconscious" (as Rachel Anderson-Rabern suggests, "Aesthetics of Fun" 94), the Nature Theater – which is not from Oklahoma, but takes its name from the theatre featured in Franz Kafka's unfinished novel *Amerika* – dedramatizes the performance of *Romeo and Juliet*, using the peculiar "scenic *écriture*" of performance as a mode of inquiry into the status of "Shakespeare as literary dramatist" in contemporary American culture (Lehmann, *Postdramatic Theatre* 74). Like many companies – Complicite, The Wooster Group – whose work addresses, rather than assumes, the constitution of "theatre" and "performance," the Nature Theater of Oklahoma is not a "Shakespeare company"; its work on *Romeo and Juliet* explores Shakespeare through its ongoing investigation of a specific form of aleatory dramaturgy. And yet, sidestepping the textual mimesis conventional in Shakespeare performance, onstage the Nature Theater of Oklahoma *Romeo and Juliet* precisely interrogates the consequences of understanding theatre as a mode of authorial inscription, the interpretive performance of "literary drama."

The performance falls into three parts. In the first part, two actors take turns telling the story of *Romeo and Juliet* as recalled by eight sources, culled from the "approximately 30" different people interviewed by the company's co-artistic director Pavol Liska via telephone (*Romeo and Juliet* Program).[33] The actors don't impersonate and individuate these subjects; that is, they don't enact realistic, individuated portrayals of Linda Cooper, Teresa Gridley, or the other interview subjects (who are unidentified in performance), in the way Anna Deavere Smith impersonates Angela Davis or Lance Armstrong, registering the codedness of their vocal, gestural address in a meticulous act of *Verfremdung*. Instead, the actors are marked by costume, diction, gesture, and movement as "actors," performing each of the transcribed and edited monologues – which they hear onstage through unconcealed earbuds – in the same rather exaggerated manner, purposely recalling the imagined acting conventions of the nineteenth-century American stage.[34] Following the eighth monologue, "Anne" (Gridley) and "Bobby" (Robert M. Johanson) – identified in the script, the theatre program, and the DVD credits but unnamed in the performance – come onstage together and speak to one another, taking up an informal meditation on love, neediness, acting, and the challenge of performing Shakespeare today. Finally, "Bobby" climactically confesses that he has never read *Romeo and Juliet*: blackout. Applause, curtain calls. Blackout again. The two actors recite the balcony scene in the dark, invisible. Lights up on the empty stage.

For Huck Finn, the Duke "just knocked the spots out of any acting ever *I* see before," and the eight monologues, four by "Anne" and four by "Bobby," are assertively American in their performance and cultural texture. Like Twain's novel, they deploy familiar phrases of contemporary American speech to lay claim to a democratic, demotic Shakespeare. In "American," Shakespeare is imprecise ("There's somethin' about somebody kissing somebody with poison on their lips, and that – " [78]), repetitive, slangy, cool rather than learned (the Capulet family are "Sort of the hipsters of the town" [89]), often crude ("Romeo's still got a – Raging hard-on – For Juliet" [94]), and full of ums, ands, ahhs.[35] Though each monologue tells the entire story of *Romeo and Juliet,* they're arranged asymptotically, curving increasingly close to, but never fully capturing, the narrative and tonal vector of Shakespeare's script. Not surprisingly, what remains in the memory are the play's key scenes: the Capulet ball and the meeting of the lovers; the balcony scene; a contrived plot involving poison and feigned death; the final scene in the tomb. Some respondents recall the Nurse (often identified as a maid), others Paris, the Friar, the apothecary, Tybalt, and/or the "guy with a very – Flourishy name like – Like – uh. . . EURISTHEPISS!" (90). Some are more focused on whether or when or how often Romeo and Juliet have sex; some remain baffled by the logic of the poison intrigue. Yet even when reduced to mere narrative, to plot, *Romeo and Juliet* is remembered as an intrinsically verbal organism, its action bound to specific lines of dialogue, regained through a manifest effort of memorial reconstruction:

> "What light –
> Through yonder window
> Speaks?
> It is the East!
> And Juliet is the West!"
> (*cough*)
> Something like that. (84)

How does this *Romeo and Juliet* represent Shakespeare at the intersection between literary drama and the embodied work of performance? The dramatic action of Shakespeare's writing is (literally) recalled to the stage, but does not determine the process, the texture so to speak, of the event. This *Romeo and Juliet* alienates the "plot" of Shakespeare's play, which is represented at the confluence of individual memory and sustaining social institutions: literature, the schools, the stage. So, too, the performance – underlined as historical burlesque – is also alienated from its conventional dramatic function, "interpreting" dramatic language. Taking up Lawrence Levine's complaint that "historians and critics" have "arbitrarily separated the 'action and oratory' of Shakespeare's plays from the 'dramatic and poetic artistry' with which they were, in reality, so intricately connected" in the nineteenth century (*Highbrow/ Lowbrow* 35), the Nature Theater *Romeo and Juliet* reproduces the historical institutions – the school, the stage – of Shakespeare performance as a means for the transmission of that essentially "poetic" artistry.

Romeo and Juliet locates the encounter with Shakespeare as contact narrative: Shakespeare in school. Though it might seem to "catalog an utter failure of literary education" (Keithley, "Uncreative Writing" 70), it would be fairer to say that *Romeo and Juliet* charts the fortunes of the "all-but-compulsory exposure" to Shakespeare in American secondary education, a Shakespeare conceived less in terms of a specifically "literary" or "theatrical" pedagogy than more broadly as "the locus of pedagogical experience for Americans" (Albanese, *Extramural Shakespeare* 69, 67). The essentially "popular" nineteenth-century Shakespeare – widely performed, routinely excerpted, extensively burlesqued, sharing the bill with music, skits, acrobats, and animal acts – celebrated by Lawrence Levine (and more recently by the National Endowment for the Arts' Shakespeare in American Communities project) has been succeeded, Denise Albanese argues, not by the elite, academic, "highbrow" Shakespeare of academic scholarship, but by a Shakespeare retailed through "the *culture of mass education*, an institution whose production began [. . .] with the rising to prominence of industrialized capitalism at the turn of the twentieth century" (70), and bears with it the social and cultural impulses of its inception. As Joseph Quincy Adams pointed out at the Folger Shakespeare Library in 1932, public education expanded just as "the forces of immigration became a menace to the preservation of our long-established English civilization," situating Shakespeare as "the cornerstone of cultural discipline," as indeed "the chief object of their [students'] study and veneration" (quoted in Bristol, *Shakespeare's America* 79). Evoking anxieties about the impact of immigration in the United States, Adams's still familiar rhetoric pinpoints the stress-line running through Shakespeare's alleged function in the culture of American teaching and American theatre. Shakespeare is certainly good for (disciplining, legitimizing, humanizing, homogenizing, globalizing) *us*, but are *we* good enough for Shakespeare?

The celebration of school Shakespeare as an instrument of potentially transformative class ambition structuring mass education cannot, however, overcome the inherent mystification of the project, at least according to *Romeo and Juliet*'s informants: "I don't know why, but this is the first Shakespeare play you read, generally" (85); it's "the überplay for high school, And then once you hit college – It becomes *Hamlet*" (86). School assimilates and disciplines its potentially distracted and rebellious flock to the Shakespeare curriculum, leading it for some reason, "I don't know why," from *Romeo and Juliet* to *Hamlet* and then . . . out – out of school, out of Shakespeare. While several of the respondents remember reading the play, they don't seem to "remember reading it" with, say, veneration, or even much interest. For one informant, what lives in memory is not reading *Romeo and Juliet* but watching a girl reading it in gym class ("I think I fell in love with HER a little. [. . .] I remember being really impressed – By her!); in the end reading the play didn't have "much of an effect on me" (87–88). Perhaps surprisingly, the Nature Theater experimental performance asserts Shakespeare as a literary event, an event of reading; and yet, *pace* Berger and Bloom, the purposes and pleasures of that performance are finally as fugitive as its words.

The Nature Theater's "in your own words" *Romeo and Juliet* stages an ambivalent regard for the literary drama. Performing the playwright's words, his language, as a "literature" beyond reach, beyond comprehension, *Romeo and Juliet* evokes a pervasive – if pervasively disowned – genre of instructional performance: the translation to an idiomatic Shakespeare text as a means of preserving any Shakespeare at all. We're a long way, now, from New Criticism's heresy of paraphrase. As the teacher's guide to the National Endowment for the Arts' Shakespeare in American Communities project suggests, contemporary "study and veneration" of Shakespeare requires a contemporary lexicon: in one assignment, students should "write their own versions" of selected Shakespeare monologues, "modernizing the diction and the situation, but preserving the structure, themes, and emotions" of the original (*Teacher's Guide* 17).[36] Of course, the verbal "modernizing" – "repurposing" is Thomas Cartelli's apt term ("Doing it Slant" 33) – of Shakespeare's plays dates back nearly to Shakespeare's day, taking in cultural landmarks from Nahum Tate's *King Lear*, to the Lambs' *Tales from Shakespeare*, to the highly edited and emended text of Laurence Olivier's film *Hamlet*, to popular burlesques from Twain to *Gilligan's Island* and beyond. The Nature Theater of Oklahoma *Romeo and Juliet* addresses the desire to preserve Shakespeare's play as a "cornerstone of cultural discipline," while also performing what Cartelli has called "the rapidly diminishing legibility" – and performativity – "of 'original-language Shakespeare'" (27).

And yet this need to repurpose the words is not merely a literary, reading problem. The performative dimension of Shakespeare's words has also been lost, the sense of the range of animating circumstances that might lend them – regardless of lexical meaning – significant force to conceive and contour behavior. This "performative" dimension of modernizing translation not only informs teaching projects (rewriting monologues), but sustains the purpose of the several enterprising publishing series – Shakespeare Made Easy, Side by Sides, No Fear Shakespeare – that offer "THE PLAY *PLUS* A TRANSLATION ANYONE CAN UNDERSTAND" (*No Fear Shakespeare: Romeo & Juliet* cover). These books translate a conviction about the principally verbal nature and value of Shakespearean drama into a marketable commodity, instrumentally extending the purchase of Shakespeare's writing on "cultural discipline." As books, though, they nonetheless also materialize the challenge posed by the drama's representation of and dependence on conventions of social and theatrical behavior, how verbal language gains its point and purpose through changing means of action, performance. Like the Nature Theater of Oklahoma *Romeo and Juliet*, this literature at once asserts the transmission of a legitimate work and an anxious regard for its necessary "transformission" (Clod, "Information on Information" 246) into words and action that rewrite the literary origins of the "original."[37]

Moreover, this literature precisely reciprocates the resistance to performance summoned by the return of the "literary dramatist," by coupling vernacular performance to an essentially literary regard for Shakespeare.[38] Translating the words, and so performing the recondite value, of Shakespeare's "literary drama" to the target audience, these books nevertheless underline the fact that reading the early modern text is less a verbal problem (understanding what the words say) than a behavioral one (understanding how the words gain force in action in an unfamiliar culture of corporeal and social signification).[39] The dense wordplay of the opening moments of *Romeo and Juliet – coals, colliers, choler, collar* – precisely epitomizes this writing/embodiment challenge. Although the outline of the scene's action is relatively straightforward, the verbal register sustaining the motive and tenor of the fight is more distant, footnote reading.

SAMSON Gregory, on my word, we'll not carry coals.
GREGORY No, for then we should be colliers.
SAMSON I mean an we be in choler, we'll draw.
GREGORY Ay, while you live, draw your neck out of collar.
(Norton Shakespeare, *Romeo and Juliet* 1.1.1–4)

SAMPSON
Gregory, I swear, we can't let them humiliate us. We won't take their garbage.

GREGORY
(*teasing* SAMPSON) No, because then we'd be garbage-men.

SAMPSON
What I mean is, if they make us angry we'll pull out our swords.

GREGORY
Maybe you should focus on pulling yourself out of trouble, Sampson.
(*No Fear Shakespeare: Romeo & Juliet*)

SAMPSON They'll not rub our noses in the dirt, Gregory, believe me!
GREGORY No, because then we'd be as grimy as miners.
SAMPSON I mean, if we get hot under the collar, we'll fight!
[*He grips his sword, to show he is ready to draw it*]
GREGORY [*agreeing*] Okay. Don't put your neck in a noose. It would be more than your life's worth. . .
(*Shakespeare Made Easy: Romeo and Juliet*)

SAMP: *Gregory, really we'll not put up with insults.*
GREG: *No, for then we should be mere servants.*
SAMP: *I mean it; and if we be angry, we'll draw our swords.*
GREG: *Yes, but while you are alive, escape the Prince's noose.*
(*Side by Sides: Romeo and Juliet*)

The opacities here are visible enough: neither carrying coal nor working as a collier has much resonance with many contemporary readers, and *colliers* and *choler* are perhaps unfamiliar words. Even without recourse to miming the hangman's noose to illustrate *collar*, the problem here is performative: how to render a verbal translation in which the *new* words recognizably motivate the complex slights of Verona's rigid status culture as accessible, modern performatives. The wounds are surely familiar – daily life for high-school readers – but the words, vehicles for the compressed violence and bawdry that drive the pulse of early modern masculinity, have not so much lost their meaning as their visible agency, their power to "do things," as J. L. Austin might put it. *No Fear* more or less retains *coals/colliers* by reiterating "take their garbage" as "be garbage-men," nicely reworking the injurious drift from servant to collier as a decline from servant to garbage-man, metonymically to garbage itself. *Shakespeare Made Easy* keeps the mining notion, and effectively if prosaically animates the experience of status loss, how it feels to be soiled by an insulting slight.[40]

Like kneeling, swordplay, hat business, the force of Shakespeare's language in its early modern social context is finally untranslatable, in part because, like all scenes of the performative, it lies outside the text. When Samson comes up with the idea to bite his thumb at the Montague dogs ("which is disgrace to them if they bear it" 1.1.37–8), *Shakespeare Made Easy* translates the gesture: "I'll thumb my nose at them. They'll be disgraced if they put up with that [*He makes a quick rude gesture*]." Though we may well wonder whether thumbing one's nose is legible either, what's clear is that the actor's gesture must be visibly insulting. *No Fear* helpfully notes, "Biting the thumb is a gesture of disrespect." But a different disrespect is encoded in translating "Do you bite your thumb at us, sir?" as "Hey, are you biting your thumb at us?" Although the gesture is readily made insulting and aggressive enough, *No Fear Shakespeare* lends verbal assistance, deleting the apparently useless *sir* in favor of the colloquial *Hey*. Granted, the social power encoded by polite forms of address may be unfamiliar to some American youth, but *No Fear Shakespeare* illustrates the underlying problematic of modernizing translation: to understand language as gesture, a gesture whose force – like that of the words themselves – will finally be invented as performance.[41]

These books speak, as announced on the *No Fear* frontispiece, to a performance anxiety, the fear that reading through the footnotes leads to the failed performance of reading, the loss of what Mihaly Csikszentmihalyi calls "flow" (see *Beyond Boredom*).[42]

> **FEAR NOT.**
>
> Have you ever found yourself looking at a Shakespeare play, then down at the footnotes, then back at the play, and still not understanding? You know what the individual words mean, but they don't add up. SparkNotes' *No Fear Shakespeare* will help you break through all that. Put the pieces together with our easy-to-read translations. Soon you'll be reading Shakespeare's own words fearlessly – and actually enjoying it. (*No Fear Shakespeare: Romeo & Juliet* v)

As texts, *No Fear* and the other guides point to an irremediable dimension of performance: when we're staging the "past," the idiom of performance can only avail itself of contemporary codes of embodiment, action. Even "reconstruction" is a relentlessly contemporary genre of performance. When actors speak Shakespeare's English, the words are grounded, gain their force as performance, through contemporary behavior. We may not follow *coals/colliers/choler/collar*, but for the scene to achieve any purpose in action, we must feel the swagger, the volatile desire to trash these guys, without being trashed by them. Although Lukas Erne and others have been concerned by the extent to which performance has "become a central component of Shakespeare studies" (*Literary Dramatist* 20), in these "translations," a more satisfying reading performance is promoted as encouraging the fearless return to the "original" text, much as "the desire to read Shakespeare for pleasure and enrichment follows from a visit to the theater" (*Shakespeare Made Easy: Romeo and Juliet* 6). Kastan's anxiety that Shakespeare becomes "for every age a contemporary playwright" (*Shakespeare and the Book* 7) is, in this sense, a legacy of print, appearing to preserve a reading work whose performatives can be – imaginatively, perhaps – reconstructed. Modernizing "translations" reciprocally perform what Michael Bristol has called an "idealization of the literary material," sanctioning "a 'return to the text' as the decisive ethical move, conceding authority to Shakespeare and then moving directly to the question of what the great author has to say" (*Shakespeare's America* 91). The problem is that we don't know what the great author has to say unless we can animate the theatrical circumstances in which his actors and characters say – and *do* – it, circumstances that continually change what we can say and do with the words on the page.

Although its verbal register is resolutely "American," like the modern language "translations," the Nature Theater *Romeo and Juliet* stages Shakespeare as book-learning, as "literary drama." Performance may help several of the informants recall the events of *Romeo and Juliet* – one person remembers "more from *West Side Story*" – but they regard these memories as illicit: the musical is "just – BASED – on it. It's not anything exactly like" (80). And while the vernacular may be a way to Shakespeare, in these accounts performance only points to the absence of authentic engagement with "Shakespeare," to what's not there rather than to what is:

> And you know what's sad is that I read it in high school,
> And really what I'm remembering is the movie!
> Which one?
> The Leonardo DiCaprio . . . Claire Danes movie!
> 1999 or something?
> It's really sad that I'm basing my information on that –
> But –
> There you go. (85)

There you go: the "literary drama" that should live in the book and volume of the brain has been swept away by the trivial recordings of performance, a sadly inferior version of the "information" of the play, hardly anything at all. As "information," and as cultural capital, *Romeo and Juliet* appears to degrade when moved from its generative medium (print) to another medium (performance), and most of the monologues struggle to return the author to his proper prominence through quotation. The Nature Theater of Oklahoma stages *Romeo and Juliet* as loss, as lost writing, a phantom document in the personal history of reading. When Romeo "serenades her. While she's – up. On her balcony," the trick of memory may not be the misremembered serenade, but the betrayal of poetic purity by the misleading purposes of performance itself: "(Or maybe that's just for – like theater purposes. I'm not really sure about that)" (89). Faced with performative "information," there's only one thing left to do: "Jeez! Now you got – I'm gonna have to go back and READ it!" (77).

The Nature Theater *Romeo and Juliet* positions the play as a "public object," and Shakespeare's function across a range of differential cultural and social hierarchies is both "more elusive and more pervasive" than a highbrow–lowbrow paradigm might suggest (Albanese, *Extramural Shakespeare* 3, 1). *Romeo and Juliet* implies that the purchase of *West Side Story* or Luhrmann's aggressively titled *William Shakespeare's Romeo + Juliet* – recalled also by the production's sound design, which scores the finale to the strains of Luhrmann's delicate theme – or any "theater purposes" on our memory, or on *Romeo and Juliet*, is a melancholic one, the introjection of loss, an unhealing wound, the scar left when the true artwork is withdrawn. *Romeo and Juliet*, Shakespeare, are sites of shaming failure: the failure of the memory to store a culturally licensed narrative more completely, with more accurate quotation from the text. Although reading the words requires their translation to a legible scene in which they might have conceivable performative force, the book – not the stage or the screen – is the source of Shakespearean mastery. *No Fear*, after all, promises that we will soon be "actually enjoying" Shakespeare.

Thematically, the Nature Theater *Romeo and Juliet* explores the complex cultural division of modern Shakespeare – authorial text versus deauthorizing performance. And as *The Murder of Gonzago* reminds us, nothing looks more like theatre than obsolete conventions of performance: while the dialogue of this *Romeo and Juliet* emphasizes the irrecoverable absence of the text, the performance renders a decisively "Shakespearean" acting perhaps all too present (see Figure 1). Recalling Twain's mockery in *Huckleberry Finn*, in *Romeo and Juliet* a grandiose theatricality displaces and replaces Shakespeare's dialogue. The two actors – Anne Gridley costumed in an ill-fitting, peach-colored, empire-waisted frock, with a plastic coronet of garland and flowers; Robert M. Johanson Hamlet-like, black tights, sleeveless frilly black doublet, street shoes adorned with large, fake buckles – each strike poses reminiscent of the high-rhetorical style of the nineteenth-century stage, often with little regard to the words they are actually speaking.[43] An oversized attitude of supplication – arms raised to the heavens, face clenched with outsized passion – is as likely to embody "Ummm" as any of Shakespeare's scripted words. The gestures are large, sweeping, grandiloquent; facial expression is impassioned, muscles taut, teeth bared, eyes flaring. The vocal register, especially Johanson's, is deep, thrilling. Perhaps again recalling Twain's satire, the "theatrical" character

Figure 1. Anne Gridley in The Nature Theater of Oklahoma *Romeo and Juliet* (Photo and Design: Peter Nigrini).

of the actors' physical performance is emphasized by what we might call its semiotic independence from the script or from acting conventions of psychologically expressive character. The prompt-box center stage is inhabited by a prompter, who actually prompts the performance (she also exits on to the stage twice, dancing around in a chicken costume). But rather than hissing forgotten lines, the prompter (Elisabeth Conner) sits before a Kafkaesque ledger (placed flat on the stage before the prompter's box), which has the script on the left, and on the facing right page several columns of notation: ILLUSTRATION, for grand "Shakespearean" gestures; EMOTION, which lists the psychological register of the action; and BEHAVIOR, small, somewhat out-of-character acts. Reversing the sense of the dramatic text as metaphorically scoring the actors' performances, in *Romeo and Juliet* it's the prompter who "is a conductor reading a very complex score" (Nature Theater of Oklahoma, Talkback), evoking the actors' movement and gesture from a book that only she can read, in a performance only the actors are privileged to see. As Elisabeth Conner notes, "I am giving them every gesture they make through the entre production" (Talkback).

Romeo and Juliet is not "scored" by the Shakespearean text, understood as an anticipatory digest of appropriate subsequent performance; the prompter conducts the performance in the discourse of performance, the conventions of embodiment native to her stage. At the opening of "Anne's" second monologue, for example, the prompter has a range of ILLUSTRATION to choose from ("R. arm higher, L. arm back, hand at hip," or "R. hand way UP, L. hand way UP. Drop both") as well as EMOTION ("Ecstatic," "Serious," "Lovely," "Dancing," "Towering"), and BEHAVIOR ("Smooth eyebrow," "Adjust bra strap"). During each performance, the prompter directs a new combination of gestures to the actors: they know more or less when they will be prompted, but not what gesture they will perform (Copper, Message, 6 July 2010). Perhaps the most fascinating performance is hidden from the audience, as the prompter signals Gridley and Johanson both by miming the gestures (raising her arms, smoothing her eyebrows) and by making the facial expressions (ecstatic, serious) that the actors will then imitate (see Figure 2).

In much of its work, Nature Theater explores the interplay between theatricality and textuality, often by reframing "the text" and the kind of work it's made to do in and by performance: in *Poetics*, they have a "chart for each actor with a grid and mathematical coordinates and time signatures, indicating where they should go at what time"; for *No Dice*, they use "edited sound files of [. . .] recorded phone conversations," something like the recordings that Gridley and Johanson hear throughout the performance of *Romeo and Juliet* (Lee, "Nature Theater of Oklahoma"). In *Life and Times, Part 1*, the actors sing a long autobiographical narrative, while the prompter uses flash cards to direct a series of largely abstract gestures, movements, and choreographies, shuffling the deck before each performance, while the actors facially mirror different members of the audience. *Life and Times* continues to expand its parts (to an epic six, at

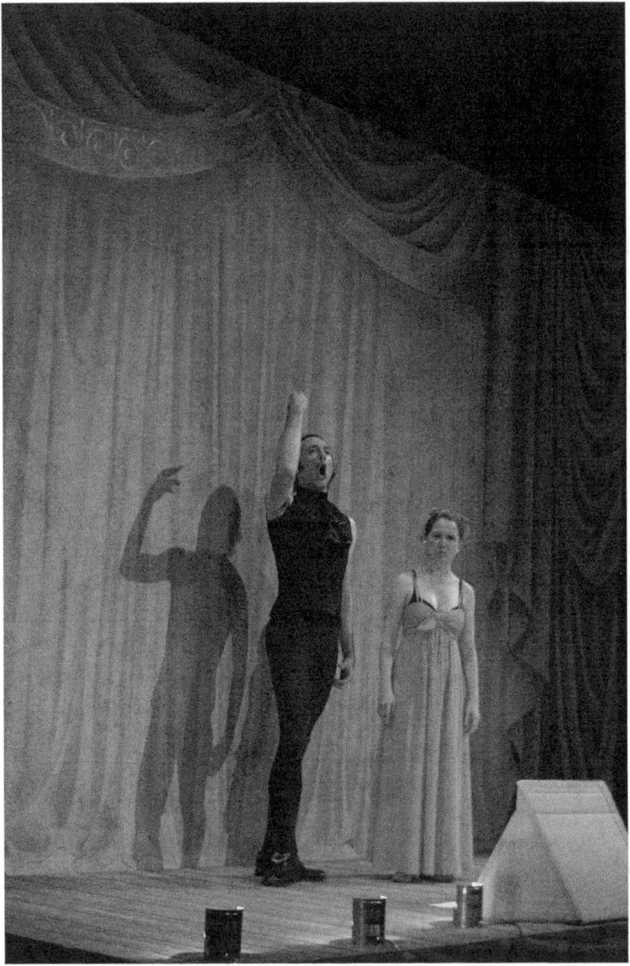

Figure 2. Robert M. Johanson and Anne Gridley rehearsing The Nature Theater of Oklahoma *Romeo and Juliet*. In this image, the footlights and the prompter's box are still under construction, showing the handmade character of the set. The prompter's box was unchanged in performance, other than being painted to resemble – very distantly – wood (Photo and Design: Peter Nigrini).

this writing), each of which stages a different relation between writing, narration, embodiment, and scenography, witnessing the company's effort to "use the readymade material around us, found space, overheard speech, and observed gesture, and through extreme formal manipulation, and superhuman effort, [to] effect in our work a shift in the perception of everyday reality that extends beyond the site of performance and into the world in which we live" (Nature Theater, oktheater.org). This experimental orientation toward the function of writing in performance imposes a formally rigorous aesthetic of chance on the narrative, in part by using an assortment of textualities – charts, graphs, tables, ledgers, flash cards – to qualify the determining force attributed to the verbal script, that listing of spoken words, in the practices of conventional theatre. Not surprisingly, Nature Theater is also involved in a distinctly literary enterprise, writing an ongoing epic through similar serial/chance techniques (see Nature Theater, "Pentameter"). In *Romeo and Juliet*, this postdramatic encounter with the text disrupts the role attributed to Shakespearean writing in the culture of performance, as the behavioral text displaces the functions often imagined to arise from the verbal script: directing the physical, psychological dynamics of performance.

The traces of Shakespearean narrative and poetry evanesce from the speakers' memories, but the signs of "Shakespearean" theatre are overwhelmingly, absurdly present onstage. While the diction is contemporary American, the appropriate accent of Shakespeare performance is exaggerated, rather British-inflected. The high style of an earlier era tends at once to magnify the "theatrical" character of the performance – recalling a moment in American theatre when declamation was closely associated with social improvement (see Roach, "Emergence of the American Actor" 351) – and to ironize it, as well as its incoherent, stammering, clearly "American" script. The accents of this *Romeo and Juliet* are not so much blemished by what Poe called "an occasional Anglicism of accent" (quoted in Roach, "Emergence of the American Actor" 342), as they are – hilariously – the invention of the stage: "balcony" becomes "bal-cOny" (rhymes with "phoney"); interrogatives are heavily aspirated ("Hwhy" "Hwhen"; these are marked in the ledger in yellow highlighter, and a note at the end marked "TASKS" reminds both prompter and actors "WH'S"); words like "HHHonest" are given an almost Cockney haitch.[44] Consonants are stressed in surprising ways ("sword" becomes "sWWord"; "dead" is almost always "dea-duh"). When in doubt, diphthong: "doomed" becomes "dee-yoomed"; "moon" is "mewn," and so on. Some sounds are clearly at home only on the stage: "morgue" becomes "MOR-gwah," "poison" and "potion" become "POI-see-on" and "PO-see-on." Perhaps inevitably, an "actor" is always an "ac-TOWR." Shakespeare's *Romeo and Juliet* lives in the book, in lines shamefacedly misrecalled from high school, as "information" sadly displaced in memory by the noise of popular films. It requires elaborate modern translation for fearful readers, and while it provides a useful vehicle for performance, it's rendered ineffably ludicrous by the outsized discourse native to its stage.

As Pavol Liska remarked in a talkback following a 2103 Berlin performance, "I was never interested in Shakespeare or *Romeo and Juliet* ... It's really more of an archaeological than a literary project" (Nature Theater of Oklahoma, Talkback). Although the language of this *Romeo and Juliet* is contemporary, its performance métier is assertively obsolete, locating Shakespeare in a traditional, theatrical past. And yet, as Richard Schoch observes of Shakespeare burlesque more generally, such "parody in fact preserves the continuity of literary traditions" (*Not Shakespeare* 19). For Kelly Copper, who conceived and directed *Romeo and Juliet* with Liska, the experience of touring abroad and being told by European audiences that the company's idiom seemed very "American" prompted an interest in the history of American acting. The competition between Edwin Forrest and William Charles Macready that ignited the Astor Place Riots in 1849 inspired the performance style of *Romeo and Juliet* (Copper, Message, 6 July 2010; Keithley, "Uncreative Writing" 68), and an interest in the scenography of American traveling theatres informed the scenic design, a foreshortened wooden stage, six footlights obviously fitted up from coffee cans, a wood-painted cardboard prompter's box, a stained and tattered backcloth of beige and blue curtains.[45]

Characterizing how the "cultural work that actors do often nominates them as caretakers of memory," Joseph Roach describes the contradiction "at the heart of many American self-conceptions, between nostalgia and progress" ("Emergence of the American Actor" 338, 339), a contradiction extended and reciprocated here, as *Romeo and Juliet* invokes the nostalgia for the democratic impulse of nineteenth-century touring Shakespeare that haunts the modern American theatrical imaginary. Produced by a traveling company (Nature Theater more often performs in Europe than in the US) who pack up the show in a bag, *Romeo and Juliet* decisively occupies the intersection of a network of Shakespearean representations – in literature, theatre, history, pedagogy – and so evokes the wider cultural field of the "return of the author." As school-inflected, Twainesque, Shakespearean Americana, it oddly reciprocates the most visible effort to restore the fantasy of nineteenth-century democratic Shakespeare to American arts and pedagogy, the National Endowment for the Arts' Shakespeare in American Communities project, which sponsors both touring Shakespeare productions and an extensive pedagogical apparatus. For all that this project may have been designed to preserve the NEA from financial and ideological assault under the sign of Shakespeare, it clearly functions as an instrument of ideological retrenchment, as Roger Kimball suggested in 2004, lauding then chairman Dana Gioia for turning the NEA away from "Robert Mapplethorpe, photographs of crucifixes floating in urine, and performance artists prancing about naked, smeared with chocolate, and skirling about the evils of patriarchy." Shakespeare in American Communities expresses a distinct vision of the appropriate purposes of the NEA: to "cut out the cutting edge and put back the art" ("Farewell Mapplethorpe, Hello Shakespeare").[46] Yet what is striking about the project is less its timid refusal to conceive of art as a means of producing new perspectives, new knowledge, than the ways its Shakespeare articulates a vision of the appropriate function of cultural (presumably as opposed to technological, medical, or scientific) subsidy: to support the "preservation and transmission of artistic culture" in an "enlightened and life-affirming way." Not surprisingly, perhaps, this sense of the proper mission – of subsidy, of the arts – is sustained by a sense of the proper function of performance as well. As Kimball puts it, Gioia "has instituted an important new program to bring Shakespeare to communities across America. And by Shakespeare I mean Shakespeare, not some PoMo rendition that portrays Hamlet in drag or sets *A Midsummer Night's Dream* in a concentration camp" ("Farewell Mapplethorpe, Hello Shakespeare").[47]

The Shakespeare in American Communities project asserts an unexperimental, antielitist Shakespeare, transmitting an image of nineteenth-century popular performance as the sign and instrument of normative American culture. Distracting facts of the nineteenth-century democratic Shakespeare tradition are simply cast in the shade of a bright and urgent nostalgia – Charlotte Cushman's famously erotic Romeo of the 1840s (played opposite her sister as Juliet) and her later celebrity as a "Hamlet in drag" come to mind. Like all acts of surrogation, the NEA revival of lost "traditions" performs a politicized forgetting, in order to denounce a history in which Shakespeare's "work gradually came to be seen as part of high culture rather than popular culture," a mandarin literature to which "everyday people could hardly relate" (*Shakespeare in American Communities: Teacher's Guide* 14). To restore this everyday Shakespeare, the project aims to "revitalize the long-standing American theatrical tradition of touring" (National Endowment for the Arts, "Shakespeare in American Communities" 3), represented here as a strategy of free-market, American, democratic "choice" rather than – as it has been throughout history – a "choice" enforced by the vagaries of the market, by laws prohibiting settled theatre companies, by the plague, and so on (perhaps the most familiar vision of the consequences of this "tradition" is Eugene

O'Neill's portrait of the tragic Tyrones in *Long Day's Journey Into Night*). Using a familiar trope of American neoliberal political rhetoric (identifying economic with political structures, the market with democracy), the project revalues business practice (touring, both then and now) as a vehicle of cultural democratization and improvement, which has been mysteriously displaced by suspect, specialized performance forms that do not cater to the broader republic: "Specialized theaters evolved that catered to distinct interests such as avant-garde theater, theater of the absurd, and musical theater" (*Shakespeare in American Communities: Teacher's Guide* 14). As Amanda Giguere notes, the nineteenth-century stage provides the focus for a "collective desire to return to simpler times, with no terrorism, no fear of attack, and no moral ambiguity" (*Shakespeare in American Communities* 60).[48]

The past, Robert Frost knew, is made simple by the loss of detail ("Directive").[49] Setting aside misinformation, the project's teacher's guide represents Shakespeare as the founding father of the republic of American theatre, asserting the undocumented claim that "When the English colonists sailed for the New World, they brought only their most precious and essential possessions with them, including the works of William Shakespeare" (*Shakespeare in American Communities: Teacher's Guide* 13).[50] By 1750, after half a century of colonial theatre, Shakespeare was numbered among both original American works and popular British hits – Farquhar's *The Recruiting Officer*, Otway's *The Orphan*, Addison's *Cato*, among others (see Wilmeth and Curley, "Timeline") – which, like Shakespeare, may also have been associated with royalist rather than patriot taste.[51] Like their British counterparts, great American actors of the nineteenth century, including Edwin Forrest (1806–1872), were as well known for their non-Shakespearean roles as they were for their Shakespearean ones (Forrest played blackface comedy before his celebrated Othello, and – in another act of racial appropriation – starred in the "aboriginal" drama he commissioned, John Augustus Stone's *Metamora*). Ira Aldridge (1807–1867), the "African Roscius," played Rolla in Sheridan's *Pizarro* before undertaking a brilliant career performing Othello, Lear, and other Shakespeare roles in commercial and court theatres from London to St. Petersburg to Łodz, Poland, where he is buried, a racial exile from playing Shakespeare in the American communities of his day. The teacher's guide features a photograph of Paul Robeson as Othello, remarking that "Shakespeare's plays were performed by well-known film actors in the twentieth century" (14), but takes no note of Robeson's own history of racial and political struggle in the United States, his blacklisting as a "well-known film actor," or that his first performance as Othello opposite a white actress took place in London (with Peggy Ashcroft in 1930); the American community waited until the 1943/1944 season to see Robeson play Othello to Uta Hagen's Desdemona.[52] As Ayanna Thompson notes, while the "new generation" learning Shakespeare in school is depicted in the Shakespeare in American Communities teaching DVD "as something that is not surburban and white, the NEA mentions ethnicity, and specifically refers to Native American populations, but eschews engagement with explicit dialogues about race" (*Passing Strange* 133).

The NEA's revisionist cultural politics is clearest at the few moments when the nineteenth-century stage is addressed, at least by literary proxy. Predictably enough, the sign that "Shakespeare was so integrated into American culture by the nineteenth century" is Twain's famous scene, in which "Twain had his young hero Huckleberry Finn travel along the Mississippi River by raft with a pair of rogues who tried to pass themselves off as Shakespearean actors to earn money in riverbank towns" (*Shakespeare in American Communities: Teacher's Guide* 14). Despite Twain's double-barrelled satire (the actors and their audiences are both impostors here), the teacher's guide takes this incident to epitomize the loss of an "oratorical mode of entertainment and education that was prevalent throughout the nineteenth century," a loss which now makes Shakespeare's "words alien to a people who once so effortlessly understood their power," if not – to judge by the Duke, the Dauphin, their audiences – their meaning (15).

Shakespeare in American Communities restores a theatrical "tradition" buffed clean of inconvenient detail. Typically rewriting and restructuring the plays to suit its own stage practices and a host of burlesque, artistic, racist, economic, and nationalist purposes, the nineteenth-century American theatre routinely violated the sacred "words" of Shakespearean drama.[53] The materiality of the nineteenth-century stage, even the hardship of theatrical touring, isn't that important to the project because theatre, finally, is significant only as a vehicle for the assertion of literary value and the cultural norms said to be enshrined there. How does performance figure in its touring mission and in the scene of pedagogy? Despite the fact that seventy-seven theatre companies from thirty-nine states have performed in over two thousand municipalities in all fifty states, the "educational materials [. . .] used by more than 20 million students to enhance their understanding and appreciation for the language and theatricality of Shakespeare's plays" provide no guidance – indeed provide no mention – of how the "more than one million high school students" who "have now seen a professional production of Shakespeare" should engage with it critically ("Chairman's Message," National Endowment for the Arts, "Shakespeare in American Communities" 1). Performance is not an object of study, Shakespeare is. Performance is merely the means to "bringing the best of live theater to new audiences" (Gioia, quoted in "Shakespeare in American Communities" 3).[54]

When performance does appear in these materials, its purpose is to immerse students "in great thoughts and great language," typically through the practice of "Modernizing Monologues" (*Shakespeare in American Communities: Teacher's Guide* 17), and rewriting the sonnets as prose love letters (18), a practice which traces its own gesture of nostalgia, replicating the nineteenth-century tradition of decontextualizing passages for moral and rhetorical instruction, oratory as a means of identifying a spiritualized literature with evangelically troped notions of national identity.[55] Snippets of Shakespeare isolated for moral and oratorical instruction: the fantasy of nineteenth-century theatre sustains the restoration of nineteenth-century pedagogy. When students do perform, performance is articulated as a competitive program of textual delivery, a recitation contest in which students listen to passages recited by well-known actors on CD, study them, and perform them; teachers have a grading chart taking in volume, speed, voice inflection, posture and presence, evidence of understanding, pronunciation, and eye contact. "Two winners from each school will be sent an official award document from the National Endowment for the Arts, signed by Chairman Dana Gioia" (National Endowment for the Arts, *Shakespeare in American Communities: Recitation Contest* 5).[56] Alternatively, students are invited to perform a "Scene outside the Globe," improvising social interactions from a one-paragraph biography of various real and imagined figures – Queen Elizabeth I, the Earl of Essex, Sir Francis Drake, Boy Apprentice Actor, Wet Nurse – in order to "demonstrate their understanding" of "the social structure of Elizabethan England" learned from the essay of about 1,300 words provided in the teacher's guide (20).[57]

As Kimball's remarks suggest, the project has little to do with the discourse of experimental performance; more to the point, it resists taking performance *as* experimental, as a means to new knowledge, creative insight. Performance is understood as predicated on the "literary drama" it supplies, identifying "the power of live theater" entirely with "the wonders of the English language, and the masterpieces of William Shakespeare" ("Shakespeare in American Communities" 5). The adjectives tell the story: performance does its proper work when it offers "a production of serious drama" ("Chairman's Message" 1), a "professional production of

Shakespeare" (1), the "best of live theater," "superb live theater," "art of indisputable excellence" ("Shakespeare in American Communities" 1, 3, 5). Shakespeare in American Communities highlights a vision of appropriate performance; either as history or as contemporary practice, performance works to assimilate the values inherent in the artwork to contemporary cultural norms. The ersatz "history" it recounts, the "modernizing" pedagogical performances it directs, and presumably the "superb" performances it funds are understood as "preserving the structure, themes, and emotions" of the Shakespearean original in quintessentially American ways (*Shakespeare in American Communities: Teacher's Guide* 17).

In the conjunction of nostalgic performance surrogation, textual modernizing, and an anxious regard for the potential loss of Shakespeare's words, the Shakespeare in American Communities project and the Nature Theater of Oklahoma *Romeo and Juliet* occupy a common cultural terrain, a terrain shared by the "return of the author" as well. Unlike the polemically antielitist rhetoric of the NEA, the touring NTO refuses an organic linkage between the popular and the populist, framing a surprisingly nuanced inquiry into Shakespearean performance as a means of cultural reproduction.[58] Invoking Shakespeare as a "locus of pedagogy" visualized through the performance of imagined Shakespearean Americana, *Romeo and Juliet* critically reframes the rhetoric shared by the American Communities project. For while it at once modernizes and historicizes Shakespeare "in American," the Nature Theater of Oklahoma *Romeo and Juliet* locates performance less as a means of transmission than of instigation, engaging Richard Schechner's sense that performance "is behavior itself," and what it restores is performance ("Collective Reflexivity" 51).[59]

Fittingly, then, the ethical, rhetorical, historical, and personal challenges of performing Shakespeare in the contemporary theatre take the stage in the final scene. *Romeo and Juliet* closes with the two actors giving yet another "in their own words" performance to reframe the dynamics of contemporary Shakespeare – the Shakespeare that must appear in theatrical performance. The scene opens with a relatively frank discussion of the often distant relation between love and sex, and the extent to which people sometimes sacrifice themselves to impersonate what someone else might find attractive, desirable: "That's kinda what actors do, right?" as "Bobby" puts it (106). "Bobby's" anxiety evokes a complex dis/identification between what the actors do here and the remembered experiences of the earlier monologues. After all, the actors' introjection of Shakespearean language is useless (however much it might contribute to their understanding of Shakespeare) unless it can be incorporated into an act, the action that sustains the peculiar relations of theatre. As the welter of guides to acting Shakespeare suggest, performing Shakespearean drama in the modern English-speaking theatre produces problems analogous to those facing readers of Shakespeare's plays: how can this foreign language and the behavioral complex of an alien culture gain theatrical force as a legible genre of modern performance? Much like the anxiety of schooled Shakespeare, acting Shakespeare engages a deeply ethical concern arising in part from the value attributed to Shakespeare, and more immediately from the sociability of theatre: for actors, the audience is not an absent collective of passive spectators but a resonant, active collaborator whose "power of associating and dissociating" contours the event (Rancière, *Emancipated Spectator* 17). After all, too little association (sleep, early exit) or too much (enthusiastic repartee, rioting) destroys the performance. Perhaps the actor should speak to the audience in his own voice, using the exposure, the defenselessness intrinsic to performance as a means to invite sympathy, association: "Oh couldn't a LITTLE NEEDINESS WORK?!?" "I mean – what's the difference between needy – neediness – ??? And being vulnerable?" (108). Understood as both the means and signifier of successful contemporary Anglo-American acting, *vulnerability* is also the literal register of the professional actor's condition, accentuated by the fact that the public pays to see something that – to judge by the evidence here – perhaps can never appear on the stage, the "literary drama," Shakespeare. More than in the competitive classroom, where reciting the text can be calibrated to a grade, performance appears to be a losing proposition. In the theatre, it isn't a competition with classmates; it's a competition with a transcendent, ever evanescent, wordy presence – it's "a competition with Shakespeare" (112).

As the reciprocal enthusiasm for the "return of the author" from the grip of performance and the liberation of "postdramatic" theatre from the clutches of the literary drama imply, competition is the substance of contemporary Shakespeare performance, which struggles to wrest the drama from its literary moorings into living behavior. Wrapping his arms around "Anne" from behind, fondling her, kissing and licking her ear, "Bobby" asks,

> What does OUR scene have?
> (*pause*)
> That could compete with – Shakespeare's. (112)

Everything and nothing: the seduction of the body seems to stand apart from the discussion, as "Anne," more or less ignoring him, points out that contemporary actors are "PROBABLY – a little OLDER? Than – most

Shakespearean actors were," and so able "to bring something different? – to the performance? (*pause*) Than the actors of Shakespeare's time would have brought to it?" What we have, of course, is not only women onstage ("For ONE thing, they were all MALE!"), but an alienated perspective, "a MODERN SENSIBILITY" that distantiates the drama: "we get the JOY! – of – trying to figure out – why this play still works today! Or why it CAN still work today!" (112–113), or, to put a finer point on it, whether what works today is "it" at all – Shakespeare's *Romeo and Juliet* or its charismatic, inalienable, uncanny (*No Fear*) double. The task of making *the play* work today differentiates us from Shakespeare: "What is it about the WORDS – that Shakespeare chose to use? – the language that he used? – that makes the play so compelling?" (113) and, evidently, so resistant, to memory and to the stage?

It's difficult to know how to take this question, especially as it is voiced – ShakesPE-AH, LANG-wadge – in this production, which opens a melancholy gap between writing and performing, and seems to long for an impossible fidelity that would transcend the accent of theatre altogether. The Nature Theater of Oklahoma *Romeo and Juliet* stages a performance "about the WORDS," but shows that words – the substance of written literature – are inevitably transformed into something else (action, behavior, performance) by the vagaries of memory, the manifest conventions of the stage, the vulnerable yet dynamic activity of actors and audiences. Using words to frame behavior is the performative challenge, to undertake a legible embodiment in which doing things with words can gain the complex provisional force of action onstage. To recall Kenneth Burke for a moment, theatre necessarily redoubles the *ratios* of dramatic action, sustaining the purposes, agents, and agencies of the drama with its own. "Bobby's" purposes – like those of any actor – can never be fully aligned with Shakespeare's, or Romeo's, a point perhaps implied by his answer to "Anne's" question, "What is it about the WORDS?" of the play: "I don't know. I haven't read it."

BOBBY It's not time yet. That's what I know.
ANNE All right...
BOBBY I shouldn't read it yet.
ANNE All right...
BOBBY 'Cause then talkin' to you would be pointless! (113)

"Bobby," perhaps, wants to keep his eventual performance in the play fresh, alive, but in this moment *Romeo and Juliet* is the instrument of his continued conversation with "Anne," a version, perhaps, of the extended double sonnet joining Romeo and Juliet hand to hand and lip to lip, structuring their mutual performance at the Capulet ball – a scene much remembered, in principle at least, by the play's informants. "What is there to keep me here? – The dialogue" (Beckett, *Endgame* 120–121). In theatre, the script is the means of present action. Lehmann notes a "fundamental *shift from work to event*" (*Postdramatic Theatre* 61) in the transition from dramatic to postdramatic theatre, but while "Anne" longs for a theatre of the literary work, "Bobby" represents the scripted drama as an instrument of the occasion, part of an event that necessarily redefines the literary work for its own seductive purposes.

Blackout. Applause rises, the house lights come back on, and Anne Gridley and Robert Johanson and Elisabeth Conner take their bows. The play is over, the audience begins to stir from its seats and head for the exits. And then blackout again. Over the PA system we hear a highly edited version of the balcony scene from "But soft!..." through "Sleep dwell upon thine eyes": it's Gridley and Johanson, in a delicate, nuanced performance, low-key, intense, contemporary Shakespeare, "in American" (in the 2010 performance at the Kitchen in New York, this dialogue was piped over the sound system; in the 2013 Berlin performance at the HAU, Gridley and Johanson spoke it from the stage, in the dark).[60] In contrast to the play we've witnessed onstage, where the theatrical body and its resources are always out of scale to the apparent expression of the script, here "Shakespeare" speaks directly to us out of the darkness, idiomatically, unmarked by troublesome bodies, their movements and gestures, the actor's failing memory and stagey rhetoric.[61] The actors no longer act, they "recite in the dark" (113). There have been other voices, mediated "into" the actors, so to speak, via their visible earbuds, and "out" of them too, as words signally held apart from their incarnation as acting by the stagey theatricality of posture, gesture, movement, and intonation. Closing with a voice-over, this *Romeo and Juliet* perhaps implies that Shakespeare performance today leaves no place for actors to inhabit. And while we still inhabit the theatre, our relation to the now invisible actors is no longer theatrical – we have been transformed from agents of the scene into its objects, consumers of performed LANG-wadge. The voices sustain, ground, clarify, enrich the script; it's a lovely, moving, troubling moment, one that perhaps reinforces a familiar sadness, the forlorn sense that Shakespeare is so purely identified with "the WORDS" that Shakespearean play can transpire now only in words. And yet, the reading also foregrounds its own style in a performance in which *style* has been very much at stake, the extent to which even (mere) reading, recitation, depends for its effectiveness on conventions of emphasis and delivery, volume, speed, voice inflection, and so on. The actors may finally speak "in American," in a modern, Shakespearean voice, but that voice too, for all its native intimacy, is now marked, located in the history of Shakespearean representation, a history that, as Kidnie observes, has tended to make the "text seem fixed, outside of history, to the same extent that performance, pulling in the opposite direction, comes to seem provisional, irremediably contaminated by, or lost to, history" ("Where is *Hamlet*?" 105). *Romeo and Juliet* is, finally, exiled from the stage.

Surrogating the populist, oratorical, American performance derided by Twain and celebrated by the NEA, *Romeo and Juliet* finally summons another nineteenth-century specter. Sitting in the dark, listening to *Romeo and Juliet*, it's hard not to recall Charles Lamb's famous essay on *King Lear*. For Lamb, *Lear* decisively marked an insuperable division between the sublime performance of reading Shakespeare and the disheartening performance of Shakespeare in the theatre: "On the stage we see nothing but corporal infirmities and weakness, the impotence of rage; while we read it, we see not Lear, but we are Lear, – we are in his mind" ("On the Tragedies" 136). Or, in this case, Shakespeare is in ours. This final scene "interpreting" Shakespeare's words perhaps provides a consummation devoutly wished: the return of the author, through direct communion with his words. And yet, like the typically unstable relation between writing and performance, scripted language and stage action, this final scene of textual delivery, recitation, seems to unsettle a sense that writing can and should determine its use onstage, not least by avoiding one of the theatre's defining resources: the physical embodiment of actors. Perhaps dramatic theatre is always about the loss of drama, at least in high print culture; from this perspective, "Authenticity, in other words, always already present in the text, inevitably eludes performance; performance is measured in relation to the text in degrees of *in*fidelity and *in*authenticity" (Kidnie, "Where is *Hamlet*?" 104). Actors may be "caretakers of memory" (Roach, "Emergence of the American Actor" 338), but here they surrogate and so memorialize a remembered mode of performance, all the while urging the disimbrication of acting from subordination to writing. *Romeo and Juliet* locates the "return of the author" in the context of the pedagogical and political uses of Shakespeare. While the notion that the "literary dramatist" needs to be restored to academic critique and education is urgent in that literature, on the stage, it seems that the author has hardly wandered off.

Dedramatizing *Romeo and Juliet*, Nature Theater suspends an organic narrative channeled through naturalized performance conventions that assert a coherent ideological closure between "the text," the fictive whole worlded on the stage, and our own passive consumption of it. To speak in this way is, of course, to render Shakespeare if not a "contemporary playwright," at least in the idiom of contemporary theatre; for Pavol Liska, the production is "an essay about theatre. Or THEE-a-tah" (Talk-back). And yet, this *Romeo and Juliet* is preoccupied with Lamb's question: is there a Shakespeare beyond the book? For the Nature Theater "characters," Shakespeare is a testament both to loss and to desire. *Romeo and Juliet* is, for them, a kind of stigma: the vitality of performance is illicit, mere "theater purposes," and the lapsing memory of the stabilizing text elusive, embarrassing. For the actors, theatre is a site of competition, at once the instrument of their extraordinarily affecting energy and discipline and a monument to the tawdry, the tired – terrible, not terrific. And yet, however evacuated by convention, the generative practice of this performance instantiates theatre as an instrument for making something new, something that takes Shakespeare into its own project of self-invention, something that will happen in this way only once, here and now, with us. Perhaps performance can only bring us farther away from Shakespeare, if by "Shakespeare" we mean the experience we might achieve by reading. That Shakespeare can only arrive in the theatre by undoing theatre, by replacing the stage of an always provisional embodiment with the darkened cavern of a readerly consciousness. The "interpretive" theatre of the master's voice is surely seductive, powerful as an image and instance of the cultural, political, even nationalist endowment of "Shakespeare." Yet, as the Nature Theater of Oklahoma *Romeo and Juliet* shows, however much that theatre may claim to return the author to us, it's finally not theatre at all.

CHAPTER 3

"The written troubles of the brain": writing, character, and the cognition of performance *Punchdrunk Theatre,* Sleep No More

> Canst thou not minister to a mind diseased,
> Pluck from the memory a rooted sorrow,
> Raze out the written troubles of the brain,
> And with some sweet oblivious antidote
> Cleanse the fraught bosom of that perilous stuff
> Which weighs upon the heart?
>
> *Macbeth* (5.3.42–47)

March 2011. We wander up a pitch-black, narrow, winding corridor, stumbling in utter darkness until we meet a light or two, then "seeling night" again (3.2.47).[1] Eventually, *a curtain, and through it a large, red, vintage 1940s hotel bar, with empty bandstand, and a somewhat smarmy maître d', Maxim; he tells us to get a drink. People fill the bar, milling about until Maxim calls all those who were dealt aces at the door. He takes us to a small room, where we're told to don masks – they're white, plastic, cover the entire face, a kind of cross between* Star Wars *stormtrooper, Area 51 alien, and Venice carnival – and informed that the guests of the McKittrick Hotel value their privacy: we're not to speak, and not to remove the masks. Into the elevator: up. Stop, the door opens, and one or two are allowed to exit. Doors close. Down, up. Doors open, we get off, exiting into a dark hallway, turn right into a long, dark room, low mounds of dirt flanking a central pathway. They're studded with crosses: a cemetery. An intense, loamy smell. Thunder, wind. It's entirely creepy. Slowly walk to the end of the cemetery, turn right, into a slightly more illuminated, massive space, divided into dozens of small brick cells of various sizes, the largest perhaps ten feet by ten feet, some with walls four to six feet high, some just a foot or so. Religious statuary in several of the cells. The bluish lighting, soundscape, and imagery are stunning; I'm wondering whether I'll be able to sleep when I get home. We move errantly through the space, eventually coming to the opposite corner: French doors lead into a glassed-in room, large, polished wooden floor. A bathtub, center, on a dais; a banquette on the wall opposite, flanking a bed in the corner, to the left dressing tables and luggage piled to the ceiling; a glassed-in space at the top of the furniture pile. Yet to see a soul. Out into a stairwell, up a floor, into a long corridor: Horvick's poster, candy shop, and the first colleague, someone else in a white mask. Past the candy shop, turn right on to – apparently directly over the cemetery below – a long cobblestone street with "shops" off it, set to a different soundscape, Glenn Miller's "A Nightingale Sang in Berkeley Square." On the right, a tailor's shop (print trays adorn the walls filled with white thimbles), down farther the entrance into a dirt-floored bar, walls of corrugated cardboard boxes, a pool table. The bartender (unmasked – a performer!) is wiping the bar, watching. In the space perhaps thirty minutes, but it's still a little too spooky to sit down, though he makes a kind of wilted gesture toward a table. Back out, on the other side of the "street," opposite the tailor is a room full of taxidermy; a kind of tea shop (a woman, another performer, drinking tea), with a room of some kind behind; an office; another room (the door now locked); and another office – the front room has two desks, a typewriter, hundreds of letters and notes tacked and taped to the walls, filing cabinets, disconsolate old electric fans, and just behind it some kind of ornithological study/darkroom: reddish light, pictures of birds, feathers, and women. "A Nightingale Sang in Berkeley Square" is still playing. While we're studying the birds, the woman from the tea shop comes in, 40s dress, unmasked, agitated but deliberate. She looks through papers around the desk, ignores us, and the two or three (masked) others who have followed her in, leaves.*

It is difficult to overstate the overwhelming impact of space in Punchdrunk Theatre's *Sleep No More*, which opened in New York in February 2011. Staged in the "McKittrick Hotel," an environment installed in three warehouses, *Sleep No More* occupies over 100,000 square feet of playing area (Kennedy, "Success in Jaded New York"), divided into about a hundred richly imagined rooms, spread over six floors (Goodman, "First Look" 2); determining the precise number of rooms is difficult, as some locked rooms have been opened during the run, new spaces have been added, and the producers are understandably reluctant to provide information (Kennedy, "Success in Jaded New York"). Directed by Felix Barrett and Maxine Doyle, designed by Barrett, Livi Vaughan, and Beatrice Moss, choreographed by Doyle, with a soundscape by Stephen Dobbie, the architecture and overall design generally relocate thematic elements associated with *Macbeth* to a 1940s setting, recalling Alfred Hitchcock's *Rebecca* (1940) and the later *Vertigo* (1958) – remember the McKittrick Hotel.[2] Without the title, it might take some time to engage the spirit of *Macbeth*, which is – like the voice Macbeth hears "cry 'Sleep no more, / Macbeth does murder sleep'" (2.2.33–34) – ghostly, ethereal.

Each floor is large and flanked by stairwells marked E and W – the only orientation received in the evening. On the top floor, the fifth (there is, apparently, a sixth floor, but I haven't been taken there; a rooftop bar and themed restaurant have opened as well), is a huge, leafless hardwood forest, blue-lit, rumbling and windy, adjoining a series of hospital rooms: one with eight beds and nightstands (one bed has a "body" of potatoes under the covers); another with tubs and an altar facing a crucifix made of soap bars; a doctor's office, the desk strewn with medical reports and a cabinet filled with hundreds of carefully catalogued hair samples; an examining room, scary Victorian examining chair; a vine-covered padded cell; a laundry; an empty operating theatre (see Figure 3). The "street" level below (fourth floor) also includes a "dead" replica of the "Manderley" bar through which we entered, covered in dust and cobwebs. Just off the "street," behind the taxidermy studio – where one of several stuffed deer peers out through a window – is "Hecate's Apothecary," overflowing with dried flowers and seed boxes, plants hanging from the ceiling, jars and bottles, a magic book, and Satanic runes scrawled on the walls. The "cemetery" level (third floor) is divided into two spaces; the empty room with the tub is the Macbeth suite, adjoining the brick garden, and to the east across the cemetery are the Macduff rooms – a parlor with various

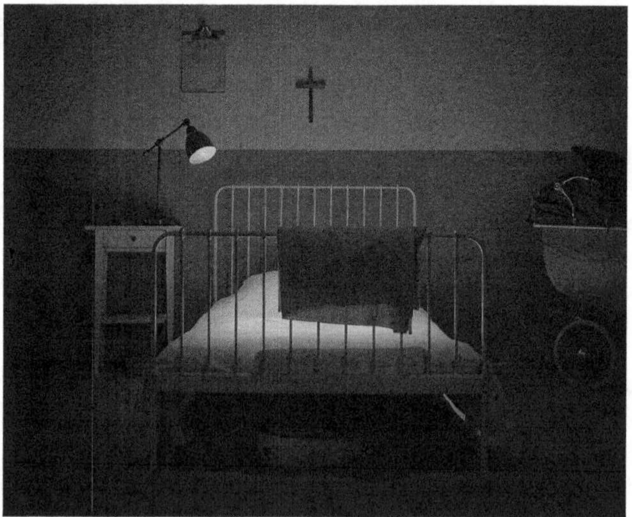

Figure 3. The hospital suite in *Sleep No More* (Photo: Alick Crossley).

mementoes on the wall and sideboards, a child's room, an office, a bedroom, a small library alcove, a nursery. On the level of the "Manderley" bar where we first entered (second floor) – which remains open and running throughout the evening – is the hotel reception desk, and a charming breakfast area, another deer standing in the corner in a bank of salt. Below the second level is a gallery – paintings of forebears, piano, small reading rooms, library, chapel – overlooking the first level, a red-floored ballroom with a black design in the center, an elevated dais and banquet table along one side, and several large evergreens on wheels – Birnam Wood – scattered around, which move and are intermittently illuminated with white lights; one stairway leads directly from the ballroom to the hotel lobby, but another goes by a small chapel, and to a bedroom off the gallery library, where Duncan is smothered by Macbeth. Sound everywhere: thunder, wind, Glenn Miller, or Bernard Herrmann's mysterious score from *Vertigo*.

This brief catalogue hardly does justice to the richness of the space, which over two hundred volunteers spent months detailing and continue to restore and improve, writing the letters that fill the desks, inventing the medical reports – Lady Macduff's obsessive cleaning; Lady Macbeth's sleeplessness – and the charts by the hospital beds, making wallpaper, arranging the decorated living spaces (Piepenburg, "Room in Chelsea"). Whether it's the dead bird in the detective's desk, the edible candy in the candy shop, the mysterious grotto enfolded among a maze of packing cartons off the poolroom bar, the vase of pickled eggs in the Macduff parlor, the space is itself a performance, and one of the pleasures of this "immersive" experience is simply moving through it slowly, taking the time to soak it in. Beyond the press coverage, there's been a relentless stream of tweeting, often from the event itself, and Barrett and Doyle work to keep the eventness of the performance fresh: "If ever the work becomes too familiar, and it becomes too easy for an audience because of the wealth of information on the Internet or word-of-mouth, that's the day when we pull it. It needs to have that fresh shock and to have that sense of apprehension" (Barrett, quoted in Kennedy, "Success in Jaded New York").[3]

Both in its ambiance and in its apparently – only apparently – casual performance structure, *Sleep No More* resembles something like living history events or historical reenactments, to say nothing of *Wunderkammern*, *Prospero's Books*, and a range of contemporary art installations. As "immersion," *Sleep No More* seems to resist the frontal, objectivizing epistemology of modern proscenium theatricality: you are in the event, aware of seeing only part of it, aware – when the actors come into view at the end of a long hallway and disappear – that the event transcends the perspective of any of its participants. (A disclaimer here: having seen *Sleep No More* five times, I'm well aware both of the tricks of my own memory and of many changes made in the performance itself, as casts change, new props are introduced, and new rooms – to me, at least – opened.) And yet, *Sleep No More* creates an overwhelming sense of foreboding, of ... *Macbeth*. First performed in London in 2003, and more or less entirely leaving the spoken text behind, *Sleep No More* stages various scenes between Macbeth and Lady Macbeth, Macbeth and Banquo, the murder of Duncan, the banquet, the witches' prophecy scene, and a dazzling range of solos as richly choreographed dance. As the assistant director of the 2009 production in Brookline, Massachusetts put it, "every line of Shakespeare's *Macbeth* is embedded in multiple languages – sound, light, design, and dance" (Piepenburg, "Room in Chelsea").

A virally marketed meditation on *Macbeth* and a response to the function of Shakespeare in contemporary performance culture, *Sleep No More* complicates the fatigued distinction between "text-based theatre" and "performance." On the one hand, few conventional theatrical *Macbeths* so richly concretize the play's language, the rich imagery of death, darkness, guilt, and infanticide. And yet the audience enters the space rather than observing it, and each spectator's progress creates an associative narrative: the haunting maze of leafless hardwoods leads directly into the hospital bathtub room, where the "written troubles" of Lady Macbeth's brain are inscribed in the scenery, and enacted in her frantic, mostly wordless performance. *Sleep No More* stands apart from a totalizing, prescribed narrative, materializing a rather depoliticized vision of Jacques Rancière's active, emancipated spectator: "in a theatre, in front of a performance, just as in a museum, school or street, there are only ever individuals plotting their own paths in the forest of things, acts and signs that confront or surround them" (*Emancipated Spectator* 16). Nevertheless, the audience acts in a manifestly determined event-structure, plotting its path through a "looped" performance, repeated three times in the course of the evening, though this structure is only peripherally sensible, if sensed at all. As Felix Barrett describes it, "We run the show in three repeat cycles so that you can choose to revisit incidents, or stumble across them again by chance. Each time you come across the action you will see things from a different angle" (Barrett and Doyle, "Interview" 26). Despite *Sleep No More*'s intricate, stopwatch-precise choreography, the "plot" of any individual performance is predicated on the awareness that there are other events happening elsewhere, that there is no single perspective gathering the event into a unified, explanatory narrative.

Asserting an "immersive" epistemology, *Sleep No More* multiplies the practice of our performance as spectators. It is possible to stumble into a "scene," and then follow a performer and "write" a kind of embodied plot: Lady Macbeth, in a clingy ballgown, staggers up two or three flights of stairs to the hospital area, dances a fitful solo through the ward, strips and huddles in a bathtub, the water reddening around her as she scrapes furiously at her flesh with her fingernails. Malcolm bears the body of Duncan with Banquo, Macbeth, and others to the small chapel adjacent to the first-level ballroom, then flees up a staircase, tripping (every time – and in every performance I've seen, regardless of the actor playing Malcolm) on the landing, racing across the hotel lobby and up the west staircase. The performance seems designed to be caught on the fly, in bits and pieces, choreographed in such a way as to make following a single performer for the duration nearly impossible (in fact it is impossible: performers occasionally exit through a door closed to us). Whatever narrative logic sustains the actors' work – the cast consists of a Duncan, Malcolm, Macbeth, Lady Macbeth, Lady Macduff, Macduff, three witches (two female, one male), a nurse, a doctor, a taxidermist, and others, several roles double-cast – it is not a "dramatic" logic accessible to the audience, though the strands do come together two or three times: a ball involving most of the cast in the lower-level ballroom; the witches' prophecy scene, a rave in the "dead" bar; the banquet scene also performed in the ballroom (the banquet provides the finale of *Sleep No More*, though not all spectators manage to see it; one of my students was wandering upstairs towards the end of the evening, wondering when it was time to leave). The souvenir program published several months after the opening did provide a "relationship diagram" identifying the fictional milieux of several groups of characters: the *Macbeth* group, a "Supernatural" group, "The King James Sanitorium," "Townspeople of Gallow Green" (the village street), and "The McKittrick Hotel." Yet these "characters," like the locations of the set itself, seem to bleed into one another. Played as a kind of detective, Malcolm is drawn from the world of film noir; "Maxim" at the "Manderley" bar and other details of the set recall *Rebecca*; the McKittrick hotel, the detective theme, and much of the soundscape are from *Vertigo*.[4]

No words, no plot, no stage, no Shakespeare. *Sleep No More*'s "immersive" aesthetic locates its *Macbeth* off the map of "legitimate" Shakespeare, offering "little insight into *Macbeth*" (Ben Brantley, quoted in Piepenburg, "Room in Chelsea"); constituting "90 minutes of wandering" that didn't add up to a play, let alone Shakespeare's tragedy (User Reviews, New York Magazine). For Ben Brantley, *Sleep No More* was "not the place to look for insights into Shakespeare," in contrast to Cheek by Jowl's production of *Macbeth*, running opposite *Sleep No More* at the Brooklyn Academy of Music in April 2011, "in which the emphasis is on interior worlds instead of the World of Interiors" ("Shakespeare Slept Here" C5).[5] A performance of *Macbeth* is justified for the quality of its "insights into Shakespeare"; *Sleep No More* appears to work in a different direction, to invoke *Macbeth* as a means to creating a distinctive event, one that clearly depends on *Macbeth* but that exceeds, displaces, or avoids reduction to Shakespeare and his words. It is and is not *Macbeth*.

Indeed, while it seems precisely to illustrate the "fundamental *shift from* [the dramatic] *work to* [the postdramatic, "immersive"] *event*" (Lehmann, *Postdramatic Theatre* 61), *Sleep No More* claims a more complex imbrication in the practice of Shakespeare performance today, its "immersive" aesthetic putting a reciprocal pressure on the critical history, situation, and practice of those terms of the art: *Shakespeare, performance*. Asserting an "immersive" epistemology, *Sleep No More* nonetheless articulates a surprisingly conventional view of dramatic performance, of Shakespeare performance, and of *Macbeth* in particular. It frames Shakespeare performance as a genre of performance in which the spectator's experience and activity are principally defined as *about* one of the most familiar, and most contested elements of Lehmann's "dramatic theatre": dramatic character.

"Character criticism" is sometimes associated with a bygone attitude toward Hamlet and Rosalind and Prince Hal as unmediated apparitions of the real. Yet, from Mary Cowden Clarke's *Girlhood of Shakespeare's Heroines* (1851–1852) to A. C. Bradley's *Shakespearean Tragedy* (1904) and revived again both in the "new character criticism" and implicitly in many "cognitive" studies of Shakespeare, the sense that Shakespeare both writes "characters," and that they embody inalienable properties of "human nature" transmitted directly in performance has hardly waned. *Sleep No More*, despite its apparently eccentric regard for Shakespeare's words, focuses precisely on a significant issue in Shakespeare Performance Studies: the function of character as an object, a medium, and an effect of performance.

Nonetheless, the definition, even the principle of "dramatic character" locates a trajectory of disciplinary dissent, from the emergence of a more rigorously "scientific" literary study in the 1930s (marked by L. C. Knights's "How Many Children Had Lady Macbeth?"), to a more assertively politicized conception of the dramatized "subject" in the 1970s and

1980s, to a "new character criticism" arising today (see Yachnin and Slights, "Introduction" 1). Taking in the notion that the response to Shakespearean drama "is underwritten by the shared complexity of our human nature," so that we "learn about our own complex human nature by thinking about and coming to respect Shakespeare's characters" (Bristol, "Confusing Shakespeare's Characters" 38), the "new character criticism" approximates to the predominantly *realistic* perspective on dramatic performance emergent in another trajectory of Shakespeare critique: "cognitive theatre studies." Whether privileging basic "image schemas" derived from the work of George Lakoff and Mark Johnson, assuming the spectator's unconscious empathetic neuronal mirroring of the represented character as definitive of his/her cognition of performance (Amy Cook, Bruce McConachie), instrumentalizing our "evolved cognitive architecture" for reading "other human beings" (Vermeule, *Why Do We Care* 15), or conceiving the audience's intellectual work as the process of "cognitive blending" laid out by Gilles Fauconnier and Mark Turner, cognitive theatre studies also takes the spectator's encounter with character to define the purposes of dramatic performance. Taken together, "character" and "cognitive" critique reciprocally illuminate a shared network of value, a common perspective on the theatre of human nature and of Shakespeare's proper function in it.

Against this background, perhaps, wordlessness may be the most deceptive aspect of *Sleep No More*. Spatializing *Macbeth*'s discourse of character, it reifies both literary character and a kind of experiential theatrical realism, at once challenging and complicating the "instincts" of conventional dramatic theatre, and our understanding of how the medium constructs its players, especially those reciprocal phantoms hedging the work of acting: dramatic characters and theatrical spectators. Inscribing "character" in performance space and insisting on performance conventions that confirm and resist realist "characterization," it charts the ways long-standing, largely "literary" conceptions of theatricality both affect and impede the making of "new" performance. In its dynamic foregrounding of text, character, space, and audience, *Sleep No More* opens a series of intertwined questions about the apparent emancipation of the spectator, the function of "character," and the character of "cognition" offered by a theatrical "immersion" in virtual experience, a surprisingly apt definition, it turns out, of the realist traditions of the modern stage. Largely cancelling speech as a mode of textual reproduction, the production in a sense removes the distraction of dialogue, enabling us to attend more directly to the work of bodies, movement, design, and space – the framing "distribution of the sensible" – as they instantiate a specific instance of, and inquiry into, the cognition of performance.

"A deed without a name": the "comeback" of character

As Shakespeare studies has witnessed a "return of the author" – restored both from the apparent depredations of "performance criticism" and the decentering of the category of authorship in theoretical critique of the 1980s – so too has it witnessed a summons for the return of "character" as an analytic category in professional scholarship. As Paul Yachnin and Jessica Slights put it, introducing their provocative collection, *Shakespeare and Character*,

> Character has made a comeback. Having all but disappeared from Shakespeare criticism as an analytic category in the second half of the twentieth century, the idea of character has now begun to emerge as an important – perhaps even an essential – way of thinking about the political, ethical, historical, literary, and performative aspects of early modern theater. ("Introduction" 1)

Both the polemic and its tact are important here; Yachnin and Slights step away from the long-standing association between "character criticism" and the impressionism of A. C. Bradley's *Shakespearean Tragedy*, and marshal a "new character criticism" (1) both incorporating and resisting what they regard as the privileged terms of recent Shakespeare criticism and theory. Like the "return of the author," the "comeback" of character is framed as a corrective to decades of critical misprision, and so involves a reframing of the critical practice that will restore an accurate view of the durable object of Shakespeare studies, dramatic character, and restore an accurate understanding of dramatic performance as well.

As most critics note, *character* itself is historically predicated on writing. Deriving from its usage in Greek, as "a figure (letter or symbol) stamped onto a wax tablet," *character* "can also be the object that stamps that figure. It thus comes to mean a readable sign in a very general sense – the mark by which something is known as what it is" (Burns, *Character* 5). "Used as a verb," Michael Bristol observes, "character means to engrave or to write. This really is a *literal* usage of the word, since it refers to the idea of written marks or letters of the alphabet" ("Confusing Shakespeare's Characters" 33), as in Othello's interrogative characterization of Desdemona: "Was this fair paper, this most goodly book, / Made to write 'whore' upon?" (4.2.73–4). Recognizing the fundamentally literary conventionality of character can have, as Stephen Orgel once remarked, a powerfully "liberating" force: as an analytic category, characters "are not people, they are elements of a linguistic structure, lines in a drama, and more basically, words on a page" ("What is a Character?" 8). Dramatic character occupies the nexus of a range of discursive patterns – poetic, economic, political, psychological – that may have little directly to do with character as the sign of a verisimilar, psychologically motivated agent.

Phrasing character as a function of formal design resists a strictly mimetic conception of dramatic character, the sense that dramatic agents are necessarily conceived to encode *people* in thoroughly verisimilar ways. The "literariness" or conventionality of character also aligns otherwise divergent trends in modern Shakespeare criticism, the New Critics' definition of Shakespearean drama as *poetry* in the 1930s and after, and the New Historical/Cultural Materialist relocation of the dramatic text within a wider *poetics* of culture in the 1980s, in which the verbal design resonates with other means for representing force, power, and identity in a "textualizing" reading of early modern English life. The New Critical impulse, famously exemplified by L. C. Knights's unavoidable "How Many Children Had Lady Macbeth?" of 1933, locates character as a function of the verbal design of the "dramatic poem": it is "merely an abstraction" – like "'plot', 'rhythm', 'construction' and all our other critical counters" – from the overall design of the work, whose purpose "is to communicate a rich and controlled experience," a "total response in the mind of the reader or spectator, brought into being by written or spoken words" (Knights, "How Many Children" 48).[6] While various ideological, political, and theoretical engagements with Shakespeare in the 1970s and 1980s tend to refuse Knights's articulation of the purely aesthetic origin and consequence of this verbal function, they share a sense, as Alan Sinfield puts it, that mimetic character is "an altogether inappropriate category": "what is recognized in our cultures as 'character' in a play must be an effect of 'the entire culture' and a 'point of intersection of a range of discourses,'" discourses interacting "intertextually" with and so redefining the purport of the verbal, poetic discourse of the text ("When is a Character" 58). For Knights, character is part of the network of poetic construction, internal to the scripted drama; for Sinfield, character lies on the interface between the text and a network of constructions external to the drama that motivate its values and render it legible *as* drama. Whether absorbing character to the function of a universalizing poetics, or seeing it as an anachronistic construction of the text's alien early modern, densely ideological poetics in the individualist language of a modern "liberal humanism" (see Belsey, *Subject of Tragedy* 51), both cases understand the significance of "dramatic character" – as an object of analysis – less as the unmediated representation of persons than as an interpretive effect of the interplay of discursive categories and conventions for representing the causes, purposes, and effects of human agency.

And yet, dramatic character has a powerful pull beyond the script. Sancho Panza, Emma Woodhouse, Stephen Dedalus, Tyrone Slothrop are made of words, immersed in the texture of the narratives that contain them, but dramatic characters – virtually on the page and materially on the stage – appear onstage in action. In the theatre, as Bert O. States suggests, however "text-bound character may be, it is a phenomenon that loses its fictionality because it is designed to evoke impressions like those evoked by real people" – people, it should be noted, we only know through their actions, taking all acts of speaking onstage as behavior – "for whom we can also imagine unlived, or fictional scenes on the principle of 'consistent continuation'" (*Hamlet* 24). What's experientially and analytically powerful about character is its worldliness, however ideologically invested that claim (or disclaiming) of worldliness may be. Even when the psychological mimesis assumed by Maurice Morgann, A. C. Bradley, or Harold Bloom is repudiated as a critical strategy, a generically realist, common-sense view of characters as unmediated people appears to have "the advantage of opening the plays, relatively, to the ways nonprofessional audiences and readers think and live" (Sinfield, "When is a Character" 57), a political commitment to recharging art as "equipment for living" (Burke, "Literature as Equipment") that sustains an ethical vision of literature, of theatre, and of critical practice:

> [Shakespeare's] characters are like us, but sometimes they are more courageous than most of us manage to be. They are people who live in a world we can understand. We don't need any specialized historical knowledge to understand Constance or Shylock or Lady Macduff if we are really alive to our own feelings and capable of empathy with other people – the real ones, I mean. Our response to these dramatic moments is underwritten by the shared complexity of our human nature. Engagement with a character has a moral dimension; it corresponds to the imperative of respect for our human vulnerability to loss and grief. We learn about our own complex human nature by thinking about and coming to respect Shakespeare's characters. (Bristol, "Confusing Shakespeare's Characters" 38)

What kind of work do works of art (enable us to) do? Bristol's account here is doubly contestatory: it at once urges a temperate universalism (Shakespeare's characters are "like us") and a primarily mimetic conception of drama and performance as well ("They are people"). For Bristol, Shakespeare's plays represent individual subjects consistent with the Enlightenment humanism of which we are still a part, subjects understood as we understand ourselves, as moral, empathetic, interiorized, psychological agents. While both New Criticism and New Historicism position the text and character as functions of various motivating poetic and political discourses, the "new character criticism" demands a mimetic, even a realist, perspective that stands apart from a Foucauldian sense of the liberal, psychic subject as an ideological, historically determined and changing event.

Were early modern subjects "like us," or do they and their textual avatars evoke an alien mode of agency or subjection? Francis Barker, for example, resists a realism of character in which Shakespeare stages people "like us": in the case of *Hamlet*, at least, "Rather than the plenitude of an individual presence, the text dramatizes its impossibility" (*Tremulous Private Body* 34). So, too, Catherine Belsey argues that "liberal humanism" – the interpretive regime of modern literary and theatrical criticism – reads character as a means of filling the "gap between the subject of the enunciation and the subject of the utterance" (*Subject of Tragedy* 48) with an ideologically laden thing, a present, interiorized, motivated, individuated *self*: "a full subject, a character" (51). For Barker, "interiority remains, in *Hamlet*, gestural" (32); not surprisingly, in the "'comeback,' of character," Barker and Belsey are routinely condemned for undervaluing the experience of "interiority" that makes Shakespeare's "people like us."

While this kind of materialist critique tends to deprivilege the sense of a determined, interiorized subject as the cause of dramatic action, Sinfield nonetheless hopes to find "a way of talking" about Shakespeare's representation of a "continuous or developing interiority or consciousness" that "does not slide back into character criticism or essential humanism" ("When is a Character" 62).[7] Plays need agents, after all, and it is how we constitute those agents – how, in a sense, we engrave them as *characters* or with *character* – that the "'comeback' of character" brings into focus. In the theatre, though, dramatic character emerges less as a thing than as a transactional opportunity, a site of what Benjamin Bennett calls "interpretivity," where the categories of *agency* are negotiated through the specific means of a given performance – acting and dramatic style, structure of narrative, the disposition of the audience. A mimetic representation of familiar human beings like us; an organizing contour in the poetic design of the verbal dramaturgy; an ideologically motivated incision in the enunciation of agency: whatever we take it to be, in the theatre character emerges in the *transaction* of the densely ideological relations of performance.[8] And yet, while materialist criticism resists aligning character with a psychological subject in favor of "larger and more stable entities – such as dramatic genres, texts, or social structures" (Yachnin and Slights, "Introduction" 4) – the "new character criticism" aligns dramatic character with another larger and more stable entity: "the historical fact that character, defined more or less as self-same, capable of autonomy and change, and possessed of some measure of inwardness and inscrutability," has "stood at the center of the literary and theatrical engagement with Shakespeare for at least the past 350 years" and "has come to form an integral part of what Shakespeare means, and of how his plays connect with and influence the world" (5). As an "organizing principle of Shakespeare's plays," character replicates the intentional and textually determined status it had for A. C. Bradley, though now inflected toward the making of performance: "Shakespeare builds a gestural, kinesthetic, and vocal dimension into how he writes his characters" (6).

The New Criticism, the ideological critique of character, and the "new character criticism" all share a common investment in the scriptedness of "character." What distinguishes the "new character criticism" is an urgently *realist* conception of theatrical performance, the sense that an unproblematic mimesis – "character" as "people like us" to whom we relate in the theatre as we do in life – provides "the principal bridge over which the emotional, cognitive, and political transactions of theater and literature pass between actors and playgoers or between written texts and readers" (Yachnin and Slights, "Introduction" 7). When Yachnin and Slights aver that "much greater attention needs to be paid to the contributions made by the theater and the performance environment as we attempt to re-articlulate a notion of character in the twenty-first century" (3), this theatre is – as perhaps it must be – a familiar modern stage, the stage of an empathetic, fundamentally Stanislavskian realism, in which the coherent, conjoined "arc" (8) of narrative and character (that indispensable cliché of contemporary acting and directing) position the theatre and our engagement with it as a reflexive metonymy of a coherent, naturalized social order, of the nature of theatre, of nature itself. Reading, or seeing, for "character" is, finally, part of the audience's inborn physiology: theatre galvanizes "the *instinct* to connect observations about dramatic characters and communities to their own life experience" that "are common among both readers and audience members" (3, my emphasis).

Despite the effort to distance character criticism from manifestly ideological designs, a "realistic" perspective in the theatre nonetheless promotes a specific vision of theatrical conduct, one that not incidentally conceives "interpretation" as the constitutive activity of its readerly spectators. Realism promises an interpretive perspective – a word chosen with care – closely identified with theatrical modernity and even modernization: the projection of a distinct field of aesthetic objectivity, and an appropriate act of legitimized consumption, one that tends to displace the material conditions and practices of performance from the regulated field of the just "interpretation" of the artwork. As Belsey argues, this theatre positions both spectator and spectacle in a specific manner: when "the whole stage retreated behind the frame of the proscenium arch, the perspective theatre thus offered an internally coherent and unified spectacle to a single and unified point of view which was outside the autonomous world of the fiction," constituted *as autonomous* by the rhetoric of that fiction (*Subject of Tragedy* 25). Proscenium realism distinctively identifies the spectator's absence from the scene of art with the epistemological power and privilege of interpretation, the "pleasure of an imaginary plenitude," a pleasure – in what Rancière might call the overdetermined "distribution of the sensible" (*Emancipated Spectator* 12) – that identifies the imagination of interpretive power (to know through seeing) with the practice of passive concealment.[9] Rendering the means of performance aesthetically irrelevant, transparent, realist theatre urges the spectator's virtual immersion in the represented fiction as the purpose of the performance.

Understanding character within a realist agenda has several important consequences. The principle of agency that defines a realist dramatic role must be filled in, identified: in practice, rather than merely noting the possible projection of "interiority" as one complex but inessential element of that agency, the problem of "interiority" becomes – as it did for proscenium realism's first generation of masters, Ibsen, Strindberg, Chekhov – the definition of the worldliness of "character," its successful mimesis of people "like us." What makes them "like us," interpretable as "people" from the darkened confines of our offstage seats is that their actions appear to externalize internal – if veiled, contradictory – psychological motives, motives the actor's performance clarifies and expresses through a manifest technique that belongs entirely to the stage. The drama of character depends on the crisis of (the possibility of) the self, a crisis some commentators locate as part of Shakespeare's "invention of the human" (Bloom). More to the point, while Shakespeare performance today, from the Globe to any local summer festival in the park, may well not be framed by the proscenium, the aesthetic and ideological persistence of realist "objectivity" remain pervasive in theatrical performance, however much actors may wink and nod to the house. By emphasizing the production of a coherent character, theatrical realism renders "character" as an object, a thing to be revealed rather than an effect of the performance mediated between the actor and the spectator. Beyond that, realism asserts the transparency, even the absence, of its means of production, the manifest performance conventions through which the specific effects of character are practiced. And, much as it does in Stanislavsky's conception of the "actor's work on his role," character itself must exist outside performance, have a perdurable identity in the world – and the text – beyond the stage, an identity the actor works to reveal through a delicate act of illusory disappearance.

Trevor Ponech offers a sophisticated account of this notion of the fictional character as a "*public agent-concept*," so that a character can have – as many clearly do – a long-term cultural being beyond the instantiation of a single text or performance ("Reality of Fictive Cinematic Characters" 42). As Ponech argues, this notion both takes in the possibility of change (our understanding of Macbeth changes over time, and Macbeth appears differently in various performances) and the persistence of identity (he's still somehow Macbeth). Yet Macbeth also exists in distinct media and temporalities of publicness – texts, theatre, film – that are reconciled through a mimetic notion of performance, what Ponech calls "copying." The different film Macbeths of Kurosawa and Polanski, for example, "are imperfect copies, their content and ontogenesis departing in countless ways from one another and from Shakespeare's public concept" (57). Yet, "at least some facts about MACBETH's identity – about its content and connection to Shakespeare's relevant creative activities" – are essential to the "realist premise" (57). Putting the case in its starkest terms, even an unusually innovative film, like Roman Polanski's 1971 *Macbeth*, "treats *Macbeth* as what it is: explicit instructions for and constraints on the realization of a right performance of a theatrical work. Subsequently, the public MACBETH concept he prescribes by cinematic proxy is similar to the one Shakespeare prescribes by textual proxy" (57–58). However distinct from the related ideological "objectivity" of stage realism, Ponech's philosophical "realism," an "ontological thesis" in which to "be a realist about something is to believe it exists and is what it is independently of how one takes it to be" (41), defines character within a specific hierarchy of text and performance. Granting that early and late modern notions of character cannot neatly overlap, Ponech nonetheless alleges a "privileged psychohistorical relationship between certain concepts":

> Arguably, Polanski's MACBETH effectively though imperfectly copies Shakespeare's MACBETH. This claim's truth requires the former stand in a nondeviant causally-historical dependent relation to the latter. Its truth is also a matter of the degree to which their prescribed contents overlap. Given this sort of identity relation, Macbeth can persist indefinitely as a familiar item in ordinary reality, Shakespeare's public agent-concept being made available to audiences time after time, across media. (58)

Since media themselves are apparently irrelevant, what mediates public agent-concepts across history? As in theatrical realism, it is the notion of the independent existence of a naturalized social background, in which we understand which "prescribed contents" are relevant and what it means for them metaphorically to "overlap" through the asserted transparency of the medium: the fourth wall and behavioristic acting, for instance. In this starkly naturalizing agenda, the public agent-concepts "are to a degree functionally equivalent to agent concepts acquired more directly via encounters with real people" (58). Writing about film "character," Ponech sets aside the force of the medium, the extent to which, sitting in the dark, observing huge light-borne images through the intermediating agency of the camera (and editing, design, and the dramatic conventions specific to film), we do not in fact encounter "characters" in the ways we encounter "real people." The driving rhetoric of aesthetic realism (the alleged transparency of the fourth wall, for instance) remains powerfully in place: the notion that the productive conventions – the *medium* – of art bear a negligible impact on our engagement with the art object, rather than being the tissue of our practice as readers, consumers, spectators. Ponech – who, to be fair, centers most of his discussion here on Kurosawa's *Throne of Blood* – is well aware of the force of convention in the construction of "character," but for him it is precisely this opacity that disappears in the "realistic" encounter.

Regarding the medium as transparent to character reinstates a familiar understanding of theatre, a sense of performance as "merely interpretive rather than constructive – a pale shadow, in other words, of the printed text" (Hartley, "Page and Stage" 79). "Character," in this regard, is a principle of containment rather than of agency, an object "struck out *whole*" (Morgann, *Dramatic Character of Falstaff* 154) and stamped into the text, rather than a fictive effect of doing these things in this way before and with these people (onstage and offstage in the house). When Yachnin and Slights see Shakespeare as building "a gestural, kinesthetic, and vocal dimension into how he writes his characters," this "dimension" reinstates a determining role for writing in performance, a role

Shakespeare's writing has regardless of the gestural, kinesthetic, or vocal practices of any specific theatre or performance medium. To conceive of writing as instrumental is to threaten the erasure of the *whole* character, replaced by the "grotesque" even "ghastly" opportunity to create character in the intermittent relations of performance. The role of the Porter evidently provides such an opportunity, and Bradley carefully distinguishes the paradigm of this role from the deeper vision of character that "Shakespeare intended": "I dare say the groundlings roared with laughter at his coarsest remarks," but Shakespeare "despised the groundlings if they laughed" (*Shakespearean Tragedy* 395). Bradley's character commentary may be extrinsic to the poem's design (though, *pace* Knights, contemporary actresses are absorbed by Lady Macbeth's lost children), but the notion of character as an object to be transmitted rather than an instrument of performance process is as intrinsic to the New Criticism as it is to Bradley; Cleanth Brooks, after all, asks, "Does Shakespeare mean for pity or for fear of retribution to be dominant in Macbeth's mind?," a question to be addressed not by undertaking the Method actor's visit to the asylum to experience the psychology of murderers first-hand, but via the fearsome imagery of the babe striding the blast ("Naked Babe" 390).

In performance there is no character apart from acting, from what an actor is doing onstage; different regimes of performance constitute both "acting" and "character" through very different means. Rather than striking *whole* the constitution of characters to be delivered to spectators, in the theatre dramatic character arises within a specific praxis, as an instrument in the making of performances, an instrument whose affordances – the relationship between its "perceived and actual properties" (Norman, *Design of Everyday Things* 9) – emerge in the changing circumstances of performance.[10] How do we register the "contributions made by the theater and the performance environment," then, in a mode of critique that both emphasizes the agency of dramatic character as prescribed by the author and invokes a realistic conception of mimetic theatre that erases the performance itself from the field of aesthetic awareness, an erasure nowhere more evident than in the casual alignment of "readers or spectators" (Yachnin and Slights, "Introduction" 3).

William Dodd promisingly explores the "character effect" by analyzing *Othello* as a series of *performatives*: here, the text doesn't determine character as much as frame a set of performance opportunities limited only by the "interaction script," a virtual interpretive constraint that blends the context of dramatic narrative with the ideal circumstances of implicitly realistic performance, a psychologically consistent "journey" or "arc" for the character-agent. Dodd argues that the "'post performance'" quartos include a range of contextual pointers, words – *marry*, *tut*, *alas*, *why* – which imply that the actors were ad-libbing in an effort to ground the conversation between "characters" by locating it more realistically within the performance between the actors ("Character as Dynamic Identity" 71). This byplay implies that the actors' interactions with each other *as actors* shape character in performance. Yet, in "a play script," taken here as interchangeable with performance, "the outcomes of verbal (and nonverbal) interactions become the basis of subsequent actions, thereby acquiring objective existence. Later interactions retrospectively select a limited range of acceptable executions and uptakes of speech acts" (70). So, for example, if "on a whim, Burbage performed Othello's greeting to Desdemona on landing in Cyprus *merely* as bloated, self-regarding rhetoric [. . .] the exchange would soon be 'corrected' by the scripted words of Iago" (70). Bradley's notion of the text of Macbeth divided between a literary and a theatrical agenda – between Macbeth and the Porter as strategies for appealing to an audience – is reciprocated here: Shakespeare's text may require a performative supplement to prove theatrically lifelike, but that supplement is hardly Derridean: its effect is to shape the purpose and function of acting to the delivery of an inscribed Shakespearean object, a script that finally regulates the interactions of performance.

As an instrument of performance, a role has different affordances in different theatrical systems, and so is susceptible to different kinds of work, provides different opportunities for making character (or not), opportunities that dramatize the dialectical interaction between "character" as an effect of reading and of theatrical performance. As James Berg notes of *King Lear*, "All character *is* property, where property represents not just what persons seem to own, but the *things* that properly belong *with* them. And all property is character, symbolic *reading material*" ("Properties of Character" 99). Berg licenses a notion of character constituted at least minimally in performance, in which the "properties" belonging to character are inseparable from those through which character is asserted, including the physical, gestural, and movement dynamics of a given actor. And as the teapot stance and the Method actor's crouch should remind us, the properties of theatrical character don't arise merely from author and actor; they are also inseparable from the conventional discourse by which character is materialized between actor and spectator historically, the shared technology of effective acting.

While dramatic texts can be read as generating a processual, self-correcting map of the "properties" of character – "that great property which still should go with Antony" comes to mind – in performance, "character" is not a thing; if it exists at all, it is "filtered through the body of the performing actor who is himself transformed by it" (Leiblein, "Embodied Intersubjectivity" 123), a conception that significantly exceeds the notion of Shakespeare as an engineer of speech, that "what actors do, after all, is not perform actions but recite lines, and the character is the lines" (Orgel, "What is a Character?" 8). Character – recognized since Aristotle as a property of the theatrical experience – is shaped by distinctive conventions of performance work (acting), and within the specific relations of theatre. And yet, perhaps especially where Shakespeare is concerned, it remains difficult to keep this "relational" understanding of character from collapsing back into the theatre-as-textual-delivery-system. For instance, working together on scenes from *The Winter's Tale*, Paul Yachnin and Myra Wyatt Selkirk discussed with student actors the effect of opening their performance out to the audience, especially the effects of delivering soliloquies directly to classmates (the set-up here is important: this was a class, so the audience and actors were well known to each other, and the experiment took place in an illuminated classroom). For Yachnin and Selkirk, moments of "metatheatre" – as in Cleopatra's "boy my greatness" speech – operate in a specific way: when the spectators, addressed directly, "feel strongly" that the performer "is being put at risk by what the text is making her say, then they will apprehend the presence of the playwright as well as the presences of the character and the actor" ("Metatheater" 140). Here, that is, collaboration between actor and spectator reifies the "presence of the playwright"; more widely, when encouraged to deliver a speech directly to a specific spectator, the actors report that "direct address to specific audience members did alter the character from how it had been rehearsed" (144). Stanislavsky was concerned that actors not understand themselves as mere commodities, giving their artistic creation over to the control of the public; when reporting the consequences of this exercise, the actors spoke not of their own relationship to the audience, but of "what the character wants from the audience. This is very much the same way that they would discuss what they [the characters] want from other characters in the play" (145). Relating to the audience only through the objectified character, and the character's through-line of action, the actors incorporate the audience into the given circumstances of the dramatic "scene," circumstances that conjure the presence of the playwright who invented it and all of "us" – the characters, the actors, the audience.

Despite the transactional dimension of the role, and the visibly historical and cultural determinants of "acting," "character" remains iconic, deeply encoded within a basically literary ethos. Moreover, in its common-sense appeal, its resistance to the ideologically and theoretically laden perspectives of the 1980s, and its realistic orientation toward performance – in which the dramatic text bears the traces of human nature to the stage, transparently realized by the actors and instinctively grasped by spectators – the "new character criticism" tracks closely with a parallel, but considerably more ambitious effort to transform the objects and practices of performance critique (and of humanities research more widely): the application of methods, insights, and models drawn from contemporary neuroscience to the "cognitive" critique of culture and the arts. This relationship is neither causal nor coincidental; yet, depending on an "instinct" for character satisfied by Shakespeare, the "new character criticism" resonates with the naturalizing impulses of the divergent application of research in cognitive neuroscience to the work of performance. This double perspective extends well beyond the presumed functioning of character onstage. Articulating a model of theatrical "cognition," it coordinates actor, character, and spectator in a regulatory account of the proper disposition of theatrical performance.

"my dull brain was wrought / With things forgotten": character, cognition, and performance

> . . . we are now entering an age in which the key intellectual goal is not to celebrate the imagination but to make a science of it.
> (Gilles Fauconnier and Mark Turner, *The Way We Think* 89)

> Confusion is what we have now in the realm of literary criticism. The naturalistic ("Darwinian") literary critics have an unbeatable strategy to replace it. (E. O. Wilson, "Foreword" vii)

Character and cognition are casually linked by many commentators; the question is whether we take "character" – both as an object/construction of reading and, more important here, as a process of performance – to confirm and require the application of a basic human nature or as a means to reconsider "the nature and position of 'the human'" (Burns, *Character* 205). The astonishing range of scientific work on the background of "cognitive" approaches to literature and theatre has given rise to a consequent range of arguments in psychology, linguistics, and various cultural fields, notably literary and theatre studies. It has also provoked an assortment of interpretive practices developing – with varying degrees of critical and "empirical" rigor, despite frequent rhetorical recourse to their warrant by "science" – an array of accounts of the relation between human perception, cognition, understanding ("mind"), their interplay with the physiological structures and process of the brain, and their implication in and through the processes of theatre.

Cognitive cultural studies is sometimes afflicted by a "self-congratulatory tone" (Fletcher, *Evolving Hamlet* xv) – younger scholars in the field are routinely described as "brave" (Vermeule and McConachie, "Preface" x), as "would-be Columbians. Embattled, even scorned, by tenured constructivists" (Wilson, "Foreword" viii). But what it shares rhetorically with the "new character criticism" is a triumphant sense of determined historical change.[11] Much like the "*dated*" materialist critique of Shakespearean character (Yachnin and Slights, "Introduction" 4, my emphasis), the work of various "poststructuralist" or "constructivist" critics – Judith Butler, Jacques Derrida, Michel Foucault – is now, due to a reliance on elements of Saussurean linguistics, "predicated on an *outmoded* and untenable science of language" (Hart, "Performance, Phenomenology" 30, my emphasis), in which critics of the "cognitive turn" merely restate "*outdated* dualisms" (Tribble, *Cognition in the Globe* 16, my emphasis), fortunately replaced by the emerging clarity and certainty of the "empirical assumptions and self-correcting procedures of cognitive science," which not only offer "empirically tested insights" (McConachie, "Preface" x), but are capable of opening "*the* cognitive structure of drama and performance" (Cook, *Neuroplay* 19, my emphasis), and so *Reinvigorating* the apparently moribund *Study of Dramatic Texts and Performance through Cognitive Science* (Cook subtitle).[12] More radically than the "return of the author," which only relegates "performance criticism" to a benighted past, "cognitive" theatre studies briskly sweeps alternative forms of the "study of dramatic texts and performance" into obsolescence.

As Johnathan Kramnick has suggested of "Literary Darwinism," some of the enthusiasm for interpretive practices derived from evolutionary psychology arises from "a weariness bordering on hostility to the current state of the humanities" ("Against Literary Darwinism" 317), a resistance to a "radical postmodern perspective" that foregrounds both the "philosophical assumptions" of scientific inquiry and its networks of material support and academic prestige (Lakoff and Johnson, *Philosophy in the Flesh* 74). While some cognitive cultural critics urge a rapprochement between "contemporary cognitive literary theory – particularly those subfields within it that integrate insights from poststructuralism, cultural historicism, feminism, and performance studies" – and cultural studies more generally, this integration nonetheless depends on taking cognitively oriented approaches as the ground of critique, as "the epistemological foundations of what we do" arising from an understanding of "the 'evolved human brain'" (Zunshine, "Introduction"). As Bruce McConachie puts it, in this view cognitive theatre studies offer ways of *knowing* not merely *interpreting* or *criticizing*, "Not just another framework in our bag of theoretical tricks" (*Engaging Audiences* vii). "Science" (and perhaps this is where the sense of unjust discrimination comes back in) provides an instrument for "correcting what the humanities get wrong" (Tribble, *Cognition in the Globe* 9), for policing the field, a means to ensure "valid" interpretation of the purposes, operation, and legitimate "meanings" of literature and performance. After all, "lacking good theories, scholarly differences cannot be adjudicated and resolved; with the result that knowledge in our discipline cannot be consolidated and advanced" (McConachie, *Engaging Audiences* 13). In this view, the application of scientific methods to the humanities – methods often taken to confirm a "common sense" conception of theatre (8) – will lead to "plausible, provisional, and falsifiable statements of truth" (14), statements that will allow us to deploy "species-level commonalities" as analytical instruments (or, at the very least, as interpretive constraints), so that an understanding of "how a play has worked for contemporary audiences can usefully inform how plays engaged historical spectators" (17), and so, presumably, *any* human spectator. And while "cultural and individual differences will also abound," differences that McConachie also attaches finally to inborn schemata, accepting a "cognitive" paradigm of critical practice is clearly intended to liberate us from the relativistic contingencies besetting humanistic inquiry, allowing objective knowledge to be "consolidated and advanced."[13]

For McConachie, scientific "standards of evaluating evidence, comprehensiveness, range, contextuality, and empirically responsible paradigms can guarantee a high degree of reliability" ("Cognitive Studies" 60), and the notion that the deployment of terms, methods, and procedures associated with the "cognitive turn" guarantees a more coherent foundation in "truth" for humanistic inquiry is widespread, even among those for whom some dimensions of contemporary literary or philosophical critique can be accommodated to notions of species adaptation.[14] I want to step away from this rhetorical barn-yard for the moment, though, to concentrate on one or two aspects of the application of cognitive cultural studies to drama and theatre, focused through the lens of acting and "character." Like the neuroscience it often asserts to warrant (sometimes rather distantly) its claims, cognitive theatre criticism is richly various in scope.

The interpretive horizon of studies in distributed cognition and its image of the extended mind coordinates with practical and institutional elements of theatre in ways quite different from studies attempting to locate a text's verbal imagery as the implementation of a universal set of primary thinking instruments, metaphorical "image schemas," which differ, too, from studies situating artwork within the "adaptive" logic of a broadly evolutionary and sometimes physiologically determined process.[15] As F. Elizabeth Hart suggests in "The Epistemology of Cognitive Literary Studies," "cognitive" work in the humanities itself traces its own manifestly ideological spectrum, from work invoking "evolutionary theory as an antidote to literary theory" (329) taking "an actively polemical stance against postmodern critical schools and against poststructuralist literary theory in particular" (317), to studies in which an indefinite boundary between the biological genesis of, say, conceptual metaphors and their cultural deployment, produce an accommodation with cultural theory, an "integration of viewpoints, leaning closer to relativism or toward the middle of the continuum and thus more toward social constructivity" (328–329). This tension – which, it should be noted, assigns potentially "relativist" contingency only to non"scientific" analysis and interpretation – is enacted across the spectrum of cognitive theatre studies. While for Bruce McConachie, the "general goal of all spectator-evaluators is the same as the goal of every human being: to maximize pleasure and minimize pain, the two foundational values of our biological lives" (*Engaging Audiences* 100), in Mary Thomas Crane's more delicate framing, the assumption that "human brains share biological and chemical components" does not "prevent a consideration of the ways in which material culture interacts with, shapes, and is shaped by those physical attributes" (*Shakespeare's Brain* 10).[16]

"Evolutionary" arguments tend to see cultural difference as a merely superficial expression of a universal human genetic endowment more or less determined in the Pleistocene era, leading to what Kramnick characterizes as a "pyramid of explanation" in which the "kind of claim you can make about natural selection puts limits on what you can say about psychology and what you can say about psychology limits what you can do with literature" ("Literary Studies and Science" 434).[17] So, too, cognitive approaches to theatre have tended to depress the differential proliferation of the medium, the extraordinarily varied conventionality of "theatre" historically and culturally, instead taking a philosophically realist perspective on theatre that is implicitly normed to the historical aesthetic dynamics of the nineteenth- and twentieth-century European and American stage.[18] Much as "cognitive" approaches to language are held to invalidate "poststructuralist theory," here "cognitive" theories of meaning militate against "constructionist" perspectives, in favor of what Tobin Nellhaus terms a "critical realism," asserting the active interplay between an objective or given real which nonetheless cannot determine the categories of its perception, interpretation, and understanding, themselves governed finally by the biological properties and physiological processes of the human brain.[19] Having "no use for an epistemology of total subjectivism and/or relativism" (McConachie and Hart, "Introduction" 6), this "realism" mediates between epistemologies of positivism and constructivisim, objective realism and relativism (and, not incidentally, between motives that continue to distinguish historical and literary analysis). As George Lakoff and Mark Johnson put it, this "experientialist" vision "varies from classical objective realism in the following basic way: Human concepts do not correspond to inherent properties of things but only to interactional properties. This is natural, since concepts can be metaphorical in nature and can vary from culture to culture" (*Metaphors We Live By* 181).[20]

As the history of theatre makes clear, "interactional properties" are not determined by the object alone, nor are they purely determined by an individual mind, especially where questions of signification are concerned. Lars Eidinger's performance demonstrates that *Hamlet* now affords us opportunities for action (eating dirt, playing the Player Queen among the audience), "interactional properties" that it did not offer to Laurence Olivier, let alone to David Garrick; it clearly offered Garrick (his mechanical fright-wig comes to mind) opportunities it no longer seems to offer to us. Does the specific environment in which image schemata are formed afford the development of different, or differently nuanced schemata? As might be expected, moving "experiential realism" into the theatre tends to emphasize the apparently "universal" character of performance practices over their historically and culturally conventional dimension, much as the notion of a universal verbal image schema tends to depress "the influence of the 'specificities of physically diverse and differentially marked bodies'" on their production, or indeed the influence of the material environment in which they are first produced.[21] The conflict arises precisely at the point at which the biological – the unconscious, preconscious paradigms of metaphorical image schemas, for instance, or mirror neuronal simulation – engages with culture, with the politics of language, with the politicized association of specific bodies in space and time, and with specific, often behaviorally abstract signifying activities.

When the discussion of theatre is at hand, the "realist" philosophical agenda of cognitive cultural studies – "to identify causal mechanisms, and determine how they work and how they generate particular outcomes" (Nellhaus, *Theatre, Communication* 26) – often assumes a relatively narrow slice of theatrical practice as normative, both of theatre and so of its engagement with an intrinsic human nature. While Tobin Nellhaus carefully distinguishes "aesthetic realism" – "the effort to create the appearance of reality" onstage (134) – from the critical realism of a cognitively inspired critique, the generically verisimilar "realistic" performance enacted behind the proscenium of the darkened commodity theatre of the past century is typically assumed as the "distribution of the sensible" intrinsic to theatre, and definitive of theatrical cognition (Rancière, *Emancipated Spectator* 12). The consequences of this assumption are particularly visible in one dimension of cognitive theatre studies: the analysis of "character." Cognitive discussions of character are, on the one hand, profitably processual; character is understood as an instrument arising in relations of the stage rather than those of the book. At the same time, the grounding of this process in a *realist* conception of theatre tends to ground character in a specific, and surprisingly narrow, model of performance.[22]

In Gilles Fauconnier and Mark Turner's account of "cognitive blending," for instance, "character" provides an indispensible element of cognitive processing, a way to particularize an agent, to attribute intention, and so to draw inferences about his or her current or future behavior: "Characters, like frames, are basic cognitive cultural instruments. We may dispute every aspect of their accuracy or legitimacy or invariance, or even their very existence, but cognitively we cannot do without them" (*Way We Think* 250). Fauconnier and Turner hew surprisingly closely to Burns' framing of "character as a mode of perception and a discourse" (*Character* 4), yet seem largely uninterested in the discursive, cultural dimension of character, the extent to which common models of behavior – or notable "characters," the trickster, Macbeth, Richard Nixon – inflect this process, however clearly they model character on a literary paradigm:

> In *The Odyssey*, Odysseus works through nearly every situation conceivable – fighting, sailing, disputing, womanizing, hiding, pleading, persuading – and remains Odysseus throughout. It is a central aspect of human understanding to think that people have characters that manifest themselves as circumstances change. When someone acts in a certain way in a novel situation, we might say "That's just like him. I would never have done that." Character transports over frames and remains recognizable in all of them, to the extent that we can ask "What would Odysseus do in these circumstances?" despite the fact that those circumstances are unknown in Odysseus's world. (249)

We can ask, but there's no answer, at least no compelling one outside the dynamics of literature. For as L. C. Knights might have observed, questions such as these (How many children had Lady Macbeth? What would Odysseus do?) mistake literature for life much as Morgann did, "by his preposterous references to those aspects of a 'character' that Shakespeare did not wish to show" ("How Many Children" 55). A character, Odysseus can hardly remain "who he is regardless of his situation" (Fauconnier and Turner, *Way We Think* 251) because "he" is the creature of his situations; indeed, myriad-minded Odysseus seems designed, as a character, to surprise in every situation, to be repeatedly recreated anew by new circumstances. Readers or listeners of *The Odyssey* develop a provisional "character" for Odysseus, but that character belongs to us, and is not detachable from the situation in which Odysseus performs: new situation, new Odysseus.[23] This "subject – the stability of character across different activities – is immensely complicated and infinitely explored in the world's *literatures*" because it remains so problematic outside literature (251, my emphasis). Hamlet reviling Ophelia in the "nunnery" scene, Pozzo blind: in dramatic performance, character is not merely reiterated in new situations, but invented by them.

I don't mean to deny the importance of character in the developing history of literature and drama, nor to deny the figuration of an "agent" as an aspect of human cognition, nor even the potentially "adaptive" consequences of the arts – characters from proud Achilles, to Oedipus and his famous complex, to Hamlet and his problems, to absent Godot provided their originating and successive cultures with paradigms of behavior. But I do mean to suggest that merely laminating literary to cognitive notions of character specifically occludes the most intrinsically cultural dimension of artforms: their conventions of representation and representational practices. Fauconnier and Turner, of course, are not concerned with literature. They use the notion of character as a means to describe a principle of cognitive functioning, an ability to register the persistence of an intending human agent over time as s/he performs in changing circumstances in order to interpret and perhaps predict his or her future actions. Yet while character may be an indispensible instrument in our cognitive arsenal, the "character" we attribute to others – to stabilize and render interpretable the blend of agent, action, intention, and scene – does not, strictly speaking, arise in narrative, if by "narrative" we mean a purposeful design of events. Literary and theatrical character are not only inseparable from the narrative or event that constructs them, but from the representational conventions of medium and genre as well, conventions that necessarily recede into the background of Fauconnier and Turner's vision of innate cognitive functions.

Or do they? For in taking literary character as an instance of a cognitive universal, Fauconnier and Turner take a specific modern representational convention – the practices of the realistic stage – as its (universal) vehicle. "Dramatic performances are deliberate blends of a living person with an identity. They give us a living person as one input and a different living person, an actor, in another." To sustain this understanding of performance, a "character" must have the status of a "living person": "The character portrayed may of course be entirely fictional, but there is still a space, a fictional one, in which that person is alive." In performance, then, the actor is visibly blended with a perceptibly alternative identity, as "In the blend, the person sounds and moves like the actor and is where the actor is, but the actor in her performance tries to accept projections from the character portrayed, and so modifies her language, appearance, dress, attitudes and gestures." Since for "the spectator the perceived living, moving, and speaking body is a supreme material anchor," it's only natural that, "for example, a middle-aged female character will be played by a middle-aged female actress" (*Way We Think* 266).[24] We might ask how the character projects anything apart from what the actor does, but for Fauconnier and Turner, the spectator "lives in" the blend of these two factive entities.

In this familiar account of acting, theatre preserves a basically literary structure of dramatic performance – delivering the "living" person of the author's creation to the spectator – and is evidently troped on a specific paradigm of modern realist practice: age- and gender-(race-? cultural-? ability-?)specific casting. In many performance traditions, including European traditions like *commedia dell'arte* (or boy actors in Shakespeare's company, or most secondary school and university Shakespeare today, for that matter), physical resemblance between actor and represented character is not strikingly relevant, and other performance practices are so highly abstract or ritualized as to bear little direct relation to the real-life attributes of the actor or the presumed attributes of the character: the movement and vocal style of Noh performance come to mind (even the monologues performed by "Anne" and "Bobby" in the Nature Theater of Oklahoma *Romeo and Juliet* are not assigned to the actor on the basis of the informant's gender). Modern conventions such as "color blind" or "multicultural" casting are designed to foreground and undo the politics implicitly inscribed in Fauconnier and Turner's theatrical "nature."

This vision of dramatic character as living person reflects a specific understanding of theatrical practice, purpose, and propriety. For the spectator's ability to maintain the "integration in the blend" (*Way We Think* 266) has in considerable measure to do with an understanding of the appropriate practice of theatrical competence:

> Experiencing a dramatic performance requires further complex blends. We will not look at these in detail, but they have remarkable properties. Perhaps most notably, the spectator will live in the blend only by selective projection: Many aspects of her existence (such as sitting in a seat, next to other people, in the dark), although independently available to her, are not to be projected to the blend. Her normal animacy and agency, her motor powers and her power of speech, her responsibility to act in response to what she sees, must all be inhibited. The actor, meanwhile, is engaged in a different kind of blend, one in which his motor patterns and power of speech come directly into play, but not his free will or his foreknowledge of the outcome. In the blend, he says just what the character says and is surprised night after night by the same events. (*Way We Think* 267)

Living in the blend is living in the proscenium house, with all the material support it provides to a specific conception of performance: for the spectator, a piece of real estate to call his/her own for a while, a physical and ideological abstraction from responsibility in or for the events of the stage, an understanding of performance as delivering a repeatable fiction; for the actor, a sense of service to the text, and of acting as the appropriate delivery of a competently shaped product – the character.

Of course, in other forms of theatre, different blendings might well be possible. Yet what makes the realist machinery of modern western theatre useful to Fauconnier and Turner is its precise means for segregating actor from character, stage from audience, the fictitious from the real, production from consumption, the constitutive (realist) erasure of the structure of representational conventions that make *blending* possible. But if character is relational or transactional, then the circumstances in which this transaction takes place are critical to the kind of character that emerges, if any emerges at all. In the classical Athenian theatre, for instance, we might well imagine that – for male citizens seated among the tribe, and so among the military cohort, watching an acting competition – the material experience of performance in *this* audience would be essential to "living in the blend." Would watching a masked actor competing for a prize skew the notion of character as an independent living identity toward a sense of the role as an instrument for victory? Amy Cook suggests that "blended space is like a stage set with props and characters, a commedia scenario awaiting enaction and improvisation" (*Neuroplay* 12), but the stage is never an empty space, mental or otherwise: its properties are configured with value and possibility, affording uses that appear, disappear, change as new demands arise. But for Cook, as for Fauconnier and Turner, the theatre is understood to afford a relatively narrow practice, one dependent on the inscription of character: "The performance shows us *how to read what's within the text* based on an embodied language," and – however text-driven this notion of performance – a director will "stage the play better" if he or she is informed by cognitive blending theory (92, my emphasis).

In the effort to locate a physiological-cognitive essence motiviating the cultural experience of theatre, cognitive theatre studies tends to discount the conventional dimension of performance, framing it as a largely transparent vehicle for the innate cognitive processes it sustains. This tendency is particularly visible in the analytical framing of the relationship between actor, character, and spectator, a framing visible enough in Fauconnier and Turner's work, but more urgently posed by studies based on notions of "empathy" loosely derived from research on mirror neuronal simulation. In McConachie's evolutionarily determined theatre, for instance, "Audiences often seek emotional extremes in the theatre, using emotional baths of laughter or tears to restore the body's sense of equilibrium" (*Engaging Audiences* 19). It is not surprising to discover that in this theatre the spectator is constrained to engage with character in a specific way: the empathetic response of mirror neurons warrants the "empathetic" logic of the entire spectacle.[25] In its most restricted neuroscientific sense, "empathy" denotes only the fact that an observer's neurons fire in the same areas of the brain when s/he observes a certain kind of motor action as when s/he performs the action; some studies argue that a similar process applies both to "goal-related motor acts" and – through a different neuronal system – may also translate "observed emotions into a viscero-motor pattern that expresses the same emotions" (there may be another a neuronal "mirror system for phonemes"). When the monkey sees the researcher reach an arm toward the banana, the same areas of the monkey's brain are activated as when the monkey reaches for the banana. Although these impulses operate at an unconscious level, too rapid and subtle to be engaged directly by conscious experience, neuronal simulation – a less loaded term than "empathy" – appears to play a significant part in instigating human emotional responses and the rational processes of interaction, judgment, decision inseparable from them (Rizzolatti, Fogassi, Gallese, "Mirror-Neuron System" 625). While we may not be conscious of the mirror neurons firing, a display of hostile behavior or a threatening look is first simulated in the mirror neurons, which initiate neurochemical transmissions instigating reactions we can recognize: fear, an urge to fight or flee, a more deliberate decision to deflect the anger, to be more wary next time, and so on – acts that appear to flow from this initial unconscious physiological response.

Like "the preconceptual image schemas," empathy operates as preconscious simulation; in cognitive theatre studies, however, it blends rapidly into a specific and familiar understanding of theatre, that what "works" in the performance is shaped by the conscious, specifically empathetic identification between spectator and character.[26] In McConachie's account, theatre not only exists to provide opportunities for such response, it does so in a familiar manner, through the kind of emotional and physical behaviorism associated with Stanislavskian realism and now pervasive in American theatre training. In a pivotal scene in *Uncle Vanya*, for instance, "Smart directors will block the scene to enhance Yelena's exhausted, yet captivating trudge across the stage as she leaves to attend to her husband's needs" (*Engaging Audiences* 25); and so "most viewers will directly experience Yelena's exhaustion, irritation, and embarrassment through their mirror neuron systems and also get a sense of her vanity as she enjoys the effect of her beauty on the men" (27). To McConachie, expanding neuronal empathy from an unconscious reaction to a conscious form of identification, the "empathetic process is mostly automatic" (27), though (as Stanislavsky thought) the spectator's "unconscious" reactive empathy is actively led by the actor and the director. McConachie's sense of what "works" in the theatre at once naturalizes Stanislavsky's practice and urges its "cognitive" origins as a principle of regulation: it encodes a specific sense of theatrical viability, of artistic success, and of proper theatrical signification.

For Stanislavsky, "*the actor's conscious psychotechnique*" is hardly a native talent; the audience's automatic experience of Yelena's (or is it the actress's?) embodiment of exhaustion is the result of a richly developed technique, an emotional sensitivity conveyed through a precisely calibrated understanding of the overdetermined purposiveness of dramatic action in the theatre ("Jumps and gaps in the line of a role are inadmissible"), harnessed to a set of aesthetic goals and interpretive practices (given circumstances, bits and tasks, emotion memory, the supertask, through-action) conveyed through the development of privileged psychological and physical skills and sustained by a specific understanding of dramatic action, now widely promoted in the West as the sign of stage success, of what "works" (Stanislavski, *An Actor's Work* 347, 289). While this "technique" urges a transparent blend of actor and character, the fact that it is constructed by both actor and director is important to recognize here: this "natural" neural responsiveness is implicitly guided by the stage picture, pacing and tempo, and by the vocal and gestural register of behavior taken as appropriate to the stage now. This "automatic" process depends on a specific way of perceiving, interpreting, and enforcing the affordances of the stage.

For McConachie, identifying cognitive processes provides a means to determine the aesthetic practices and goals of the stage, because those goals are the goals of stage realism. Since "Cognitive psychologists have discovered that most people can only integrate about seven pieces (or 'chunks') of information in a single conscious gestalt, and only about four if those chunks are in motion," then "If several characters had been moving or talking during Yelena's exit, for example, the focus of the scene would have been fragmented and viewers, presented with too many chunks of moving information, might have missed some of her important qualities" (*Engaging Audiences* 32). Perhaps the purpose of *Uncle Vanya* is to enforce a monocular attention to the affective qualities of the play's principal characters, though Chekhov himself typically resisted a fateful empathy with his main characters, much as his revolutionary verisimilitude often depends on the buzz and hum of several distracting events happening at once. For McConachie, though, theatre is less an event than a means of communication, a way to signal the text's mimesis of emotion to an audience. Interpretation generates regulation: "All of this is common sense for actors and directors," especially for those, trained in the US, native to this notion of an emotionally centered – one might say emotionally capitalized – theatre for the consumption of character (32).

The production and the reception of theatre are highly redundant systems, and the assertion of performance conventions as invisible, as happens in McConachie's work as well as in Fauconnier and Turner's, provides a means to identify legitimate interpretation and limit it to the "common sense" encoded in the paradigms of American realist theatre and the training programs that have sustained it for nearly a century, a "common sense" we are now urged to understand as fully warranted by adaptive evolution. Since for "Most spectators most of the time," empathizing with characters is what they should, and must, desire to do (McConachie, *Engaging Audiences* 55), then this innate propensity is best satisfied when performance displays these coherent, purposeful, familiar beings. Evidence is hardly called for, and none is supplied, since, "make no mistake – empathy begins as animal instinct," and so interpretation-through-simulation is "basically a *natural process* controlled by our hard wiring" (McConachie, "Cognitive Studies" 55); "audiences generally 'blend' the actor and the character together into one image, one concept of identity, to enable their affective immersion in the performance" (*Engaging Audiences* 42), the affective immersion that defines performance, and the iron rule of what "works." This "blend" is plausible to anyone whose sense of performance derives from the immersive dimension of film or from the realist traditions of fourth-wall verisimilar theatre. But one need only recall the predominance of theatre forms (and even some individual works) that foreground the performer's skill as a performer – Beijing opera, Kabuki, American musicals, *commedia dell'arte*, even the extraordinary combination of verbal and gestural articulacy characteristic of Shaw's plays – to understand how partial and tendentious this understanding of the spectator's cognition really is.

Noting that empathetic and cognitive "simulation" depends both on the spectator's understanding of his/her likeness to or difference from the person observed, and on the "imagination and cognitive knowledge" that would enable the observer fully to put him/herself in another's situation, McConachie surprisingly observes that "A person who has not experienced extreme grief or great physical pain, for example, will have difficulty empathizing with someone who has undergone these experiences" ("Cognitive Studies" 57), signally confusing technical empathy with the self-conscious function of affect in American actor training (a term chosen with care here, to avoid the technical distinctions between "emotion" and "feeling" in neuroscience research). These remarks, though, perhaps allow an alternative conclusion to be drawn from this narrowly empathetic vision of theatre: if most spectators most of the time can't actually get into Philoctetes or King Lear or Miss Julie, perhaps that's precisely the point. Theatrical "empathy" takes place in a highly conventionalized environment, one that – even on the stage of Ibsen or Chekhov – must work to differentiate its constitutive behaviors from those that take place onstage. Decaying Philoctetes suffers outrageously; self-absorbed Lear curses outrageously; elegant Algy and Jack duel no less outrageously, with muffins: not only are these dramatic situations unique, the skill that creates them in the theatre is unique, and uniquely visible as well. Fauconnier and Turner suggest that blending is focused on the "anchor" of the actor, but stage acting often prevents a "transparent" identification of the actor with the character. Think of the "cheating out" required in the realistic theatre, of elocution and diction, of masks, formalized movement patterns, kothurnoi, dance, dividing a character between actor and narrator, multiple actors playing the same character, role doubling, and so on. Theatrical acting involves a distinctive, visible display of technical skill, and physical behavior that occurs no place else, and affords another distinctive behavior – spectating – that occurs no place else, too. McConachie raises the obvious problem of masked performance, asking: "where masks were conventional [of course, they remain conventional in much contemporary performance worldwide], such as the classical Theatre of Dionysus, did the wearing of masks by the actors interfere with spectators' empathetic engagement? Probably it did, to a degree, but it is likely that the actors knew how to compensate for the loss of their facial expressiveness through other means that encouraged empathetic mind reading" (*Engaging Audiences* 75).[27] There is, of course a simpler conclusion. Masks obstruct the everyday means of reading for "character" through the agent's facial expression; foregrounding the actor's technical vocal and physical performance, masks draw attention to what the actor is doing *as acting* as well as to a fictive "identity" arising from his playing. Masked performance underlines the theatrical specificity of *acting*, and implies the theatrical specificity of its dialectical counterpart, *spectating*. The protagonist was, after all, not a "character," but the principal contestant in an *acting* contest.

As in the "new character criticism," "cognitive" accounts of character, actor, and spectator promote a regulatory blend of philosophical and theatrical realism. McConachie's theatre rests on the unquestioned (and unsupported) "truism that most audiences go to the theatre to be moved emotionally" (*Engaging Audiences* 92): "empathy is *el camino real* linking the emotional entanglements of actor/characters to the mirror neurons and chemical changes in the brains of audiences. We experience actor/Blanche's PANIC and feel PANIC ourselves. Voinitsky is enRAGED at the professor and many spectators will share the actor's RAGE with him" (95). As a result, "Smart directors" (25) should structure a clear "empathetic process" (27) for their audiences, in effect raising empathetic neuronal simulation to the warrant of conscious experience.[28]

Yet, while cognitive approaches to apprehension, attention, and cognition rightly emphasize the mutual reinforcement of emotion and intellectual judgment, "cognitive" approaches to theatre have tended to emphasize the transparent role of empathy and sympathy at the expense of other ways of characterizing the work of performance. McConachie explains that the "Brechtian desire to elevate a spectator's rational over her or his emotional response was misplaced" because "a modest level of emotional engagement is necessary to sustain all rational attention in the playhouse" and elsewhere (*Engaging Audiences* 3). Of course, some rational attention is *also* required to render emotional engagement meaningful; otherwise, in the terms of much cognitive cultural studies, human responsiveness would be restricted to the basic survival motives – *fight*, *flee*, *feed*, and, not least, *fuck*. Yet Brecht hardly "discarded empathy as a welcome response in the theatre" (76), regardless of whether he sometimes confused empathy (feeling what the other feels) with sympathy (feeling in response to the other). The lesson of the experience of "alienation" often has to do with Brecht's savvy use of direct affective arousal to provoke analysis and judgment of the causes and significance of that arousal: Galileo's scientific team celebrating his resistance to inquisitorial torture, at least until the bell tolls; Kattrin's suicidal drumming, which saves the town but changes nothing. *Terrible is the temptation to do good*: we cannot understand, participate in, be fully entertained or changed by Brecht's theatrical logic unless we are to some degree tempted by Andrea's delight, knowing all the while Galileo will fail, unless we are irrationally seduced by sympathy as Grusha is. This mutually reinforcing, dialectical experience of emotion and judgment is the lesson of Brecht's most excoriated – and most brilliant – *Lehrstück*, *The Measures Taken*. Rotating the role of the Young Comrade among the actors, the performance instructs each of them in the pull of feeling; the point is not that we don't feel for the coolies struggling ineffectively to haul their barge (in the theatre, their rope is fixed to the stage: the theatre rationally demonstrates the destructive futility of their labor, while arousing sympathy and empathy for its brutal, straining, difficulty). Instead, *The Measures Taken* seems to raise the possibility that empathy can be trained to guide a number of responses, in this case stimulating attitudes (of the actors, characters, spectators) already groomed for ineffectuality by the social status quo, and those useful for revolution. Brecht's theatre is fully coherent with a "cognitive" perspective on the interplay between empathy and demonstration, emotional and rational responsiveness. McConachie's tactical misreading of Brecht illuminates the ideological framework within which cognitive theatre studies currently operates, and the rhetorical reciprocity between the ideology of realistic theatricality and the "cognitive" theatre of human nature.[29]

It is precisely at this juncture that Stanislavsky's role as the theorist of the realistic production of character through acting gains its greatest, and perhaps most controversial, leverage. The notion that theatre operates as a cognitively redundant system, one in which the habits and processes of extratheatrical behavior sustain, explain, and justify appropriate acts of theatre by both actors and spectators, has tended to reinforce a sense of the stage as reproducing universal human traits encoded in dramatic writing, enacted through fundamentally realist formalities, an aesthetic urging the ideological transparency of the means of stage production naturalized *as* theater. As we have seen with regard to Fauconnier and Turner, this dynamic is particularly evident in "cognitive" accounts of acting. Rhonda Blair, undertaking a related line of thinking, suggests that "Current research in cognitive neuroscience" not only "provides new insights into how the structures and processes of the brain, which is a part of the body, are related to consciousness," and so bear "the potential to deepen our understanding of acting methods"; it actually "confirms some basic principles of acting's twentieth-century visionaries and master teachers," especially "Stanislavsky and his heirs" (*Actor, Image* 3). How does a "cognitive" account of the actor's work on character – the combination of the "actor's work on himself" and the "actor's work on his role" that Stanislavsky developed at the beginning of the last century – define the (human) nature of theatrical performance?

Part of a continuum embracing Irving and Antoine, Belasco and Brahm, Stanislavsky was far from the only turn-of-the-century manager to clutter his stage with *things*; where Stanislavsky's practice proved innovative was in reciprocally objectifying the actor's interiority as part of the theatrical event, signaled by an ethical commitment to the emotional exposure definitive of acting as a Romantic art.[30] "Actors should educate themselves, build up a store of learning and real-life experiences, but onstage, while they are acting, they should forget what they have learned and be intuitive" (Stanislavski, *Actor's Work* xxiv). Rather than cunningly deploying the conventional signs of character, Stanislavsky's psychotechnique develops the notion of the actor's emotional vitality in performance through the now familiar design of "emotion memory," which coordinates an actor's richly specific personal and emotional recollection and response to the stimuli of the dramatic and theatrical environment with the projection of a character's interiority, understood as the climax of an invented, linear narrative devised to advance authorial intentions unrealizable in dramatic form. In this regard, Stanislavsky's practice arose within a specific "distribution of the sensible," a regime assumed and naturalized as *theatre* in cognitive theatre studies. Yet much as Stanislavsky's common-sense approach to emotion and memory resembles, but is not fully consistent with, the psychological dynamics of his near contemporary Sigmund Freud, so too it remains distinct from notions of *self*, *mind*, and *emotion* emerging in cognitive research, which nonetheless provide the warrant for Stanislavsky's commanding authority in cognitive descriptions of theatrical performance.

Stanislavsky occupies a signal role in cognitive theatre studies in part because, as the theorist of realistic theatre practice, he pioneered a mode of performance taken as transparent to interpretive practices asserted as cognitively privileged. Yet Rhonda Blair recognizes that in contemporary "cognitive" accounts, the "self" and the "memory" used to reconstitute it act as useful perceptual fictions in ways that should complicate the blithe absorption of Stanislavskian technique to the projection of an agent, a "character." A memory is neither a location, an inscribed record, nor a data file, but a present configuration of neuronal and chemical activity which is always new, reconstructed in the present circumstances of its generation. So, too, the sense of a perdurable *self* is a useful fiction, less the cause of action than the way "the mind *attributes* causation of action to itself'" (Daniel Wegner, quoted Blair, *Actor, Image* 59). The "self" is an unavoidable contentless instrument: while the mind/brain does not possess "a single central knower and owner, [...] our experiences tend to have a consistent perspective, as if there were indeed an owner and knower for most, though not all, contents" (Damasio, *Descartes' Error* 238). Although "cognitive" cultural critique often drives a wedge between the empirically demonstrable "truths" of scientific inquiry and poststructuralist "relativism," as Mary Thomas Crane implies in her superb reading of *Hamlet*, the notion of a fungible, opportunistic, instrumental "self" has considerably more in common with Francis Barker's "gestural" interiority (*Tremulous Private Body* 32) than with Stanislavsky's objectified "character." *Hamlet* tries "out a range of spatially delineated possibilities: there is, or is not, an essential self (variously the soul, rational faculty, heart) that works as a stable locus of agency; this self can, or cannot, be altered by influences from outside; this inner self can, or cannot, be reliably expressed; actions do, or do not, create the self" (Crane, *Shakespeare's Brain* 117). Perhaps the theatre approximates to biology, but insofar as Hamlet is "a theatrical character, his dream of subjective interiority was always futile" (149). Crane undertakes here a literary reading of *Hamlet*, principally concerned with what reading the play's language against the structure of primordial image schemata might say about "what it is like to conceive of oneself as an embodied mind, along with all of the problems and dilemmas that condition entails" (4). Although we might say that cognitive models of a provisional "self" resonate with the indeterminate nature of Stanislavsky's practice – which provides an instrument for inventing (rather than finding or reproducing) the linkage between the character's and the actor's tasks or objectives – cognitive theatre studies more typically finds that "*Self* is resonant with *character*" in a more stable and stabilizing way (Blair, *Actor, Image* 60). Stanislavsky's prescription for the actor's construction of a psychobiography through an emotionally invested transformation of the "given circumstances" of the play is not merely *an* approach to acting, but *the* approach, one that precisely erases the complexity of the "self" that *Hamlet* and cognitive science, as distinct from cognitive theatre studies, openly assert.

For Stanislavsky and his American inheritors in the 1930s and 1940s, the "Method" provided a universal solvent, a means to produce a human reality within any dramatic performance:

> The realist, the naturalist, the impressionist, the cubist take food into the mouth, chew it, swallow it down the throat to the stomach. Exactly the same thing is true of the subject matter we perceive in art, the way we assimilate it, develop it, embody it, ways nature has established once and for all, and which are not susceptible of change under any circumstances. (Stanislavski, *Actor's Work* xxviii)

Blending Stanislavsky's confident assertion of the representational authority of his technique with Antonio Damasio's understanding of the role of memory and emotion in the mind's ability to portray the organism's relation to an object world, Blair readily realizes Stanislavskian acting as paradigmatic of the nature of the stage: the actor "takes on some form of the internal (mental) and external objects of the text and its given circumstances, integrates these with her own mental objects, derived from memory and personal history, and devises a pattern of behavior." The result "is typically a course of action related to the character's desire to acquire or avoid something," and so replicates the pleasure/pain dynamic driving the evolution of the species (*Actor, Image* 60).

Antigone, Noah's Wife, Viola, Phèdre, Rosaura, Gretchen, Nora, SHE who is CLARA PASSMORE who is the VIRGIN MARY who is the BASTARD who is the OWL, Betty, THE VENUS: dramatic roles assert a rich, culturally specific perspective on human action and identity, inscribed to afford specific theatrical talents and techniques, an affordance that changes as theatre and culture change. In the theatre, character is a function of the interplay between the forms, styles, and practices of dramatic writing and those of performance, conventions that shape much of what counts as our participation as spectators as well. While Blair is aware that "values are imbedded [*sic*] in a given culture, in its language, imagery, and master narratives" (*Actor, Image* 56), the rich specificity of acting practice merely marks an underlying commonality: "the 'real,' the 'natural,' the 'imitative,' the 'realistic,' the 'truthful,' character, action, and emotion," however complicated these may be "in interesting ways in our contemporary culture" (23), nonetheless signal a single determinative relationship between "an actor's creativity," "*the* actor's process," and "its relationship to biology" (56, my emphasis). Although presumptions of the "'truthfulness' or 'universality' about a particular linguistic, cultural, or personal framework can unnecessarily limit an actor's creativity" (56), there's little sense here that Stanislavsky's instruments are themselves tied to "a particular linguistic, cultural, or personal framework," the framework of stage realism that neatly reciprocates the essentialist rhetoric of cognitive theatre studies.

In this view, seizing the biological interplay between the theatre's participants was Stanislavsky's moment of empirical genius, his apparent intuition that "Consciousness is not an abstract or ethereal process of an incorporeal mind, but a process of the body that helps us negotiate our way through the given circumstances of our lives, *in the same way* that an actor has to engage a character's given circumstances consciously and physically to determine its course through the play" (Blair, *Actor, Image* 64, my emphasis). "Given circumstances" are, for Stanislavsky at least, an interpretive heuristic, a means to seizing the opportunities of a dramatic role within the specific affordances of stage realism. Given circumstances are an instrument designed to resolve a perceived problem facing actors in transforming text into action (itself a specific, historically and culturally located understanding of theatre), perhaps especially the problems posed by Chekhov's unconventional, apparently purposeless roles and the apparently plotless dramatic logic sustaining them: "the fact that the dramatist doesn't give us the whole life of a play or a role but only those moments which are presented and performed onstage. [. . .] We have to supply what the author has not created in his printed text, using our own imagination. Otherwise you won't get a continuous 'life of the human spirit' in a play from the actor, you'll be dealing with isolated scraps" (Stanislavski, *Actor's Work* 288). The notion of "given circumstances" is deeply responsive to the ideological moment of the realist stage: it points to a notion of organic dramatic and theatrical form, of authorial intention registered in performance, and of a rich coherence between motivated, individualized characters and their social surround, a *scene* that functions as an *environment*.

Stanislavsky's assumptions here help us to unpack Blair's incorporation of "given circumstances" to human biology, and more generally the realist orientation toward character in cognitive theatre studies. For the history of dramatic writing suggests that the dramatist gives us as much of the "life of a play or a role" as s/he cares to inscribe, or as can be rendered performable in his or her theatre: Oedipus does not soliloquize; Hamlet is deaf to speaking verse; Nora cannot live, or once could not live, without a letter box. Dramatic character itself is a function of interpretation – all that's *there* are lines on a page – and as the history of both literary critique and theatrical performance shows, character emerges as an effect of performance practice, practice which takes in both an understanding of agents and agency in the world, and also the specific forms of agency practiced in a given theatrical culture. As Bruno Latour might put it, "Action is simply not a property of humans *but of an association of actants*, and this is the second meaning of technical mediation" (*Pandora's Hope* 182). Insofar as "emotion memory" and the notion of a perdurable character embedded in its "given circumstances" are useful interpretive and productive instruments, they are – alongside conventions of scenography, design, architecture – *actants* of this kind, providing a means of using the actor's body functionally and rhetorically within a specific structure of representational technical mediation. "Given circumstances" are means of insisting on a specific experience of theatre and naturalizing it to a vision of the world, a vision that, here, asserts an interchangeability with the world itself.

Yet the character's "given circumstances" are also those of the actor: wherever it is that Hamlet walks in Elsinore, in the Schaubühne, Lars Eidinger's Hamlet treads on (apparently edible) dirt, in a space openly shared with the contemporary audience. In this sense the "given circumstances" of the theatre elucidate the technical challenges of performance: how to undertake *this* act in a *theatrically* satisfying, effective, significant way. For Stanislavsky, the "given circumstances" are not only the character's imagined material, psychological, and social circumstances, but also implicitly the circumstances of the modern proscenium theatre: where a performer remains "in character"; where the stage asserts itself as a coherent fictive "environment" behind the fourth wall, unaffected by the audience's presence; where the spectator is virtually immersed in the staged fiction, not the practice of the stage; where the actor shapes an artistic rather than a merely commercial (or, in earlier eras, patronized, literally servile) relation to the public; where the performance is an organic work of art like the literary ("printed") texts it realizes; where performance accents an artistically mediated verisimilitude. In the theatre, acting involves richly signifying and interpretive activities that gain their specific function and meaning from the theatrical circumstances of their use. "Emotion memory" was the instrument of authenticity for Stanislavsky, and a rather different instrument for Marlon Brando after its migration to the United States, but both versions provide a means to make a certain kind of physiological behavior register as significant through contemporary codes of enactment: it's hard to imagine Brando's work arousing the same kind of response – it's perhaps difficult to imagine it arousing any specifically *theatrical* response – in, say, the court of Louis XIV, though it might well have prompted a legal or medical one.

The old chestnut of a theatrically unsophisticated spectator – usually located on the frontiers of theatrical culture, like the Wild West – rushing the stage to save Desdemona confirms an important recognition about theatre. Although our performance as spectators has biological, social, and cultural dimensions resembling the life-world outside the theatre, it is also recognizably marked off from other kinds of activity, even when it appears to reproduce verisimilar behavior (which seems relatively unimportant to most theatre historically). In reciprocating a biological determinism, the assumption of theatrical "realism" betrays a powerful and important insight about dramatic performance, an insight that runs directly counter to the notion of a technique transparent to our biology. Though "imitation" may be, on Aristotle's authority as well as that of cognitive studies, an ineluctable human activity, "acting" is not merely doing the police in different voices. We all "act out" in that sense, but much as mimesis in Aristotle's theatre involved masks, training, special garments, a specific disposition of the audience (and the entire *polis*), so in the great majority of performance traditions acting is a practiced accomplishment, a trained and visibly asserted skill: audiences become aficionados not of Hamlet or Lady Macbeth, but of Kemble or Kean, Gielgud or Olivier, Jacobi or Branagh, Mirren or Dench, Tennant or Eidinger. Acting – even Stanislavsky's disappearing machine of naturalistic performance – provides a distinctive point of attention, and so stands in an instrumental relation to the persons of the stage, and to human "cognition" in the theatre.

In any given theatre, acting might be conceived as a structure of affordance: a means of seizing the instrumental value of the performance's (and the performer's) situation, materials, opportunities in relation to a given sense of aims, purposes, abilities, consequences, significance of the project – in relation to what counts as *work* and as "working" in the theatre. Reliance on Stanislavsky and his realistic epistemology of theatrical practice necessarily grounds performance (much as it did for Stanislavsky) in a print-based understanding of theatre, as the transmission of a whole, "realized" world to an audience, in which the structure of legitimate "choice" is determined by licensed habits of production and textual interpretation. Yet as the history of Shylock onstage suggests, this license changes. The instruments of performance (a dramatic role) gain new properties, new affordances as we insert them into changing practices (culture, theatre, acting), asking them to help us undertake different kinds of work. Not only is the role of Shylock susceptible to different labor here and now (wherever here and now is for you) than it was in 1590s London, like any instrument, its perceived uses have changed according to the work people have tried to perform with it. And while acting and watching acting may appear to be more closely determined physiologically than, say, considering a painting or reading a text, they are nonetheless constructed activities that gain their meaning – their ability to accomplish work, itself a cultural value – precisely through their instrumental distinction from the behavior they may represent.

For this reason Blair's shrewdest insight about Stanislavsky finally displaces the realist agenda assumed as normative in much cognitive theatre studies. Character, she suggests, is "a process, rather than a discrete entity, a motivated movement, rather than a gloss of feeling."

> That is, a character becomes a dance performed by the only discrete entity there is – the actor. There is no character in any fixed or pre-set sense; as in life, there is only the progress of a particular individual moving through a particular context, changing with each moment. What the actor is doing becomes simply – and complexly – that: what the *actor* is *doing*. (*Actor, Image* 82–83)

What "the *actor* is *doing*" is being done with and within a constitutive apparatus, a practice. That practice may invoke the overt display of personal emotional vulnerability; it may involve masks; perhaps drumming syncopates its rhythms and emphasis; perhaps musicians sing the dialogue. In fact, decoupling "what the *actor* is *doing*" from this naturalized practice – stage realism as the vehicle for a privileged understanding of spectatorial cognition in the theatre, empathetic neuronal simulation with the character via the actor – actually restores the cultural force of Blair's suggestive observation: that the distribution of the sensible *in* the theatre is sustained by the forms of the sensible articulated *by* that theatre, *as* theatre. If character is a function of "what the *actor* is *doing*" then the *what* matters: wearing a mask, striking an elegant teapot stance, enacting a *mie*, using a trained spontaneity signaled in the myriad nuances of physical and vocal behavior to freight a line with complex, contradictory subtexts of desire.

"*[A]s in life*, there is only the progress of a particular individual moving through a particular context" (my emphasis). Blair articulates a conception of theatre as an event rather than primarily as the representation of a work, and nearly resumes Rancière's account of "individuals plotting their own paths in the forest of things, acts and signs that confront or surround them" (*Emancipated Spectator* 16). Yet Blair largely neutralizes the *produced* character of that "context," its "acts and signs" and the "distribution of the sensible" within which the particular individual moves, subordinating it to the determining physiology of human nature (as though the "given circumstances" of the theatre were either those outside its doors, those described in the fictive drama, or both). This erasure provides a critical index of the contemporary predicament of cognitive theatre studies. Committed to a realistic epistemology as the ground of theatrical experience, "cognitive" approaches are caught between a perspective that attends to the cultural specificity of "what the *actor* is *doing*" and a longing to retain the warrant of transmitting a universal experience (once the province of the literary drama), one that can be used to ground and value the performance process in a transcendent human nature. What the actor should be doing is transmitting Yelena's saucy exhaustion, not, say, wowing the audience with her (or his?) emotional volatility, or comportment, or vocal finesse, or dancing skills. As Jonathan Kramnick suggests, "cognitive" approaches to the arts tend to invoke a "scientific rationale" for seeing them "as the repository of timeless themes and for criticizing those scholars who fail to see how this is so" ("Against Literary Darwinism" 346). Stanislavsky becomes the inventor of a physiologically "valid" means for registering timeless art not merely in the naturalistic rhetoric of early twentieth-century performance, but in ways sustained by the essential process of human cognition. Here, cognitive theatre studies coordinates with the underlying motives of the "new character criticism": its reliance on a realistic representational epistemology in the theatre, and the correlative notion that human nature provides immediate access to dramatic character which properly operates in the theatre as an "identity." Yet extrapolating again from Kramnick's succinct case, if the disposition for a realist actor–character blend were so fully innate, we might well expect a considerably narrower variance in the practice of theatre, both diachronically and synchronically. Instead, the appetite for theatre, and for the range of events formalized as character in different kinds of performance, appears to be "considerably more sensitive to environment and history" (346).

The theatre is richly preoccupied with the projection of agents, typically via a network of conventional practices (masks, idiosyncratic movement vocabularies, versified language, vocal styles and tones) specific to stage performance. Dependent on those means, character appears as a densely "performative" effect, arising between actors and spectators when the conditions specific to the event have been met. Mere utterances, as J. L. Austin suggests, must meet extraordinarily complex conditions in order to gain the "force" of action among participating speakers and listeners:

imagine the consequences of a baseball umpire calling "you're out!" at a close play at the plate, but signaling "safe" with his hands. There seems little reason to think, then, that the "force" of "character" arises in the unique signifying armature of the theatre through the suspension of the conventions of its performance, as though masks, movements, verse were transparent to character, rather than the vehicles for its felicitous appearance, its "force" in the exchange between actors and spectators.

Punchdrunk Theatre's *Sleep No More* provides an unusually instructive instrument of inquiry here, precisely because its "immersive" aesthetic appears to insist that spectators each create a distinctive, individual "performance" within the event, largely through relatively immediate practices of "cognition": exploring the space, eating the candy, shaping a performance with actors who see, occasionally speak to, and sometimes touch them. Yet while it might seem to resist the disposition of proscenium theatricality, in practice, this "immersive" rhetoric depends to a considerable degree on the ideological relations of realist theatricality, as well as on the familiar uses of Shakespearean drama found there. *Sleep No More* spatializes "character," but does so by spatializing a formalistic, even poetic *Macbeth*. Appearances to the contrary, *Sleep No More* also depends in some respects on an objectifying rhetoric of "character," and frames a familiar realist relation between actor, character, and spectator. At the same time, by multiplying its idiosyncratic movement systems, it complicates the vehicles of "character," refracting the ways an objectified "character" may or may not emerge from, and ground the exchange between, actors and spectators. That is, the "immersive" logic of *Sleep No More* is inextricably entangled both with a "poetic," language-based sense of the play its silence might seem to spurn and with the "immersion" in fictive character otherwise promoted by the spectator's apparent exile from the field of play in modern proscenium realism. Richly attending to the spectator's function in the event of performance, *Sleep No More* responds directly to the interplay between "character," poetic rhetoric and the conventions of the modern stage, enacting a brooding mediation on the implication of writing, character, and "cognition" in the performances specific to the theatre.

"Nature seems dead" (2.1.50): spatializing *Macbeth* in *Sleep No More*

> Hamlet's inwardness is an abyss; Lear's sufferings finally seem more than human; Macbeth is all too human. Despite Macbeth's violence, he is much closer to us than are Hamlet and Lear. (Harold Bloom, *Shakespeare and the Invention of the Human* 534)

A superb vehicle for actors from Garrick to Branagh, *Macbeth* is a "character" play. Macbeth looms unusually large in the action of Shakespeare's short play and speaks with horrifying precision about the fearsome process of his experience, from the "horrible imaginings" that drive the opening scenes of the play (1.3.137) through the murder that begins his intense process of alienation ("To know my deed 'twere best not know myself" [2.2.71]), through the fits and illness that bring him to the ennui of having so "supped full with horrors" (5.5.13) as to be evacuated as a subject, transformed finally into an object (that severed head), whose last lines are memorable only for their reduction of intention, interiority, "character" to mere agency: "Lay on Macduff, / And damned be him that first cries 'Hold, enough!'" (5.10.33–34). Among Shakespeare's plays, *Macbeth* is perhaps the least in need of a restorative "new character criticism": from A. C. Bradley's impressionism to the New Critical poetic syntheses of L. C. Knights and Cleanth Brooks, to a materialist critique attentive to the uses of "character" in the enactment and reinforcement of ideology, to attempts to map the play's cognitive image schemata, analyzing the processes of "character" has been the pressing agenda of much of the play's critique.[31] In performance, *Sleep No More* models a vision of theatrical "cognition" surprisingly dependent on a familiar, literary *Macbeth*, in effect marking the persistence of a "poetic" dramatic logic even in the "immersive" dynamics of theatrical production. In this regard, it underlines the cultural legacy of interpretive paradigms and practices grounded in the critical and rhetorical tradition to a "cognitive" modeling of the spectator's share.

Donald Freeman's widely discussed reading of the use of "cognitive metaphor" in *Macbeth* usefully highlights the dependence of "cognitive" on more familiar practices of character criticism. For despite Freeman's desire to render merely "literary" critique passé – "How can a cognitive-metaphoric reading of the 'To-morrow' speech be shown to be better" than other forms of reading, he asks ("'Catch[ing] the nearest way'" 706) – in practice, his essay dramatizes the interdependence of "cognitive" analysis on fundamentally rhetorical strategies of interpretation. Whereas earlier critics read verbal imagery as part of the play's design as "poetry," cognitive approaches claim some verbal imagery as foundational to our appetite for and comprehension of the drama, warranted by the functional primacy of cognitive metaphor in the transcultural processes of human understanding. In Freeman's reading of *Macbeth*, then, the familiar tropes of "poetic" analysis – blood, darkness, clothing, gender – become significant merely as epiphenomena, based on the deeper and more essential motivating structure of these "embodied" metaphors, in this case the CONTAINER and PATH tropes. As Mary Thomas Crane notes of her own work with images in *Shakespeare's Brain*, this kind of critique has several similarities with purely literary, "word-based approaches" (she cites C. S. Lewis's *Studies in Words*, William Empson's *The Structure of Complex Words*, Raymond Williams's *Keywords*, and Patricia Parker's *Shakespeare from the Margins*). Since they are "based in a different theory of meaning and emphasize different patterns and structures" (27), though, "cognitive" textual interpretation claims to avoid mere "formalism," by offering more "than a materialist or historicist supplement to formalism, providing in addition a way of tracing in the text the interactions between culture, language, and cognition" (31).[32]

Elucidating the foundational function attributed to an image schema requires much the same persuasive structure as New Critical argument: the integration of verbal imagery toward the assertion of a coherent, consistent, and organic "meaning," significance sometimes constrained less by the "data" – Shakespeare's imagery – than by the critic's rhetorical capacity to show how apparently distant acts and images can be transformationally aligned within framing structures of argument. To Freeman, for instance, both *Macbeth* and its most relevant critics rely on "two core image-schemata, the CONTAINER and the PATH," which "have been shown to exist elsewhere in language and in other kinds of perception," and so guide our perception of the play's "language, characters, and crucial entities like Inverness and Fife Castles and the witches' cauldron." Since these image schemata are "already there" in "the language of *Macbeth*," "We understand *Macbeth* – its language, its characters, its settings, its events, its plot" – not merely "in terms of these two central bodily-based image schemata." Rather, our understanding is determined by them: "The unity of the language of and about *Macbeth*" – provided we reinterpret its assertions in terms of these two metaphors – "as well as the unity of opinion about that unity, arise directly and consequentially from this embodied imaginative human understanding" ("'Catch[ing] the nearest way'" 706–707). Metaphor and metonymy denote an endless process of deferral and transformation, and Freeman's claim that these image schemata are warranted by their foundational function in human consciousness depends – like all accounts of metaphor, including those of Lakoff and Johnson – finally on a "poetic" rather than an "empirical" rationale.

Merely linking the images of CONTAINMENT is insufficient, however, to explain the play's "cognitive" grip. For these metaphors to constitute a "better" reading, they must be seen to evoke more abstract ethical and interpretive patterns, problems of character in this case. To link images of CONTAINMENT with moral value, images like the witches' cauldron must not only be connected with other images identified with CONTAINMENT – the body, the castle, the self, the country – but these images must be exchangeable through an intermediating set of values: "metaphors [. . .] arise from a mapping of the CONTAINER image-schema into various target domains," target domains "expressed in individual words, dominating themes, characters and physical and psychological settings" ("'Catch[ing] the nearest way'" 693). As we might suspect, then, the plausibility of Freeman's "cognitively" determined reading depends on a surprisingly familiar interpretive sophistication. The first CONTAINER image is an index of the challenge: "Sweno, King of Norway, for example, is characterized as 'that spring whence ... Discomfort swells.'" Fair enough: a spring contains the water before it bubbles out, though one might pause to ask whether we typically conceive the "spring" as a container or as a passage: it strikes me that the image of a "spring," a cleft in the rock or an isolated pool, connotes the site of an outflowing, rather than what's contained before it burbles forth. This may seem a cavil, yet Freeman's argument that the image network appropriately grounding interpretation is a fouled CONTAINER depends precisely on the plausibility of such alignments, a formalism that has more in common with rhetorical critique than it does with empirical demonstration. The witches' cauldron, a literal container, must "contain" in ways akin to the way murder is contained in the inhospitable castle (though the sympathetic response of the surrounding nature to the murder perhaps implies that the castle is a morally permeable container, more a sieve than a cauldron), to the way Macbeth's mind contains its skrittering scorpions, and so on. The perception of these image schemata is (always?) already shot through with value: the witches' cauldron, for instance, "perverts" its natural use, "the creation of inner nourishment" (693) in order to be aligned with other perversions of CONTAINMENT.

Any reader will be impressed by Freeman's imaginative dexterity, and most will hesitate, too. When she commands the spirits to "unsex me here," ordering them to "Make thick my blood, / Stop up th' access and passage to remorse, / That no compunctious visitings of nature / Shake my fell purpose," Lady Macbeth is said unethically to be reinforcing her containment capacity, asking to "be made watertight, proof against just the kind of influence she proposes to have upon her husband" ("'Catch[ing] the nearest way'" 694). Perhaps so, but it seems equally plausible to see this speech as a refusal of CONTAINMENT. Much as she fears the spring of Macbeth's "milk of human kindness," Lady Macbeth seems more literally to wish herself less an impermeable container than an impenetrable solid, a substance proof against the "compunctious visitings of nature" whose "access and passage to remorse" is obstructed by her now thick blood (see 1.5.38–62). Alternatively, Catherine Belsey suggests that what Lady Macbeth contains here seems to be less a "self" than its trace. She points to a reading that erodes the privilege of CONTAINMENT as the defining trope of character, suggesting that Lady Macbeth is neither a solid nor a container, but a diffusing screen: "the subject of the utterance is barely present in the speech," divided among the grammatical subject (the spirits Lady Macbeth addresses) and a long list of body parts, which seem less to express her containing wholeness than her dismemberment: crown, toe, blood, and so on (*Subject of Tragedy* 47). Although Freeman argues for the cognitive priority of a CONTAINMENT metaphor here, alternative ways of reading this speech suggest that the force of his reading arises finally from rhetorical rather than empirical foundations, from ceding an a priori privilege not only to certain images, but also to the reading practices that align them with the restricted set of alleged conceptual metaphors.

For "cognitivist" critics the "end game is not an explication of the image, but an explication of the integration network necessary to compose that image and therefore the spaces, connections, and images recruited for this comprehension" (Amy Cook, *Neuroplay* 27). Yet, this "integration network" – which, despite recalling neurons, is purely heuristic, its metaphorical "spaces" and "connections" giving the appearance of a material habitation in the brain to what would otherwise be called "conceptions or "categories" – is finally indistinguishable from the poetic tenor and vehicle it claims to supersede. As Kenneth Burke might suggest, "cognitive" critique shifts its claims of *substance*, but cannot divest the rhetorical means for asserting those claims; the paradox of substance assures that the interpretive priority of "cognitive" to ordinary metaphors will not be decidable as a function of their rhetorical power, but only through recourse to external authority, here the "science" that legitimates some metaphors as prior.[33] To the extent that the "value" of a "cognitive" approach to image schemata and their blending "lies in how it maps the likely spaces and uncovers connections not immediately apparent but maintaining power even in dormancy" (Amy Cook 41), it dramatizes the mystified character of its alleged empiricism: the paradigm exists as a conceptualized "space" and merely awaits the discovery of the "dormant" data it must contain, "data" often invented by the interpretive process by which the "space" is conceptualized. Surely the connective power of the imagery of blood, darkness, garments, and masculinity is merely lying dormant for the moment, awaiting a more powerful connection to CONTAINMENT; otherwise it would be notable that Freeman seems to scant one of the most influential treatments of imagery in *Macbeth* – Cleanth Brooks' "The Naked Babe and the Cloak of Manliness" – and the rich range of imagery it brings forward.

Ironically enough, Freeman's essay dramatizes a contemporary cultural poetics, signaling – as much else in both "cognitive" and "character" studies does – an anxiety about the state and force of the humanities, expressed here by the dual restoration of tried and true categories (character) and practices (close reading) of interpretation, now grounded not in the flighty abstractions of an obsolete continental philosophy, nor in the mandarin taste of a bygone generation of literati, but in the hard, unassailable empiricism of "science" or "biology" or "evolution." Although Freeman does not address stage performance, a similar concern for the work of metaphor animates *Sleep No More*, which, like an essay by Cleanth Brooks (or even Donald Freeman) undertakes a critical interrogation of *Macbeth* by shuffling elements of the poem in order to assert a sense of its informing verbal, imagistic, and conceptual logic. For despite the absence of Shakespeare's language, *Sleep No More* participates in the rhetoric of "text-based" theatricality, and the literary conception of character and cognition it evokes. More important, its "immersive" conceptual design not only recalls an explicitly New Critical agenda for the relations between text and performance; it depends on a surprisingly realistic theatrical rhetoric, a rhetoric at once staging the complexity of character and the specifically theatrical contingencies of spectatorial "cognition."

It's hard to know if something happens in every room. Perhaps not. Back on the cemetery floor, but at the other, east end of the building (in the stairwells, the floors are conveniently marked E and W). Getting oriented. Suite of several cozy rooms: a nursery, with a white crib, and a mobile of a dozen or more cloth dolls, Victorian style. All headless. A bookshelf-lined hall where Macduff and Lady Macduff perform an energetic dance up and down the walls; she is pregnant, but that doesn't stop her. They come down, we – the number of spectators has now swelled – part, she puts on her mink, they embrace, kiss, and depart, she down the stairs and he through a passage. I don't follow but instead explore the hallway, the Macduff family rooms to the left: there's a bedroom, a dusty office, a locked door, then a child's room. It's tidy, as if the children had been playing and just wandered out for a moment – a doll and children's book on the bed, a few toys on the floor. As I'm looking at the bed, I realize there's a mirror behind me. I turn, but I've been ghosted: the mirror doesn't reflect me, but a ghastly reflection of the child's room, with the bed soaked in blood – "Blood will have blood" (3.4.121). I wander out, breathtaken. A parlor, the wall covered with mementoes; on a sideboard, a number of period decorations, including a large inverted vase, filled with eggs. "You egg," indeed. Out again into the cemetery: two figures, Macbeth and Lady Macbeth stand at a gravesite. Macbeth stoops and scoops up a handful of earth.

Despite its avant-gardish "immersive" aesthetic, *Sleep No More* enacts a fundamentally New Critical practice, spatializing "character" by remaking a network of verbal imagery as the scenic landscape of performance, in which each spectator takes a distinctive PATH, ironically enough, through a CONTAINER materializing images of blood, babies, darkness.[34] The verbal images that guide critical interpretations of *Macbeth* are visualized here in chilling detail, and – as they are in critical practice, "cognitive" or otherwise – detached from the narrative and dramatic logic of the play, to be assembled by an individual spectator's trajectory. Although we cannot see the "thick-coming fancies / That keep her from her rest" (5.3.40–41), the nightmare is materialized as the realm we inhabit with Lady Macbeth: the hospital rooms, her bloody bath (or, if we miss that scene, the bloody bathwater she leaves behind), the punishing dance in a strange glassed-in box near the ceiling of the Macbeth bedroom. The spaces of Macbeth's and Lady Macbeth's minds – of their souls is more accurate – are also registered by the overwhelming presence of death and deadness in the space we share. The witches drain the poor sailor "dry as hay" (1.3.17), and it's all dryness here: the apothecary with its hundreds of dried plants (recalling not so much the witches' recipes – a sailor's thumb, body parts of Turks and Tartars, liver of blaspheming Jew, and a long list of animals and animal parts – as the doctor's "rhubarb, cyme" [5.3.57]); the taxidermy room, the dead eyes of weasels and pheasants staring out at us, slant reminders of the martlet (1.6.4) and the hoarse raven (1.5.36), the screaming owl (2.2.15) and the clamorous "obscure bird" (2.3.55), to say nothing of the scorpions filling Macbeth's mind (3.2.37).

Sleep No More reifies Macbeth's interior world as "immersive" performance space, materializing elements of the play's verbal texture as objects in a thematically resonant environment. Like the verbal structure Cleanth Brooks once drew from *Macbeth* (reassembling intermittent verbal imagery of the text in a new rhetoric of organic interpretation), the objects in *Sleep No More* resonate as much more than "excrescences, mere extravagances of detail" (Brooks, "Naked Babe" 391). They function metaphorically in our performance as spectators, reassembled in an "interpretive" logic taken as homologous to a deep structure in the play itself. Barrett, in fact, sees the performance spaces to be "as autonomous and complex as the characters themselves, and each one operates as a distinct *chapter* in the overall work" (Barrett and Doyle, "Interview" 31, my emphasis). Emphatically identifying the space of performance with the printed space of the book, Barrett decomposes *Macbeth* in ways more reminiscent of the practices of literary "interpretation" than of the instrumental uses of the script for performance. Indeed, Barrett precisely tracks Harry Berger's notorious dichotomy of reading versus seeing plays. Unlike actors or directors, bound in Berger's view to the temporal order of performance, readers are "free to explore the 'umbrella' potentiality of words by uncoupling them, abstracting them, and holding them over the play or transferring them to another speaker," or to another material object ("Text Against Performance" 102). These "Strange images of death" (1.3.95) betoken a world, and a mind, in which "Nature seems dead" (2.1.50), a nature we enter as the McKittrick Hotel.

Like words, objects in *Sleep No More* figure simultaneously in several registers of signification. Deer, for instance, haunt the space: beyond the mounted trophies scattered throughout, full-size specimens stand in the taxidermy studio and in the hotel breakfast room, large enough to incarnate an uncanny, unsettling deadness, tall enough to look us in the eye. Recalling the garments, blood, and children of Brooks' "The Naked Babe and the Cloak of Manliness" – or the CONTAINMENT imagery of the cauldron, castle, country, and body in Donald Freeman's reading of "cognitive metaphor," for that matter – *Sleep No More* materializes the object world of *Macbeth* through repetition, multiplicity, analogy, transformation. Ross reports to Macduff after his family has been murdered by Macbeth's henchmen: "Your castle is surprised, your wife, and babes / Savagely slaughtered. To relate the manner / Were on the quarry of these murdered deer / To add the death of you" (4.3.205–208). The deer, then, also embody a principal fantasy of adult horror in *Macbeth*: infanticide. Brooks noted a "great many references to babes in this play" ("Naked Babe" 396), and children are evoked everywhere in *Sleep No More*, too: the headless-doll mobile, the "*bloody child*" (4.1.92 s.d.) concealed in a font in the dead ballroom and birthed by one of the witches in the delirious prophecy scene (the doll remains lying visible and bloody in the empty ballroom for some time after this scene, too), the pictures of children and the children's bedrooms in the Macduff suite, the egg sculptures there and elsewhere – "What, you egg! / Young fry of treachery" the murderer gloats, gutting Macduff's son (4.2.83–84). "I have given suck, and know / How tender 'tis to love the babe that milks me" (1.7.55–56). Although

L. C. Knights thought the question of Lady Macbeth's children largely irrelevant to a poetic reading of the play in the 1930s, as Carol Rutter has pointed out, for actors, actresses, and directors, "locating the 'missing child' has become the crucial performance trope defining the Macbeths' partnership," both in performance and especially in rehearsal (*Child's Play* 171).[35] As we move through a space emptied of children (there are no children in the cast, nor allowed among the audience), their bloody, dismembered absence is palpable, physically and metaphorically memorialized in their rooms, their toys, and the objectified detritus of Shakespeare's language – the headless dolls, the broken eggs, the deer.

The sensory poetics of *Sleep No More* gather a signal element of *Macbeth*'s thematic logic, the parallel between disordered nature and the moral darkness within, into the experiential logic of the event. While some of the rooms – the taxidermy shop, the hospital bath and bed rooms – approach something verging on low-level room light, most of the set is dimly lit, tinged with blue or yellow. The doctor's office has a single small lamp (without my glasses, it was difficult to read the reports stuffed in the drawers); other areas – the small "interrogation" room and the corrugated metal hallway leading from the "street" back to the "dead ballroom" – are nearly dark. "Light thickens" (3.2.51) around us, and while we get used to the "darkness [that] does the face of the earth entomb" (2.4.8–9), it eventually becomes oppressive, inescapable, even tedious: "I am in blood / Stepped in so far that, should I wade no more, / Returning were as tedious as go o'er" (3.4.136–138). This tedium arises not from boredom but from excess, a tedium that reifies our experience with Barrett's collocation of the space with "the characters themselves": "The time has been," just an hour or two ago, when we "cooled / To hear a night-shriek," but after a time we almost forget "the taste of fears," so "supped full with horrors" have we become (5.5.9–15). *Sleep No More* works to produce a sensory experience as an index of Macbeth's experience, a kind of "empathy." It is not unconscious, mirror-neuron empathy, but something else; a performance in darkness that spurs the ambition to see everything – all that rich detail, everything happening elsewhere – and the precise "tedium" of being "supped full": "The night is long that never finds the day" (4.3.243). *Sleep No More* creates an environment in which the physical sense of disorientation, an experience that combines sensory overload with sensory deprivation, articulates with a characteristic gesture of the play's representation of character: "cabined, cribbed, confined, bound in / To saucy doubts and fears" (3.4.23–24).

Sleep No More is "text-based" in a surprisingly imaginative, surprisingly literal way: structuring an identification with the disorienting experience of inhabiting Macbeth, it also reframes a familiar critical perspective on the play. As Alan Sinfield puts it, "the distinctive quality of *Macbeth* derives from the feeling that we enter the consciousness of the protagonist" ("When is a Character" 57), the "heat oppressèd brain" of Macbeth (2.1.39). In the theatre, the "problematics of vision" registers this thematic; the challenge of "seeing and interpreting in an uncertain visible world," has been – presumably from the first (non?)appearance of the "dagger of the mind" (2.1.38) onstage in the seventeenth century – central to the play's rhetoric in performance (Diehl, "Horrid Image" 191). Running at the Brooklyn Academy of Music opposite *Sleep No More* in April 2011, Declan Donnellan's *Macbeth* with Cheek by Jowl – a production *of Macbeth,* words and all, rich with Cheek by Jowl's focused physical energy – also sustained the "problematics of vision," of seeing, as the means of the audience's activity in the performance, usefully benchmarking the "immersive" aesthetics of *Sleep No More.* In Donnellan's *Macbeth* there are no witches, no weapons, no stage blood, no murderers. For the witches' scenes, the entire cast stands upstage and produces their spooky dialogue as a chorus; the killing of Banquo, the rape and murder of Lady Macduff, the skewering of her son are mimed silently by the victims. In the final battle scene, we hear the amplified sound of broadswords unsheathed, but see no weapons. To see this *Macbeth* is to create its violent instruments for ourselves: Macbeth sees the "dagger of the mind," that "fatal vision, sensible / To feeling as to sight" (2.1.36–38), and Cheek by Jowl identifies us formally, rather than merely psychologically, with him. Seeing with Macbeth stands at the center of our experiential agency in the theatre's "distribution of the sensible," gesturally *unmasking* our pretended absence from the spectacle. As in the very different structure of *Sleep No More,* this imaginative theatrical rhetoric accomplishes a performance readily identifiable with a familiar vision of the play, one hardly aligned with either a literary or a theatrical avant-garde. As Harold Bloom might put it, "I think we most identify with Macbeth because we also have the sense that we are violating our own natures, as he does his" (*Shakespeare* 534).[36] In the Cheek by Jowl production, and arguably in *Sleep No More,* we must – like Macbeth – (de)file our minds to see the play through.

A wordless environmental performance, *Sleep No More* nonetheless hews to a conventional conception of Shakespeare's character-driven drama, and to a still powerful fantasy of "text-based" theatricality. Comments on Facebook occasionally suggest that spectators should read *Macbeth* beforehand, and Catherine Quayle notes a "sly illumination of universal truths in the text" ("Excuse Me"); Barrett not only describes the spaces of performance in bookish terms (each is "a distinct chapter in the overall work" [Barrett and Doyle, "Interview" 31]), he also frames body and text reflexively: "it was about trying to find a way of making the spoken word as experiential as the body" (quoted in Eglinton, "Reflections" 47). Not only is "The world of *Macbeth*" one "into which we *have been thrown*, a dungeon for tyrants and victims alike," but in the play "Shakespeare rather dreadfully sees to it that *we are* Macbeth; our identity with him is involuntary but inescapable" (Bloom, *Shakespeare* 517, 518, emphasis in original). "*To know my deed 'twere best not know myself*" (2.2.71). Despite the "immersive" adventure it provides, despite the absence of Shakespeare's words, *Sleep No More* spatializes a familiar and fully "literary" sense of character, incidentally repolarizing Charles Lamb's famous distinction between the distractions of seeing *King Lear* in the theatre and the authentic encounter with the work that, for him, emerged only when reading the play: "while we read it, we see not Lear, but we are Lear, – we are in his mind" ("On the Tragedies" 136). What makes us feel "we are in his mind" in this spatialized *Macbeth* is *performance*.

Nonetheless, for much of the "immersive" performance the audience performs its conventional theatrical role, overlooking scenes organized explicitly as scenes "of" *Macbeth*. After his solo in the brick garden, Macbeth returns to the bedroom (Lady Macbeth is long gone), nattily suits up, and then proceeds out and down to the gallery level: he stands motionless, peering down at an elegant ball. He watches, inscrutably: Duncan dances smoothly with Lady Macbeth, who glances up at him; another actor – who plays one of the witches – dances lovingly with Malcolm (blending Shakespeare and a Hitchcockian detective); the female witches dance as well. Sudden thunder, the ball vanishes, and Macbeth descends for a long, athletic *pas de deux* with the bald witch, throwing one another around the ballroom ringed by the silent, looming evergreens (of course, if you haven't seen the witches' scene, you don't know she's a witch, or was, or will be). The group scenes alternate dialectically with the solos, perhaps emphasizing more fully notions of fictive coherence that stand apart from the emergent plotting of our "immersive" journey as spectators. The most stunning single event in *Sleep No More* (though, to judge by many accounts, and by Twitter, not one that everyone actually sees), the witches' prophecy scene (4.1), takes place in the "dead bar" on the "street" level, a room that can be entered only through one of its doors (if you exit the other door, you can't return; there's an ominous minder stationed there). The bar is suddenly transformed: blasting techno music and strobe lighting underscore the entrance of the three witches: the male witch strips, and puts on a giant, goatish, Satanic headpiece, and when Macbeth arrives, they pull him into the fray.[37] It's loud, disorienting: the female witches suckle one another, one gives birth to the "*bloody child*," Macbeth is partly stripped, and covered in blood, and it takes place more or less right where the audience is standing – the actors occasionally stumble into the spectators, and it's easy to get bloodied. The strobe unsettles the spatial relations of the performance, which flashes in and out of view, coming right at you and then suddenly veering elsewhere, but does not undo or displace them. The banquet scene, too, involves most of the cast in an explicit *tableau vivant*: Macbeth, Lady Macbeth, Macduff, Lady Macduff, Banquo, Duncan, Malcolm, the witches assemble on the elevated dais in the first-floor ballroom, to music and brilliant, blood-red lighting, toasting in slow motion. Although individual spectators see these scenes largely by accident, in one order or another, if they see them at all, they locate a relatively traditional economy of dramatic performance within the *event* of *Sleep No More*.

It is, of course, entirely possible to see *Sleep No More* with little sense of *Macbeth*. The "character" I have assembled here depends on a familiarity with the *text* of the play (indeed, on having the text of the play open to hand while writing) and, as in much "literary" critique of performance, not on the *script* of the production. It also depends on activities that cannot be part of the performance: organizing unspoken verbal imagery, collocating absent language with the event, establishing a possibly coherent system of relations between verbal items in the text of the play and the spatial, material, kinesthetic dynamic of the performance (the structure of this chapter overtly, if perhaps clumsily, attempts to reflect this dialectic between my experience of the event and my later efforts to chart an "interpretation" of it). Encountering the space and its various practices of "immersion" is, one might say, an "interpretive" experience in Benjamin Bennett's sense (Bennett, *All Theater* 184), an effort to understand the unfolding here and now of an event we sometimes play as more or less traditional theatrical spectators, and sometimes play in other ways. The temporal structure of a spectator's performance of *Sleep No More* does not track to the dramatic narrative, and recalling *Rebecca* or *Vertigo* or the records of seventeenth-century witch trials in Scotland or the text of *Macbeth* provides only a provisional and intermittent heuristic, however useful these texts may be subsequently in rethinking the work of the performance. "Interpretation" requires taking ourselves as participants *out* of the immediacy of the event to construct something else, a verbal representation of the performance, a thing of words made in relation to that other thing of words, the text of Shakespeare's play. This is, of course, a familiar notion of theatre, confirmed in one online "tip": read Macbeth before attending the performance ("Review: Tips"). *Sleep No More* insists, as the New Criticism did, that the interpretation is not the poem. At the same time, and again like the New Criticism, *Sleep No More* frames the "dramatic" element of the performance as dependent on, derived from, the text; it is purely aesthetic, legible most clearly in relation to other artworks – *Macbeth, Rebecca, Vertigo* – and not, say, to the social life beyond its walls.

It's later in May; the run has been extended and I've come again. I go first to the top floor. There is a man in a lab coat folded on his back in the window between the bathtub room and the forest: a doctor. He rolls into the forest, and I slowly follow through the door, but while I circulate through the maze, he has disappeared. I pick him up again in an office I had not noticed before, more or less opposite the padded cell, down the hall from the office with the medical reports and the hair collection. He sits intently at a desk facing the door; to my left suspended on the wall are pages of books, with lines, shapes, razored out of them. The man is razor-cutting lines from a book, and forms a pattern with them on the desk. From time to time another masked spectator comes down the hall and looks in: I watch for perhaps twenty minutes. The doctor turns to look behind him, slowly gets up, and moves for the door – he does not look at me and I step aside. He turns left and walks quite quickly to the operating theatre, a room perhaps twelve or fifteen feet square, with an elevated seating area around the two walls opposite the doorway. He begins a long dance: he's tall, muscular, and moves slowly but powerfully over the operating table. It seems as if every body surface engages with the table, before he rolls to the floor. He finds (did he have it with him?) a piece of chalk, and begins writing on the low wall circling the table/stage that supports the elevated "operating theatre" seats. The wall is covered with writing; was it here the last time? He then proceeds out through the bed room and the bathtub room to a small room behind the soap crucifix. The room contains a glass case of small objects. He places a piece of cloth on the case, and then takes several objects out, arranging them on the cloth. Pieces of glass, several tenpenny nails. This takes perhaps ten minutes. He is impassive, controlled, concentrated. He slowly walks away. I take a nail with me.

If the spatial dimension of *Sleep No More* concretizes a "literary" vision of language and character, then Maxine Doyle's choreography takes a similar point of departure, one that readily collocates "literary" and "cognitive" visions of theatrical character. Doyle examines "the text

Figure 4. Tori Sparks as Lady Macbeth in *Sleep No More* (Photo: Alick Crossley).

closely – getting a feel for its rhythm, its structure, and its imperatives" and uses "this as a springboard," principally to "the emotional realities that are in the text": "Emotion is really the key driver in our work, and that's why I work predominantly with dancers. I think dance can express humanity more directly than any other art form" (Barrett and Doyle, "Interview" 31). Despite Doyle's notion of dance as a transparent instrument of natural human responsiveness, in some ways the choreography of *Sleep No More* resists the straightforward lamination of literary character with performer and so troubles the principal models of "cognitive" processing of character – the empathetic-to-sympathetic logic of emotional identification urged by McConachie and the blending of "character" and "actor" described by Fauconnier and Turner.

Throughout the evening the audience encounters the performers moving through the space, the men mainly in tuxedos, often without jackets, the women mainly in slinky ballgowns or 1940s suits (see Figure 4). The dancers develop a characteristic movement vocabulary or vocabularies; the solo and pair dances are muscular, athletic, dangerous, and are often "in character," though it may take some time, knowledge of *Macbeth* and Hitchcock films, and reference to the program provided after the performance, to know *who* – what character – the dancers represent, or represent at this moment as opposed to in earlier or later scenes. Lady Macbeth dances solo in the Macbeth bedroom, and then climbs up above the furniture into a small, Plexiglass-fronted box, perhaps ten feet deep by ten feet wide by eight feet tall: she throws herself against the glass for several minutes before exiting and wandering erratically out the west stairway. Macbeth, too, has a physically demanding solo, leaving the bedroom for the brick "garden" outside, where his dance also involves, well, climbing the walls. Both the solo and duet choreography tend to stress the vertical – there are dances up doorways, climbing a bookshelf, in the hotel lobby telephone booth – in ways that enact both the skill and daring of the performers, and identify the choreography with the principal trajectories of modern dance, foregrounding "gravity as a universal within and against which the body articulated its dynamism" (Foster, *Choreographing Empathy* chapter 1). In one sense, these performances are fully in line with conventional readings of *Macbeth*, and perhaps even illustrate them: as Bradley put it, "even when the speed of the outward action is slackened, the same effect is continued in another form; we are shown a soul tortured by an agony which admits not a moment's repose" (*Shakespearean Tragedy* 332–333).

The dance vocabulary is tense, the body apparently in constant struggle with itself, with gravity, perhaps with the weight of its own embodiment (or character). Our mirror neurons are surely firing, and the agitated movements and – sometimes – grimacing facial expressions do enable the intermittent attribution of character (or at least, the attribution of concentration and exertion), especially to the performers of Macbeth and Lady Macbeth. But the choreography also tends to dramatize the limitations of a theory of performance that understands spectatorial performance as a straightforward extension of nontheatrical behavior, a simple "blending" of actor and fictive "living person"/character, in which we "compress" and "integrate" the blend to identify this fictive agent, or "decompress" it to attend to the actor's performance (see Fauconnier and Turner, *Way We Think* 266), or in which we are drawn definitively by empathy along "*el camino real* linking the emotional entanglements of actor/characters" to our own (McConachie, *Engaging Audiences* 95). Lady Macbeth in the bath seems to want to claw her way out of her skin; yet although the dancers' work sometimes externalizes a gestural sense of the principal characters of *Macbeth*, the choreography often has a depersonalized quality and traces a movement spectrum from energetic contact-improvisation to generic "modern" abstraction, to meticulously focused behavior, more in line with the possibility "that dance's intrinsic appeal lies in its ability to excite viewers' interest in movement's trajectory" (Foster, *Choreographing Empathy* chapter 3).

Susan Foster's treatment of empathetic theories of modern dance is apposite here. Where John Joseph Martin "presumed that kinesthetic engagement led to emotional attachment, and [Yvonne] Rainer hoped that movement could be enjoyed simply for its physical factuality," the mirror-neuron studies used to privilege an emotional involvement with character in theatre studies have led in a different direction in dance studies. Ivar Hagendoorn's admittedly speculative work implies that what the mirror neurons may bring into focus is not empathy with the intentions generating movement, but merely an interest in the movement itself, a kind of technical attention to the movement alone, and an anticipatory attention to its possible directions (Hagendoorn, "Some Speculative Hypotheses"). As the doctor's performance – if he is a "doctor" – suggests, much as the (wandering, gathering, dispersing) audience is visibly choreographed into the spectacle, "dancing" here embraces a wide variety of activities, some in a conventional modern dance idiom and some not, but all challenging the lamination of movement and gesture to representation, to character, and to writing. Malcolm – if the actor is "Malcolm" in this sequence – has a long scene alone in the detective's office in which he types out a line, very slowly, moving back and forth between the two desks in the meanwhile; he cuts it out from the paper with a razor, opens the desk drawer, and does something with it. When he leaves, I open the drawer and discover that he has tied it around a dead bird's leg. *Sleep No More* uses writing, but cuts it from the book, rearranges and repositions it – as performance must do – into another mode of production. In performance, words signify as something else, as action. In *Sleep No More*, actions sometimes also signify simply as movement, action, a *doing*, not as the expression of character and not as the delivery of a scripted meaning.

How does behavior, movement, activity re-present literary character? Macbeth and Banquo seem to fight it out in the bar, moving across the bar, to the floor, on and off the pool table, throwing one another in wide arcs around the room; Macbeth and one of the witches (slinky blue dress) have a sultry duet in the candy shop, and another in the hotel lobby that leaves him prostrate on the floor (see Figures 5 and 6). While these events have an "emotional" quality, seeing these performances has more to do with an affective/critical response to their temperature and coloration, to the pace and scope of movement than with seizing specific motives or intentions, with characterizing these agents. A woman sits in the "dead bar" and slowly eats her dinner, occasionally rising to take a spectator out into the hall and into a sealed room; she returns (alone) and lip-syncs "Is That All There Is" to a deeply distorted voice.[38] A woman drinks tea; the taxidermist prepares specimens. A man (the taxidermist, elevator clerk, hangman – are they the same "character?"), expressionless,

Figure 5. The taxidermist and a spectator in *Sleep No More* (Photo: Alick Crossley).

Figure 6. Macbeth and Banquo duet in *Sleep No More* (Photo: Alick Crossley).

rapidly slides a heavy oak door across the gallery, ramming it into the wall. These performances are abstracted from a narrative structure, a logic that – for Aristotle as well as for "cognitive" approaches to theatre – is essential to deriving the effect of character from actions, a plot. Here, there is often only movement to respond to: abstract, contentless, detailed, blank-faced movement, part of *my* plot, perhaps, but not clearly part of another causal arrangement of incidents, and not expressing a distinctive character. Like Lady Macduff atop the bookcase, these performances do not narrate; and sometimes when they do (Lady Macduff's dance with the Nurse in the hotel breakfast room, begging for a glass of milk – of human kindness?), the narrative remains opaque, disconnected from other events, conjectural. The actors are fully absorbed, meticulously *doing* what they *do*, yet even in the scenes more overtly recalling *Macbeth*, much of what they do is not representational; it does not seem to refer to or constitute a fictive person or fictive elsewhere – *Macbeth*, *Vertigo*, *Rebecca*. This concentrated work is astonishing, and it is perhaps difficult to "characterize" because it is not about character: "what the *actor* is *doing*" is what we attend to (Blair, *Actor, Image* 83).

Spatializing character throughout its environment, *Sleep No More*'s choreography and movement enact a complex duplicity with regard to dramatic character. At times, the choreography partly depends on a textualized character antecedent to performance, the reproduction of a literary character through a psychologically illustrative, expressive dance. Yet *Sleep No More* also suggests that character and motive, intention, are not essential to our experience of theatrical performance. Indeed, "character" as an inscribed entity may well lie outside it: my sense of the actor playing a noirish detective altered somewhat when I realized that he was also (playing?) "Malcolm." The emergent cultural signification, the "interpretivity," of those acts and of our own is a function of the manifest conventions of performance, nonetheless immediate for being evidently scripted, choreo*graphed*, and repeated. In its "immersive" dimension, *Sleep No More* allegorizes the illusory immediacy of theatre, emphasizing not its transparent accommodation to the *real*, but something else: the material density and opacity of its *performance*.

It's later the same evening in May: before heading down to see the banquet finale I return to my favorite space, where I began this evening, the huge, forest of leafless hardwood under the cold blue light: it's a maze, with a white mountain goat – still, stuffed – stuck in the center. Unlike Birnam Wood, the pine forest in the basement ballroom, there's nothing moving, nothing living here: even the "sere, the yellow leaf" (5.3.24) *has long fallen and blown away. I walk slowly around the maze, not really wanting to leave. A small commotion and I see the Nurse coming in my direction – she walks up to me and looks intently into my eyes. This has happened before with other characters, and it is a bit unsettling, perhaps more so because of the mask. Then she takes my hand: THIS IS GREAT! I've heard – and seen – that the actors sometimes select a spectator and take him/her aside, into a room, where interesting things seem to happen. She takes me slowly and carefully, stroking my arm from time to time to the elevated hut in the corner of the "forest." We climb two or three steps, she unlocks the door and we enter; she closes the door behind us.*[39] *It's a small room, furnished with a table, a sink, two chairs – a bit homey. She has me sit and sits across from me, our knees almost touching. She reaches over and raises my mask: it feels astonishingly intimate, a real surge of excitement. She says several times "it's alright." She gets up, pours a cup of tea from a silver pot, puts in some sugar and extra tea leaves. She then spoons several spoonfuls of the tea into my mouth. Dabs my lips. Puts the napkin on my lap. Then she slowly, and with a strangely restrained energy, begins to tell me a story. The story is about a very sad little boy, abandoned by his parents, who needs to find a home. He travels to the moon, but it is only a piece of wood; he goes to the sun, which is a dead sunflower; he goes to the stars, which turn out to be fireflies stuck in the sky, so he returns to earth, where he sits down and begins crying. He cries forever. She then takes my hand pretty hard, pushes my sleeve back, and begins stroking the veins of my forearm, then traces lines in my palm and presses her thumb hard in the center, once. She leads me out. I turn and look back while she closes the door. She pulls the shutters down over the windows. I remember the dead animals hanging on the wall.*

Although the cast and some elements of *Sleep No More* have changed over time, in the press, social networking blogs, and Twitter feeds following *Sleep No More*'s premiere in 2011, several elements of the production have become known, perhaps the most intriguing being that individual members of the audience are taken aside, often into small rooms, where various ritualesque scenes are performed with them, one-on-one. One of my students, Emily Wallen, stumbled on Macbeth ducking through a door; she followed, to discover him showering off the blood: she remained, playing an assertively voyeuristic role ("All Within Site"). Another reports:

> Macduff was holding an egg. He stopped and looked at me like I was a freak. Then, he grabbed my hand and pulled the door shut, locking it behind us. He pulled out a cigar box and opened it up ... and made me look at these eggs (that were inside) really closely ... He took an egg out of the box and started squeezing and the egg broke and it was full of dust. He freaks out and shoved me against a wall, asking "Who are you?" and takes my mask off my face ... Then there was a crash, and the lights went out. When I looked back at him, he started shivering and grabbing me really close and he bear-hugged me and said "Me thought I heard a voice say sleep no more." Then, he was butterfly kissing my face and he kept saying "sleep no more," and then he really shoved away hard, pushing me against the wall, and he ran away. I ran after him, thinking I would follow him. He had my mask, and then he just threw my mask. People were waiting to see

> when we would come out of the bedroom and they all saw me without my mask on. (Alex Shaw, quoted in Wallen "All Within Site")

Having engaged in this one-on-one myself at a later performance, I can confirm what strikes me as the alarm of Shaw's description: the performance is physical, rather threatening, direct, manhandling. Some one-on-one scenes take place in public: I watched a spectator given a small ring by the actress sitting and eating in the "dead bar" before the witches' big scene; I watched with a very small group as a woman was brought into a kind of interrogation room and given a small amulet by Banquo and Malcolm. On Facebook, some people report being addressed as "Fleance," and Todd Barnes was taken by Lady Macduff into a room, told a story about a girl whose parents die, asked to read along with her from a book, and given a necklace with a gold locket; inside the locket was a small piece of paper with illegible writing and a few seeds of anise – "this will protect you." She then took him to a wardrobe, and they both went inside.

> Once inside, we were incredibly close. She ran her hand up my arm and began to caress my face. Then she put her face next to mine. We were cheek to cheek, and this was the most awkward part. I could feel her breath. I've never been to a "gentleman's club," but I suddenly became aware of the rules that goven that space: be touched but do not touch. Yet, this immersive theatre experience seemed to rely on my participation. I felt the need to reciprocate her affection in some way, but I did not. She put my mask back on, and then she pushed me out of the back of the wardrobe through a secret door. The room I ended up in was the one with all of the bathtubs. As I entered, Lady Macbeth and her nurse were getting into the tub. (Todd Barnes, Message, 2 August 2011)

Emily Buttner was watching the banquet scene when Lady Macbeth outstretched "her bloody arms" and yelled at the crowd: "'Take my hands!' I took them, and she led me up five flights of stairs at breakneck speed, not letting go of me even for a second to turn up the next staircase. All the while she repeated, 'What is done cannot be undone, cannot be undone what is done undone cannot undone'" (Buttner, "Restoration versus Reality"). At the end of one performance, just before the banquet, I followed Duncan to a corner behind the evergreens in the first-floor ballroom; he turned, embracing me, and said, "Don't you know the body is a temple." Emily Buttner had a more interesting experience after the banquet finale: "After Macbeth was hanged, everything around me went black, and I felt a hand grab my arm. It was Lady Macbeth, who had earlier dragged me up five flights of stairs in a mad rage. Now, though, she was smiling, and took my arm in hers placidly. She led me out of her banquet hall and into the lobby from which I had entered *Sleep No More*. She took off my mask, which had been unmoved on my face for the past three hours, kissed me on the cheek, and turned away, disappearing into the darkness."

False face must hide what the false heart doth know (1.7.82): these moments of intimacy reciprocate the most provocative element of the production, the masking of the spectators. Punchdrunk uses "the masks to encourage people to go on a journey on their own, and to create a kind of interior world" (Colin Marsh, quoted in Eglinton, "Reflections on a Decade" 51). Or, as a Twitter dialogue on the *Sleep No More NYC* Facebook page has it: "Best thing to happen in the theatre since the proscenium." Comment: "Screw the proscenium." Yet as Barrett has remarked, "Handing out the masks is like assigning seats in an auditorium. It establishes each individual as part of an audience, and creates a boundary between them and the action. The masks create a sense of anonymity." The masks also "allow people to be more selfish and more voyeuristic than they might normally be," in effect intensifying the anonymous voyeurism inscribed in realistic theatricality (Barrett and Doyle, "Interview" 26). Indeed, as Barrett has remarked of his initial inspiration to mask the audience while a student at the University of Exeter, when the spectators are masked, they "become part of the aesthetic and disappear into the whole picture" (Healy, "London Troupe").

The masks dramatize the privilege of the modern spectator, the extent to which the act of seeing is *produced*, staged in and by the ideological topography of the spectacle, its cognitive burden and possibilities intrinsic to the design and practice of that event. Unlike the masks in Stanley Kubrick's *Eyes Wide Shut* – Bill Hartford's "present fears" are also less than the "horrible imaginings" of his wife's sexual fantasies – in *Sleep No More* our masks underwrite the agency to watch, but not to act, at least not to act with the legitimate performers. Tori Sparks, a superb Lady Macbeth, likes it "when the audience gets really close, that they want to see if you have tears in your eyes or want to feel your breath – all that's fine. But don't try and steal the scene" ("'Sleep No More' but Move Nonstop").[40] The mask performs the work of the darkened auditorium and the theatre seat, separating, individualizing, and interiorizing us as a group of spectators: the "interior world" of our private consumption literalizes the commodity structure of realism, a structure so evidently on display that interior design magazines have covered the production. We can eat the candy and wander the space, but we are less the agents of the performance than its furniture.

In this regard, masking the spectators reciprocates a realist enthusiasm pervading *Sleep No More*. As in Stanislavsky's productions of Ibsen and Chekhov, the rooms are packed with stuff, externalizing and reifying "character" as an extension of a socially and materially determined environment. *Sleep No More* literalizes the physical and ideological confinement of the fourth-wall realism, surprisingly abstracting the "immersive" performance from the agency of its audience. The performance's three cycles are carefully managed, and we wander through a densely totalized, "retro" environment, operated through a concealed technological apparatus. Throughout the space, black-masked minders in black t-shirts and jeans, occasionally in black suits, intervene to police the spectacle: helping spectators with claustrophobia, holding doors closed when spectators are not allowed to enter, gesturing – or occasionally slightly restraining – spectators who talk or bring a cell-phone or camera into view (I did try), preventing access to the fabled sixth floor (where, to judge by Twitter and Facebook feeds, some spectators have been allowed). Emphasizing a transparent identification with "literary" character, *Sleep No More* also summons the aesthetic relations of theatrical realism, urging a fictional interpretive "freedom" while concealing the work of two of its constitutive agents: the means of production behind the scene, and the reciprocal means of production behind the mask. As Brecht might have said, that's the realist theatre's closest approximation to the reproduction of social life: a prison in which the guards are barely visible, and in which we "choose" to be cabined, cribbed, confined to a "nature" we assent to, assent through, produce.[41]

Samuel Weber describes theatre as "a place of fixity and unfreedom," a "prison, to be sure, but one that confines through assent and consensus rather than through constraint and oppression" (*Theatricality as Medium* 8). The scenes of "private" intimacy, however, momentarily suspend our spectatorial distance, anonymity, and apparent lack of responsibility in the event, providing the perhaps illusory sense of agency. It's hard not to hear a note of vulnerability and exposure in Alex Shaw's remark, "they all saw me without my mask on": how to "act" without the mask that defines our function in the spectacle? And yet, much as Barrett and Doyle work to "imagine the action that might have been happening off the page" of the "'unseen text,'" here, too, textuality plays an important and rather surprising role ("Interview" 23). The story that the Nurse told me was lifted from Büchner's *Woyzeck* (scene 21); several other moments of intimacy – not all – have a similar moment of textual reference: Lady Macbeth speaking to Emily Buttner as she drags her up the stairs, the illegible text Todd Barnes found in the locket, Duncan's fevered quotation from Corinthians 6:19, "Fleance" (otherwise absent from *Sleep No More*).[42] *Performance* in *Sleep No More* articulates a complex regard for textuality, recalling Harry Berger's sense that performance "invests its charismatic representation of a world with verbal traces of the hidden processes by which the communities of the play and the theater join in producing that world" ("Text Against Performance" 125). Many of its most striking spatial and movement elements, the elements with which we engage most directly as spectators, are inspired by the language of *Macbeth* but are inspired in an absence of spoken words. At the same time, those moments in the performance in which our realistic absence from the spectacle is uncannily interrupted, often involve the transmission of a "text" – sometimes even a slip of paper – as though textuality were always an unseen, secreted element of dramatic theatre.[43]

Sleep No More dramatizes the complex reciprocation between Shakespearean drama and contemporary cultures of performance. Virally marketed, tech-forward, and resolutely hip (in the week leading up to Halloween, patrons who had attended received an e-mail "telegram" inviting them to one of a series of fancy-dress performances: audiences lucky enough to land tickets would be required to wear themed costumes – all black, risqué red, film noir formal; since the winter of 2011 there have been New Year's Eve, Valentine's Day, and several other theme events as well; a sleek rooftop restaurant, Gallow Green, opened in 2012, and another, The Heath, opened in November 2013), *Sleep No More* nonetheless reproduces a range of familiar attitudes toward the cultural function of Shakespeare, and of the legitimating role of writing in performance. The role of "immersive" innovation in sustaining a reciprocal theatrical conventionality is now documented by the copycat "immersive events" that have sprung up recently in New York, including the notably slack-jawed adaptation of *War and Peace* as immersive dinner theatre, *Natasha, Pierre, and the Great Comet of 1812* (see Healy, "Care for Caviar"). A *Macbeth*, *Sleep No More* palpably replays the language of "character," often in ways resonant with a century's worth of character criticism, the notion that Shakespeare has written the gestural dimension of the role into the text, a role that – on the page or on the stage – should transport us deep inside the "written troubles of the brain." Despite its *eventness*, *Sleep No More* immerses its audience in a paradoxical practice: we write our individualized plot lines in movement, but are constructed within the spectacle as realist voyeurs, watchers, *readers*, not agents. Yet at the same time, *Sleep No More* also articulates an alternative, experiential, perhaps anti-interpretive paradigm of performance, as much of the choreography – in its abstraction, its frequently affectless behaviorism – foregrounds performance as a *doing*, here and now, a practice we share with the performers, perhaps most intensely in the unmasked "private" performances, performances which at once recall, displace, mystify the work of "writing" in the transmission of performance and dramatize the essential *theatricality*, the dependence on a "distribution of the sensible" characteristic of *theatre* – and so all cognition of others, actors, characters, and spectators – in *Sleep No More*.

Replaying *Macbeth* as an "immersive" event, *Sleep No More* dramatizes the complex *affordance* of dramatic writing in contemporary performance, as the production seems at once to reinforce a sense of textually determined character and the spectator's affective "mind reading" cherished by cognitive theatre studies and a more eccentric sense of the performance event operating through typically opaque, theatrically specific means. As theorists of both design and cognition recognize, an object's ability to be used, to do work, lies in its *affordance*, the interplay between the "perceived and actual properties of the thing" that enables us to imagine its utility in both expected and unanticipated contexts (Norman, *Design of Everyday Things* 9). Texts certainly have properties, but their ability to be instrumentalized in making significant performance depends on the application of practices that determine our perception of those properties, and so determine the properties themselves. Performance practices are not transparent to "dramatic" representation, nor to the character that may (or may not) be inscribed there; they are the historically, culturally, socially, and aesthetically contingent behaviors that remake the text, constitute the event, mediate our participation in it as performance, and, sometimes incidentally, convey an effect of representation. As Edwin Hutchins puts it, "The structured representational media in the system interact in the conduct of the activity" (*Cognition in the Wild* 373). While a realist approach to character, and to the "cognition" of performance more generally, grounds its explanatory power in the imputed force of innate social and/or biological systems driving spectatorial experience, experience valued in some cases only insofar as it conforms to an assumed evolutionary imperative (say, sociability or reproduction), *Sleep No More* enacts a complex duplicity of practice, at once underscoring its conventional formality (masks, choreography) and simultaneously claiming the "transparency" of practices associated with modern realistic performance. In a reflexive register, it recalls a familiar "dramatic" logic of textual "reproduction," yet – doing so without words – stages the essentially rhetorical contingency of the claim of any dramatic theatre to reproduce writing as performance. If we create or recognize "character," we do so at the intersection of opaque movement and notions – of Shakespeare and Hitchcock – drawn from beyond the event. And, while decisively positioned in the perspective of realist theatricality, behind the mask one is constantly aware of responding to movement without motive, to actors who are sometimes "characters" moving intermittently and exchangeably through an interrupted narrative that's at once fictive, repetitive, uncanny, and unseizable. It's a little like life, but also like nothing else: it's theatre.

In this sense, *Sleep No More* precisely occupies, perhaps even performs, a defining dialectic of contemporary Shakespeare performance. Invoking and staging a kind of experiential realism, it complicates a "cognitive" notion of "character" and performance, in part by invoking – rather than merely dismissing – the relations of realistic theatricality and the interpretive agenda it typically sustains. *Sleep No More* dramatizes the ongoing implication of a "literary" Shakespeare in the work of contemporary experimental performance while locating the familiar locution of performance as an "interpretation" of "the play" as extrinsic, perhaps irrelevant, to the conduct of our immediate performance as spectators. This "immersive" inquiry traces *Sleep No More*'s investment in the conventional tropes sustaining modern theatricality: dramatic character, the structuring relations of "realistic" representation, the overdetermined constitutive power ascribed to Shakespeare's invisible hand in our performance in/as/of the distribution of the sensible.[44] *Sleep No More* frames the theatrical event as dependent on traditional uses of the theatre; yet if we place the "cognitive" accent not on using "scientific" explanations merely to validate "the way we already read, the way our brains already are, the way that literature" – and theatre – "already works" (Fletcher, *Evolving Hamlet* xv), but on the affordance of the instruments we make, it also appears to frame performance, and to use *Shakespeare* to frame performance, as an instrument for a critical, experiential reassessment of its own conditions of meaning, an instrument opening emerging ways of knowing in and as performance.

I've checked my watch – it's getting on toward 10 p.m., I'm back more or less in the center, on the "street." Malcolm, the detective has come from the office trailing spectators, and turns the corner. Lady Macbeth appears, and I realize I've seen this before; I caught it earlier when I'd followed Macbeth from the "bar" fight with Banquo, where he met her on just this spot; and here he comes. They embrace, then move through the taxidermy room to the stairs – we all follow, down, down, down to the bottom level, the "ballroom" studded with huge trees. There's a large table on a dais, and they join the rest of the cast

Figure 7. Masks in *Sleep No More* (Photo: Alick Crossley).

there, at opposite ends. Thunder. The lights flash, catching the cast in different, grotesque postures: the Witches, Banquo, etc. Macbeth rises, comes to the center of the dais, climbs up on a chair. A noose comes down from the flies; it's fastened on his neck, and the chair kicked free. He swings out over the audience, perhaps 150 of us standing there, watching. "A Nightingale Sang in Berkeley Square" begins to play. Minders and the elevator/taxidermy/door dancing guy lead us out, upstairs to the Manderley bar where we entered, to drink, dance with the cast. The masks belong to us, now.

CHAPTER 4

Retrotech: writing, theatre, and technologies of performance *Michael Almereyda,* Hamlet

> Dead ends, losers, and inventions that never made it into a material product have important stories to tell.
>
> (Erkki Huhtamo and Jussi Parikka, "Introduction")

The contemporary intermediation of "Shakespeare" is pervasive, remaking how we read, research, write about, see, and perform Shakespearean drama.[1] In the past decade, Shakespeare online has not merely expanded; it has explosively diversified. But while information about Shakespeare, his theatre, and various forms of Shakespeare's texts has been available in digital form for some time, the major innovation in online Shakespeare in the past decade has involved performance (on my laptop, a digital environment almost always accessible to wireless, "Shakespeare" is now represented by several MP4 film files, a number of text files, and links to sites including the British Library's website Treasures in Full: Shakespeare in Quarto, Internet Shakespeare Editions, Global Shakespeares, Early English Books Online, and IMDb).[2] Theatre companies now regularly post clips of productions on their websites in addition to broadcasting full pay-per-view productions to theatres, as the Metropolitan Opera and the National Theatre have done. There are multiplayer Shakespeare games, an interactive live-and-online *Midsummer Night's Dream* was performed at the RSC in June 2013, and of course YouTube (2005) is populated not only by clips taken from stage and film productions, but is itself the site of a highly developed Shakespeare-performance culture: videos on acting Shakespeare, on early modern pronunciation, parodies, high-school and college class projects. The collaborative online project Global Shakespeares provides a compendium of clips of live and film performance from around the world, as well as a set of informative critical essays. Social networking media play a central role in Elliott Visconsi and Katherine Rowe's superb mobile app, *The Tempest* for iPad, the forerunner of a complete-works set of iPad apps; Cambridge University Press's Explore Shakespeare apps incorporate a range of performance activities. Actors can run lines, do exercises, and manage their careers from a number of iPhone and iPad apps as well. As Alex Huang notes, "the age of Global Shakespeare 2.0 – worldwide performances in digital forms – has arrived," bringing with it new opportunities "in performance theory and practice enabled by digital forms and tools ("Global Shakespeare 2.0" 41).

In 2000, Michael Almereyda's film *Hamlet* undertook a searching meditation on the transfer of dramatic "content" or "information" among the performance technologies of writing, theatre, film, and digital media, and the social networks that define and sustain them.[3] Representing and enacting digital archiving and intermedial performance, Almereyda's film now occupies a distinctive technological temporality, its "tech forward" stance now as passé as the phrase itself, perhaps even as seeing the film in the theatre, that communal platform contemporary media can emulate but not restore – *Hamlet* on a wiki, *Pong* on a browser. Assertively visualizing *Hamlet* in a technologically rich environment of mobile communications, TV sets and VCRs, desktop and laptop computers, the film nonetheless seems, and seemed when it first appeared, to occupy "the bleeding edge of obsolescence" (Chun, "Enduring Ephemeral"). History lesson: that small red plastic thing that Hamlet gives Horatio is the object represented by the Save icon – a visual skeuomorph – on your word-processing toolbar, a "floppy disk."[4]

Of course, Shakespeare's play is freighted with its own obsolescences, the Marlovian diction of the Pyrrhus speech, to say nothing of *The Murder of Gonzago*. Yet Ethan Hawke's Hamlet seems temporally marooned, as Almereyda's allegorical representation of technology and performance refuses the signal advance in digital technologies of the 1990s: wireless communications and networking. We expect to see it, and expected it in 2000, too, especially since Ethan Hawke and Julia Stiles were deeply colored by the affective and vestimentary codes of youthful cyberculture. Yet while they look hip enough to have gone to protest the World Trade Organization meeting in Seattle in 1999, where the press widely reported how flash-mob organization availed itself of wireless communications to circumvent police actions, Hamlet and Ophelia use neither cellphone, email, nor SMS.[5] And though we glimpse Guildenstern's cellphone once, *Hamlet* is pointedly offline: no Google (1996), no AltaVista (1994), no Internet. Even Ophelia's wire is an old-fashioned radio transmitter, with a broadcasting range apparently confined to the Elsinore Hotel where she meets Hamlet. Other films wear the moment of their technical innovation proudly: the magical transformation of Ariel into a monkey to dazzle

Caliban in the 1908 silent *Tempest* (*Silent Shakespeare*); Hamlet's anxious animated thoughts in Olivier's film; the digitized monuments atop the Montague and Capulet towers in Luhrmann's *William Shakespeare's Romeo + Juliet*. But *Hamlet* wears technology with a difference. Framing *Hamlet* as always already obsolescent, Almereyda's film reflects a more systematic engagement with, and concern about, the interface between dramatic writing and the asynchronous technologies of performance, which – digital or otherwise – dramatize the implication of *Hamlet* in still emerging, always emerging, regimes of "knowledge representation" (Kirschenbaum, "Digital Humanities" 419).

Almereyda's Denmark Corporation is less millennial New York than a technologically parallel universe. In the film, Hamlet obsessively records and remixes but his instrument of choice is an obsolete toy camera. Ophelia works with Polaroid images, 35-millimeter film, and a darkroom, though by 1999, when *Hamlet* was being shot, digital video and still cameras had been widely marketed for at least a decade; Photoshop dates from the late 1980s. New media tend to dramatize the cultural implications of their predecessors; at the same time, they occupy a temporal horizon alongside their predecessors, a period in which medial practices are negotiated, in ways that revise and redefine their cultural uses and meanings. Recorded performance in this sense not only created the condition of "liveness," but continues to dramatize the intermedial complexity of theatre.[6] *Hamlet* was conceived, and continues to operate, in relation to several technologies and institutions (all unknown to Shakespeare in their present form): writing and acting, literature and theatre and film and digital media, print publishing and stage performance. Almereyda's film extends a meditation on the intersection of human action with objects and technologies (writing, printing, acting in Shakespeare's era, portable digital devices in ours) that change the name of dramatic action. As Bruno Latour might put it, "Action is simply not a property of humans *but of an association of actants*, and this is the second meaning of technical mediation" (*Pandora's Hope* 182), mediation by the technologies of performance.

Hamlet seizes a defining principle of dramatic performance, not only that it is always present tense but that it stages human behavior at the intersection of its several technologies of representation. In 1600, *Hamlet* was in some measure about the interplay of writing and acting, all those "Words, words, words" digested into speech, action, books, letters, poems, and scripted – and emended – drama. The *Hamlet* of contemporary device culture is preoccupied with the changing uses of digital media, instruments understood not so much as "engines of computation as *venues* for *representation*" (Kirschenbaum, "'So the colors cover the wires'" 525).[7] In the Wooster Group's *Hamlet* (premiere 2007), the cast (surrounded onstage by screens and monitors) takes its cue from a digitally remastered – and live-edited and distorted – projection of John Gielgud's 1964 stage production of *Hamlet*, itself filmed and distributed for a "live"-like performance that year, as a Theatrofilm by Electronovision.[8] Thomas Ostermeier's *Hamlet* at the Schaubühne in Berlin (premiere 2008) is more assertively set in a kind of contemporary nowhere, in which a gleaming boardroom/banquet table rolls downstage on a trestle over the main playing area, a thrust dirtbox where Old Hamlet is buried, and which becomes progressively muddier throughout the performance; it takes place indoors, and requires electronic lighting, sound, digital projection, the entire apparatus of modern theatricality. More to the point, much as Almereyda's *Hamlet* opens with Hawke reflecting on "What a piece of work is a man" (from 2.2) in the screen of a Pixelvision camera, Ostermeier's production opens with Hamlet reflecting "Sein oder Nicht-sein" in the screen of a digital video camera, his visage projected on a beaded screen strung across the stage.

Hamlet's agency emerges today through technologies that exceed, challenge, and redefine what N. Katherine Hayles calls "the legacy systems of speech and writing" (*My Mother* 39), the legacy systems of literary drama and dramatic theatre. Creating play that's not conceivably part of the text's "instructions" for appropriate mimesis, these productions partly underscore this dimension of performance by "literalizing" the text, reciprocally recalling moments of the dramatic script absent from the performance. Scott Shepherd, the Wooster Group's Hamlet, begins the performance by casually taking the stage, checking out the equipment, turning finally to the technicians in the booth: "OK, you can play the tape." But while the performance from that moment tracks the projected Burton film, Shepherd appears to manage its progress. Bored with the "fishmonger" scene, he turns again to the technicians: "OK, we can skip to the book." Skipping *to* the book is also skipping *in* the book, both fast-forwarding the Burton film the production stages as its text, but also Shakespeare's script in which scenes are commonly labeled by key words (fishmonger, nunnery), phrases (rogue and peasant slave), locations (closet, graveyard). So, too, we see Ethan Hawke's Hamlet in a diner, composing the poem to Ophelia, a scene that Shakespeare apparently thought not worth writing nonetheless memorialized by the few lines Polonius recites (2.2.108–120). Ostermeier uses only six actors, and his Hamlet, Lars Eidinger, after playing the Player Queen in his underwear with a cardboard party-hat crown, dons a fat suit, reminding us that, by the end of the play at least, the prince is "fat and scant of breath" (5.2.269). *Hamlet* is preoccupied by the slippage between the name of action and the technology of its execution. In the theatre, in the cinema, on the pixelated screen, *Hamlet* forcibly engages us, as perhaps it has always done, with the indeterminable multiplicity of the media of dramatic performance, addressing and defining its audience through a constitutive blending of "other media and 'conventions'" (Weber, *Theatricality as Medium* 118).

Despite their engagement with digital means, productions like Almereyda's or the Wooster Group's or Ostermeier's insist that performance is not simply the transfer of scripted "information" to a different, nontextual platform of representation. These productions refuse the notion of performance as an instrument for *communicating* a textual message, and so the more familiar sense of the dramatic script as "information" ideally unchanged by the "transformission" of performance, to adapt Random Clod's [Randall McLeod] deft term for the successive performances of printed books ("Information on Information" 246). *Hamlet* occupies a representative place in the performance of cultural transformission: Q1, Q2, F, Rowe, Pope, etc.; Burbage, Betterton, Garrick, Burton, Eidinger, etc. Scott Sheperd's and Lars Eidinger's analog performances are both framed in dialogue with digital (re)production; Ethan Hawke's Prince digitizes materials from the archive to manufacture a video to torment the analog court. Foregrounding the technological temporality of performance, *Hamlet* today extends the question of "transformission" beyond the page–stage (and page–page) dialectic into technologies that are at once profoundly inscribed (though in ways, and on a scale, illegible to the human senses) and that enable the storage, display, and remaking of performance. *Hamlet* enacts the ontological complexity of artworks in digital transformission, as manuscript and print, theatre and film, even the born-digital performances on YouTube are (trans)coded for storage and (dis)play on a range of different platforms. *Hamlet* today illustrates what Hayles calls a "generative cultural dynamic," the contemporary tension between "computation as means and as metaphor" (*My Mother* 20).

At the intersection of performance technologies, *Hamlet* dramatizes the fallacy of performance as communication, of Shakespeare as information. As everyone now knows, at least since Claude Shannon's "Mathematical Theory of Communication" in 1948, "information" is not identical with "meaning," but "a measure of the disambiguation required to express an intelligible message" (Gayley, "Networks of Deep Impression" 303).[9] For that reason (and many others) it would be simplistic merely to equate "the text," *Hamlet*, with "information" in a digitally remodeled metaphor for writing and performance, as though the contemporary function of performance in any medium were merely to transmit the verbal data with as little noise as possible. The temptation to model performance as the execution of textually driven protocols – a Shakespeare algorithm – is nonetheless revealing, not least because this description sounds so familiar, so much like the "ministerial" understanding of theatre in print culture as the embodied execution of instructions delineated by Shakespeare's script. Much as performances are not books, theatre, film, and digital performances are not textual communications systems. As *Hamlet* today insists, in part by abrading the interface between the literary text and the multiple performance technologies that use it, the noise of performance remakes the "data," Shakespeare, *Hamlet*.

If, as William R. Paulson puts it, "Noise is 'anything that arrives as part of a message, but that was not part of the message when sent out'" (quoted in Clarke, "Communication" 138), then performance is *about* the noise; with regard to a model of performance as textual transformission, "the noise *is* the art" (Clarke, "Information" 164), incidentally dramatizing the difference between the theatrical and the engineering sense of the word "performance."[10] Roman Jakobson – himself indebted to Shannon – recognized that "noise" is essential to the poetic uses of language.[11] Dramatic performance – stage, film, digital – transmits a range of signals, most of them nonverbal; it also transmits (many of) the scripted words of the play, transformed by (and transcoded into) acting. In this regard, much as Anne Gridley and Robert Johanson, wired into the performance in the Nature Theater of Oklahoma *Romeo and Juliet*, can be understood as *transducers*, an understanding of the intermedial nature of performance also requires a broader understanding of its audience as "experiencers."[12] For the reception of the performance exceeds the decoding of the textual message; it exceeds a sense of performance as an embodied critique of, commentary on, interpretation of the textual message; and it also exceeds the neuronal "mimicry" of the actor/character's expressed intentions as the defining limit of appropriate theatrical mimesis. In a sense, as Clarke notes, if "the concept of information incorporates the unity of the difference between signal and noise," then "Signal *or* noise, it's all information. Or again, the bodies" – *all* the bodies – "of the technological infrastructure of information systems are always part of the message" ("Information" 166–167).

Bring in da Noise, Bring in da Funk: dramatic writing does not function like a *score* because theatrical performance is not a process for reproducing scripted "information" stored in the text. As Friedrich Kittler remarks, as a medium, "Writing, however, stored writing – no more and no less" (*Gramophone, Film, Typewriter* 7). The recognition of the "noise" factor in dramatic performance can be seen as part of a widespread critique of the metaphorical extension of Shannon's "information" to describe cultural processes, whether in N. Katherine Hayles' refusal to privilege "informational pattern over material instantiation" in *How We Became Posthuman* (2), in Jerome McGann's rematerialization of the semantic effects of the "bibliographic codes" lost in the New Bibliography's "informational" understanding of textual transmission (*Textual Condition* 13), in Alan Liu's sense of artistic work as "*information designed to resist information*" (*Laws of Cool* 179), or in Matthew Kirschenbaum's analysis of the dematerialized conception of digital technologies arising when "Western consumer culture" depicts "information as an essence unto itself" (*Mechanisms* 38).[13]

Set in the Denmark Corporation, Almereyda's *Hamlet* performs an inquiry into the transmission of drama across several platforms of production, an inquiry also concerning the objects and practices of humanistic inquiry – what *Hamlet* is and what *Hamlet*/Hamlet does – in the stuttering succession of performance technologies, both "using information technology to illuminate the human record, and bringing an understanding of the human record to bear on the development and use of information technology" (Schreibman, Siemens, and Unsworth, "Digital Humanities" xxiii). Almereyda's film displays a range of performance technologies, but less as an evocation of a contemporary technospace than as an allegory of the interplay between performance and technological change, change that bears directly on the transformission of culture and its products, represented here through the transformission of *Hamlet*. A meditation on the persistence of *Hamlet* across the obsolescence of performance technologies, the film articulates a prescient response to "debates in the digital humanities" emerging at the moment of its making, debates (now considerably more intense) about how the objects and labor of the humanities – Hamlet's work – are altered by digital instruments, and by the altered forms of cultural imagination they enable. In two central scenes of Hamlet's digital inquiry – his encounter with the Player, here played by James Dean and John Gielgud, and the performance of his own encounter with digital *making*, *The Mousetrap* film he springs on the Denmark Corporation – the film allegorizes *Hamlet* in the practices of recording, remaking, and remediating the cultural history and purposes of drama in the unending transformation of performance technologies.

Device-ing *Hamlet*

> Media cross one another in time, which is no longer history.
> (Friedrich A. Kittler, *Gramophone, Film, Typewriter* 115)

Bestriding the cusp of technological transformation, *Hamlet* is preoccupied with the tactical uses of new media. The film implicates *Hamlet* not only within the process of technological change but also within a paradigmatic cultural and critical shift, in which digital technologies alter the materials of culture and of inquiry, their implication in "knowledge representation." The emergence of "digital humanities" as a "tactical term" more or less simultaneously with this *Hamlet* implies an altered perspective on the work of the film, imagining a practice in which new performance technologies provide both practical instruments and an animating theoretical and methodological discourse for humanities work, both for thinking "humanities research" and for framing the artistic discourse that is the humanities' partner in cultural inquiry.[14] Hamlet, digital humanist.

The world of Almereyda's film is "poised," as Courtney Lehmann remarks, "on the verge of a new technology of expression" (*Shakespeare Remains* 96); with its obsessive investment in *recording* experience, Almereyda's film situates *Hamlet* at the intersection of several technologies of performance, presenting the drama as writing, film, and digital media, while nearly dropping theatre from the mix. And yet, merely to locate the film as representing and participating in its moment in technological succession – after laptops, before Facebook – is to miss its most powerful engagement with the transformation of culture by technological change. Rather than seeing performance technologies – theatre, analog recording, digital production – as instrumental amanuenses for representing the values inherent in the text, the film's deliberately anachronistic representation of technologies crossing in time instead asks how technological change alters *Hamlet*'s transformission as both an object and a practice of inquiry in performance.

Technology isn't merely set dressing in Hamlet; as *actants*, defining the name of action, different devices contour the nature of performing *Hamlet* in sometimes contradictory, sometimes convergent ways. In her rich and provocative reading of the "technologies of memory" in the film, Katherine Rowe points to the "polychronic" dimension of such change, suggesting that Almereyda's *Hamlet* responds to the ways "Shakespeare's own plays allegorize their relation to media that were both new and old at the time of their earliest performance" ("'Remember Me'" 39).[15] Shakespeare's play explores the interface between writing and playing. Although we hear that Hamlet has written a poem, and that he plans to script a short addition to *The Murder of Gonzago*, onstage Hamlet continuously exploits the ambivalent representational power of the dominant analog technology of his stage, *acting*: "I am but mad north-north-west. When the wind is southerly I know a hawk from a handsaw" (2.2.315–316). Almereyda's Hamlet undertakes an experimental relation to this technology, enacting a continuous performance of *poiesis*, of *making* enabled by portable recording media and digital editing. This performance – rather than the notably retro technology he uses – identifies Hawke's Hamlet as involved in "a methodological investment in *thinking through making*: understanding one's research by constructing digital representations and implementations of it" enabled even by his funky, outdated tools (Gayley and Siemens, "Introduction" 220).

Like all instruments of performance, the various devices scattered through the film's visual field signify within a wider understanding of technologies as social practice, "patterns of conduct through which particular desires are literally incorporated and made manifest" (Hershock, *Reinventing the Wheel* 21). The significance of Hamlet's *thinking through making* is marked by his technology of choice, a Fisher-Price PXL 2000 toy camera, introduced in 1987 and withdrawn two years later, marketed to groom children as makers of home video and so as eventual consumers of pricier adult toys. Almost instantly archaic, it later gained a small yet significant following among aficionados and video artists, including Sadie Benning and Michael Almereyda. Armed with a plastic fisheye lens, recording at high speed on an inexpensive and ubiquitous medium – *audio* tape – the PXL 2000 was technologically sophisticated; blending analog and digital technologies, this road not taken also represents the structuring ambition of capital on technological change.[16] For Hamlet doesn't merely remake a forgotten, failed technology into an instrument of avant-garde artistic practice. His creative medium embodies an alienated perspective on the embeddedness of digital media in corporate culture (Denmark Corporation), frustrating the commercial purpose of the PXL 2000 camera – its planned obsolescence as its young users "grow into" the market – by using it into adulthood, and by redefining its failure to produce video acceptable to the wider public as the sign of its utility as an instrument of privacy, for the recording of a personal diary.[17]

An apparatus of both private reflection and surveillance, Hamlet's camera is cognate with the uses of technology in the surveillance culture of the Denmark Corporation, and the corporate horizon of digital culture more widely.[18] We perform today on instruments insistently identifying privacy with the sphere of corporate (and state) surveillance. Hardware (iPhone, iPad), software (Microsoft Word), browsers (Safari, Firefox), search engines (Google), applications (Kindle) – to say nothing about transactions on any cellphone or participation in any form of social media (Facebook, Twitter) – gather data about our habits and patterns of use. The business model of Google (1998) or Facebook (2004) depends on the increasingly narrow-bore targeting of advertising enabled by this "infrastructural imperialism" (Vaidhyanathan, *Googlization of Everything* chapter 3): our eyes are for sale. In Denmark, too, "knowledge representation" takes place in the corporate sphere, and frequent intercutting between shots of Hamlet's eyes and his PXL 2000, his TV monitor, or his computer screen dramatize the interaction of the subject with corporate-driven information technology, imagery given chilling – though hardly surprising – relevance by the 2013 revelation that the US National Security Administration uses private corporations to oversee the collection of surveillance data drawn from wireless phone and internet communications. In *Hamlet*, Hamlet and Claudius engage in reciprocal acts of surveillance, the "cryptopticon" replacing the "panopticon" of Foucault's theatrically modeled surveillance society (Vaidhyanathan, *Googlization of Everything* chapter 3).

Hamlet hardly anticipated Facebook, but the film's emphasis on technological anachrony foregrounds how technologies mark phases in human history, differentiate them globally (the eras of "print," the "telephone," or the "cellphone" happened at different times in different parts of the globe, even in different parts of the same nation or province), and alter what they perform. *Hamlet* resists what Siegfried Zielinski describes as the "anemic and evolutionary model" of technological progress, a "lazy linearity" inscribed in "teleologies that simplify historical research" and subsume "the media by cataloguing its forms, its apparatuses, its predictability, its necessity" (*Deep Time* vii). As Almereyda points out, nearly "every scene in the script features a photograph, a TV monitor, an electronic recording device of some kind" (Almereyda, "Preface" x), but rather than outlining a clear purpose or process of succession (in the sense that mid-twentieth-century Shakespeare films promised a better, more realistic encounter with the play, superseding the stage), the film's various technologies of representation jostle against one another, *actants* that seem to offer – like manuscript, print, theatre, film – competing ways of conceiving, enacting, extending, recording, instigating, preserving, and understanding both *Hamlet* and its role in the history and practice of representing human action.[19]

The film was released seven years before the iPhone, and its anachrony marks a distinction between communications and recording technologies. Bracketing *Hamlet* in this way – technologically advanced, but neither ubiquitously networked nor fully intermediated – the film attends more precisely to the performance, the use and signification, of distinct representational technologies, each of which frames a different temporality of *Hamlet*'s performance. For instance, the landline telephone is the principal instrument of distance communication in *Hamlet*, despite the widespread use of mobile phones in 1999: Claudius speaks to Rosencrantz and Guildenstern mainly by telephone, using a cordless phone and a speaker-phone in his bedroom (though he does use a car-phone, and on the move as they are, Rosencrantz and Guildenstern summon him after Polonius's murder on Guildenstern's handy mobile phone). Hamlet uses a payphone in the basement of the Elsinore Hotel to remind Gertrude to avoid the bloat king's reechy kisses while he lugs the guts away. After Hamlet discovers that Polonius and Claudius have wired Ophelia, he flees, and she hears his calumny on the telephone answering machine in her apartment. Descended from the telegraph, telephone transmission is historically linked to text transmission: Hamlet sends a fax to Claudius to announce his return to Denmark, and Claudius faxes Hamlet to invite him to the duel.

The telephone reminds us of an important point made by David Golumba in his searching critique of *computationalism*, that "Networks, distributed communication, personal involvement in politics, and the geographically widespread sharing of information about the self and communities have been characteristic of human societies in every time and every place"; they have not "emerged only with the rise of computers," mobile telephony, or online social networking (*Cultural Logic of Computation* chapter 1).[20] Yet while even landline telephones convert analog voice to digital signals for fiber-optic transmission, the landline telephone also marks the film's technological temporality, a moment – clearly waning – in which to *perform* the phone call meant occupying predetermined space/time coordinates. Like theatrical performance, the telephone requires a certain kind of *being there*; at its inception, the telephone was also scripted for public use, and its migration to domestic and personal space was – like text messaging and many of the apps on contemporary mobile phones – an unintended consequence driven by its users, and often initially resisted by the industry.[21] With the arrival of mobile phones, the landline now marks this history, the incomplete withdrawal of the telephone to the private sphere (perhaps responsible for the tawdriness of Claudius and Gertrude pausing their foreplay in the nasty sty to talk to Rosencrantz and Guildenstern on their speaker phone).

The telephone, then, represents one technological step away from the spatially mediated qualities of publicness and presence represented by theatre. Ophelia's phone has an answering machine, which marks a step away from the temporally mediated qualities of the stage: the listener doesn't need to *be there* when the call is performed to get the message. As an instrument both for live communications and for recording, then, the telephone implements and signifies the process of technological *convergence*; old and new media, residual and emergent technologies (or perhaps more and less residual), obsolete and cutting-edge instruments complicate both the blithe succession of technologies, the kinds of performance they enable, and their figuration of time, place, and history. The film insists on the spatial and temporal innovation of the answering machine, and its alteration of performance: Hamlet's "nunnery" speech apparently took place over some time but is broken up into several calls to Ophelia's machine, representing an undecidable temporality to his performance, transforming the temporal structure and pace of his outburst into a series of signals, on/off, playable in the time it takes Ophelia to burn his Polaroid photo.

Hamlet's devices foreground the technological transformation of the means of *Hamlet*'s performance: text, voice, body, image. In this regard, even the modest telephone articulates with the striking transformissive possibilities of the film's dominant mode of *making*: visual recording. The film opens with a vision of corporate towers, advertising, and a stock-market crawler framed by the moon-roof of a limo, and then moves quickly to Hamlet toying around with his video diary. Taken with the PXL 2000 camera, edited on the small hand-held monitor, and displayed simultaneously on a large TV monitor, the image almost immediately asserts its fungibility, its native interplay of recording, storage, editing, and display; the screen fills with images of Hamlet, but also of Ophelia, with cartoons, and with film footage of stealth bombers in the Bosnian war. But while the avant-garde use of Pixelvision at once locates filmmaking as an art of the archive, and implies a resistance to the corporate structure of film *making*, in *Hamlet* that gestural alienation is difficult to identify with any specific instrument. When Hamlet appears at the press conference to record Claudius's opening speech, he's one among many other recording agents. The video camera is the instrument of both confession and surveillance, as well as the *actant* that celebrates corporate power. Although the business of the Denmark Corporation is not specified, its logo is a camera shutter and the media seem to be under Claudius's control, as is perhaps dramatized by Claudius's "so much for him," delivered while ripping a copy of *USA Today* and its cover photo of Fortinbras in half.[22] Published by the Gannett Company, *USA Today* precisely illustrates the convergence of corporate media, and nicely underlines Henry Jenkins's point that media "convergence is more than simply a technological shift. Convergence alters the relationship between existing technologies, industries, markets, genres, and audiences"; it is "a process, not an endpoint" (*Convergence Culture* 15–16). Gannett is the largest newspaper publisher measured by the daily circulation of its many papers, and through its subsidiaries owns television stations nationwide as well as other media properties ("Gannett Company"). Fittingly, the street boxes of *USA Today* are fashioned to recall televisions, the effort to reposition print news under the sign of performance technologies also signaled by its shorter stories and extensive use of graphics.

Hamlet's Pixelvision recording will, implicitly perhaps, repurpose the fawning news conference, but however alienated Hamlet may be from Claudius's economic apparatus, his personal technology is also fully consistent with its métier: much as political theatre is the presiding art form of Shakespeare's Elsinore, recorded performance is the art form of Almereyda's Denmark Corp. We first see the Ghost shut in an elevator on the monitor of a security camera (he finally disappears from our view into the deeper reaches of capital/technology, a Pepsi machine). Much of the "fishmonger" scene is played through the security camera's lens, identifying us – the film's viewers – with the invasive vision that oppresses Hamlet, as Bill Murray's Polonius speaks aside to the camera, knowing we are there, or will be (like the telephone and answering machine, the security camera also combines recording and transmission technologies). Hamlet's *Mousetrap* is a "film/video" composed of digitized animation and selections from ersatz home movies, silent films, advertising, and a porn film. Flying to Heathrow, Hamlet edits and saves the letter Rosencrantz and Guildenstern are to deliver to the king of England – on what appears to be an overdue-for-replacement Mac Powerbook 180c (circa 1993), another piece of nearly retro technology – and copies the original to the floppy he later gives to Horatio. On the plane he also sees the news, previously recorded, of Fortinbras ("how all occasions do inform against me") while Rosencrantz and Guildenstern read about Fortinbras in the magazine of record for digital culture, *Wired*.

The impact of recorded performance is amplified in *Hamlet* by the ubiquity of screens in the film's visual field, which often project a visual dialogue with the action of the play. The television is on in the background – showing oil fields exploding and burning – during Hamlet's scene with the Ghost, and Claudius watches Bill Clinton on the TV in his limo during the prayer scene. Hamlet seems to be contemplating the "To be, or not to be" soliloquy (3.1.55) by watching a VHS video of the Vietnamese monk Thich Nhat Hanh discussing "being" and "interbeing" on a TV monitor, he considers it again while recording himself putting a gun to his temple and in his mouth, and finally – famously – delivers it walking down the "action" aisles of a Blockbuster store, shadowed by *Crow II – The Crow: City of Angels* (1996) – playing on the monitors behind him.[23] As Hamlet dies we see a grainy, black-and-white Pixelvision replay of various images of the film, intercut with a "live" color image of Hamlet's eye. Television news anchor Robert MacNeil delivers a pastiche of Fortinbras's and the Player King's lines from a TV newsdesk to conclude the action, and the film ends with these lines scrolling on the teleprompter.

Marking an interface between writing, live performance, and recording, MacNeil's teleprompter images the film's complex engagement with the notion of dramatic performance as a form of textual communication. Unlike the dramatic script, absorbed as acting, the newsreader's teleprompted script is not transcoded but merely concealed, a digital script audibly "delivered" in the analog performance of "information"; fittingly enough, it was long-time reporter and newsreader Robert MacNeil's idea to "feed him the text on a teleprompter," which has the effect (much like the finale of the Nature Theater of Oklahoma's *Romeo and Juliet*), of ending "this image-saturated movie with a final shot of – *words*. Shakespeare's words, ascending a glowing screen" (Almereyda, "Director's Notes" 143). Positioned at the end of the film, the teleprompter simultaneously appears to reassert Shakespeare's writing (reorganized pieces of it, anyway: writing is digital) and to image the inability of writing – and of a sense of performance as *reading*, and of spectating as *imaginary audition* – entirely to capture the analog drama, live or recorded.

Hamlet seems to imply that while the era of recorded performance encodes a range of technologically identified temporalities, what's on the edge of displacement is the pre-digital intersection of the "legacy systems of speech and writing" characteristic of theatrical performance, the originary systems of *Hamlet*. Manual writing is visible, but largely inconsequential in *Hamlet*. Ophelia attempts to meet Hamlet by drawing a picture of an outdoor fountain during the opening press conference ("3:30?" she writes), but Laertes and Polonius at first intercept her message; she does pass it off to Hamlet, but he never arrives at the meeting. We see Hamlet writing in a coffee shop, inscribing the poem that only leads to Ophelia's exploitation and manipulation by her father. And we even see a theatre once: Hamlet, who has hijacked Claudius's limo and is about to shoot him when Claudius laments "Words without thoughts never to heaven go," stops the car, and flies down the street, in front of the Broadway marquee for Julie Taymor's stage reanimation of the Disney (animated) film, *The Lion King*.[24] Needless to say, the theatre is closed.

Almereyda's Denmark is visibly a *mediapolis*: "a mediated public space where media underpin and overarch the experiences of everyday life." But while *Hamlet* suggests that "we no longer live *with* media, but *in* media," it purposefully reimagines Shakespeare's typical anachrony, old media up against new, taking up a "productive approach to the lifeworld that media engender (*creativity*)" in part by staging a critical resistance to the "(inevitable) disappearance of media from active awareness (*invisibility*)." *Hamlet*, that is, interrogates the politics of "knowledge representation" in the mediapolis, questioning whether "reality is something one can zoom in on our out from as viewed through a camera" (Deuze, Blank, Speers, "Life Lived in Media").[25] For while Hamlet adapts a discarded technology for artistic and political purposes, and refashions its potentiality through digital means, if there is a victim of living "*in* media," it's Ophelia. Ophelia is more fully retro, a film photographer, taking 35-millimeter photographs during Polonius's advice to Laertes, and developing film in her darkroom while she waits for Hamlet. Ophelia's one foray into wireless technology – when she's wired by Polonius and Claudius – destroys her, and it's fitting that the flowers and herbs she scatters in her mad scene ("here's rosemary") are another recording technology soon to be drowned in the digital flood: Polaroids.[26]

Sherry Turkle pointed out in 1995 that "People explicitly turn to computers for experiences that they hope will change their ways of thinking or will affect their social and emotional lives," experience that has become more pervasive and more intimate in the decades since (*Life on the Screen* 26). Turkle's *Life on the Screen* is oddly synchronized, now, for us, with this *Hamlet*, documenting an interconnected but not yet fully pervasive moment in digital technologies, a moment before ubiquitous data, recording, social-media communications. Technologically belated at the moment of its making, *Hamlet* perhaps merely documents a moment of historical change. Yet it also frames a deeper problematic, the consequences not merely of changing performance technologies (they're always changing) but how technologies affect the changing performance of cultural transmission, as "print-based disciplines such as literature, history, philosophy, religion, and art history," and disciplines (theatre) historically understood as instrumentalizing manuscript and print texts, "move into digital media" (Hayles, *How We Think* 1). After all, Hamlet's PXL 2000 epitomizes the retrotech interface of analog and digital, the interface of dramatic performance, in which a "digital" segmentation of written language into discrete units stands against the apparently "analog" nature of speech (carried on the continuous flow of the breath), movement, and gesture. And yet, as Lydia Liu suggests, the digital is what "makes the analog appear as such, something distinct from itself" (*Freudian Robot* 24).[27] *Hamlet* tactically occupies the analog–digital interface, the place of dramatic performance, to open a wider question: what is *Hamlet* post-print, post-theatre, post-film, in the ongoing negotiation between writing and acting, digital and analog means of *making* performance?[28]

Zoom out: theatrical lossiness in digital humanities

Digital composition in sound and image (including texts) and the remediation of print and recorded visual media to digital forms of storage and representation has transformed both the understanding and the practice of the humanities and humanities research, and the practices of performance and Performance Studies as well. From the digitization of now searchable photo-facsimile texts to the editorial work exemplified by Internet Shakespeare Editions, to the kind of research enabled by the database – Franco Moretti's "distanced reading" or Martin Mueller's "literary informatics" – the understanding of the nature, history, and significance of print literature has been irrevocably altered and expanded.[29] One of the most significant aspects of this upheaval has been to remake the basic conception of the signifying armature of the book. On the one hand, materialist bibliography has attributed signifying capacity to elements of printed objects once seen as hermeneutically transparent supports for literary meaning – ink, paper, binding, layout, design, and so on. On the other, by conceiving the significance of distinct versions of a text, it has also challenged the authority of a single idealized work: *King Lear* is two early modern versions, but also Tate's and Malone's and Bowdler's and the Oxford's. If digital technologies have assisted in staging the multiplicity of print, print – emulated everywhere on screen – has also reflexively clarified the supposed mobility and transience of digitized virtual representation.

The dramatic opposition between the mobility and immateriality of "'open and interactive'" digital forms and the "'static and linear'" appearance of "traditional textual forms" is now considerably less persuasive than it appeared when texts first became widely available in computer-mediated form (McGann, *Radiant Textuality* 25).

Like all writing, dramatic writing is simultaneously a means of storage and display, but what it neither stores nor displays is performance: it is deployed in the intermedial work of theatrical production. John Guillory has noted that nearly "all works written before the sixteenth century, we should remember, are transmitted in the remediated form of print, as well as (usually) translated into modern languages, arguably a form of remediation as well" ("Genesis of the Media Concept" 322 note 2). Shakespeare's texts, delivered in manuscript and sold to the King's Men, were – this is the "literary dramatist" question – both instrumentalized in performance and remediated into print. The texts persist for most of us now in successively mediated forms as well: the scholarly or teaching edition, bristling with introductory and explanatory material, footnotes, editorial apparatus, an object and an instrument bearing little material or cultural resemblance to the early quartos or Folio or to the hypothesized manuscripts they sometimes invoke. Editions are now also reimagined as iPad apps, which can add video commentary by specialists, games, and other activities to the apparatus. "Popular" editions – even reprints of the Folio – materialize various commitments to literature, theatre, pedagogy, reading, the market, "Shakespeare," that inform how "the text" is staged *as* a text. As a document in remediation, *Hamlet* also functioned in the industrious activity of early modern theatrical production, itself a moment in an ongoing process of social and technological change continuously altering the medium. Indoor and outdoor playing, patronage and capitalism, women onstage, the Licensing Act, moveable scenery, gas lighting, electrification, the director, trade unions, film and television, onstage projection: as a medium, theatrical performance today takes in activities with a long historical legacy, as instruments with different moments of historical emergence interact with and within contemporary modes of stage production. The modern theatrical medium – temporally, geographically, and politically marked and differentiated as it is – may be historically continuous with Shakespeare's, which is to say that it is also crucially distinct from Shakespeare's, not only because it shares "Shakespeare performance" (a distinctly modern genre to be sure) with radio, film, television, and the internet, but because it is now constituted in relation to digital technologies, constituted by digital technologies, and represented – as performance and as knowledge – by digital means as well. *Hamlet*'s obsolescence images one condition of theatre, a medium in which technological succession is not only always visible (and audible, forsooth!) but continually dramatizes its ongoing ideological transformation.

But if theatrical performance is always staging technological change, where is theatrical performance – so analog – in the process of fashioning digital humanities culture? As David Saltz has noted, the environment for most theatrical performance today is one that is densely mediated. Not only are various forms of technology incorporated into the dramatic action (cellphones in Peter Sellars's 2009 *Othello*), or visible as part of the stage design (live feed video in Sellars's 1994 *Merchant of Venice*, Ostermeier's *Hamlet*, the Wooster Group), but digital technologies are incorporated into the making of the performance itself, extending from instruments onstage – stage lighting, for which computerized lightboards store hundreds of cues for hundreds of instruments – to those that manage and operate the house: ticketing, HVAC, house management, stage management, plumbing ("Performing Arts"). Yet, as a coherent artistic practice and as an object of humanistic inquiry, theatre has been at best fitfully incorporated into the disciplinary self-reflection of digital humanities. As in *Hamlet*, theatre is visible in this literature, but closed. Despite sites like Global Shakespeares that make various selections of – and some entire – performances available online, including video of live performance as well as film and video performances, in the programmatic literature defining the discipline of the digital humanities, theatre figures largely by its absence, replicating its marginality to the traditions of Anglo-American humanities.

Alan Liu's shrewd exploration of "humanities education in the age of knowledge work" (*Laws of Cool* 301), for instance, advocates for an interplay between a variety of "archaic and historical knowledge technique[s] (e.g., memorization, storytelling, music, dance, weaving and other handicraft, iconography, rhetoric, close reading)" (307–308) as part of an alliance between "such older, text-based humanities fields as literature and history" and "such newer humanities fields as film studies or media studies – fields, that is, in which historical/critical inquiry blends more easily with pragmatic approaches to the world of avant-garde and commercial art (as when artists or directors become guests in classes, participants in conferences, or employers of interns)" (318). As part of his goal to develop an institutional base in the changing landscape of the digitally reliant university, Liu does recall that the "creative arts" were "conspicuously absent from the consciousness of the humanities during the latter's recent 'interdisciplinary' gold rush toward the social sciences," the "gold rush" that was, of course, part of the definition of Performance Studies as a field in the 1980s, and of the theoretical renovation of the study of theatre in that period as well. But now, Liu suggests, in an act of mutual survival, "humanities departments would also collaborate directly with art studio, design, visual arts, creative writing, music, and other creative or performing arts programs (including the new breed of 'media arts and technology' programs)" (318). Once absent, always absent: the unnamed others of disciplinary renewal, Theatre Studies and Performance Studies remain outside the history of humanistic research, absent from its consciousness, and so absent from the way digital humanities "models the way the humanities are organized for research and teaching as well as the way they are adapting to social, cultural, and technological changes" (Voice of the Shuttle website).[30]

In effect harnessing the multimedia dimension of digital representation to a conception of *humanities* and *research* that moves beyond texts and writing as the defining objects of inquiry and (perhaps) the defining medium of "knowledge representation," Liu's gesture here – and Liu is deeply engaged with forging an institutional synergy between the "arts" and the "humanities" – is echoed across a disciplinary literature striving to accommodate the critical perspective of fields analyzing sound, movement, and visual imagery, and also to engage the acumen of *makers* in those media. This encounter with "*thinking through making*" represents a defining element in the emergent disciplinary ideology of digital humanities (Gayley and Siemens, "Introduction" 220), the replacement of an instrumentalized "service" function – in which digital technologies and their "technicians" were assigned the role of "serving client disciplines, which tend to initiate collaborations, set the agenda for the research and take academic credit for the result" (McCarthy, "Telescope for the Mind?" 117) – with a research practice. As McGann puts it, the "next generation of literary and aesthetic theorists who will most matter are people who will be at least as involved with *making* things as with writing text" (*Radiant Textuality* 19).

On the one hand, as is the case in contemporary cognitive theatre studies, this emphasis on *making* and methodology is sometimes represented as "providing a welcome relief from the radical skepticism of contemporary humanistic thought"; since the computer is "wholly intolerant toward equivocation and uncertainty," it "represents an emancipation from the ironic imprisonments of postmodern excess" (Ramsay, *Reading Machines* "Preconditions").[31] On the other, at least in the practice it ascribes to other *makers* on campus, the rhetoric of digital humanities sometimes tends to reproduce a familiar "humanities" perspective on the "arts" as uncritical and unreflective, guests at the seminar table. Kathleen Fitzpatrick also notes a "long separation" between "studio artists and art historians or between literary scholars and creative writers," an evocative "theory–practice divide" that has been overcome in some quarters of media studies by bringing the "two modes together in a rigorously theorized praxis, recognizing that the boundaries between the critical and the creative are arbitrary" ("Humanities, Done Digitally" 14). So, too, Anne Burdick, Johanna Drucker, Peter Lunenfeld, Todd Presner, and Jeffrey Schnapp disclaim the division that "emerged over the course of the 20th century that separated humanities knowledge into study and analysis on the one hand and practice and application on the other," a division in which the "criticism, hermeneutics, and close reading" associated with the former are distinguished from the "design, collaboration, and performance, often stretching across media and involving multiple agents, producers, and authors" of the latter, so that "the process of 'how' became separated from the content of 'what'" (*Digital_Humanities* 76). However, while the boundaries that distinguish between critical and artistic creativity may be arbitrary, their institutional configurations are not, an institutional configuration that the disciplinary rhetoric of the digital humanities appears to replicate with an acceptable cultural and historical "lossiness," at least as far as theatre is concerned.[32]

For while the model of "practice-based research, long integrated into the sciences," may be "relatively new to the humanities" (Hayles, *How We Think* 19), at least in art history and literature departments, both "practice-based research" and the "theory–practice divide" have defined daily academic life and, more intermittently, participated in a "rigorously theorized praxis" for decades in that unthought corner of the campus, and of the humanities, occupied by the Theatre department. One illustrative consequence of the theoretical surge of Performance Studies in the 1990s, which strategically incorporated artists such as Guillermo Gómez-Peña and Holly Hughes as *makers* of its critical disciplinary discourse, was to habilitate *performance* as an object and practice of inquiry in the humanities. At the same time, since Performance Studies often took shape against conventional definitions of theatre and formal theatre studies, it was hardly capable of, or interested in, displacing the antitheatrical prejudice common in fields like literary studies, history, and so on. Theatre Studies occupies an eccentric orbit in the humanities in the United States, its critical and theoretical methods and objects of study largely derogated (surely literary history and philosophy can take care of that) and its artistic activity (directing, acting, design) deplored as merely professional, too pragmatic, too commercial, too stagey, too *uncool* to join the "avant-garde and commercial" artists invited as guests to humanities class, or to participate in a conference. Despite projects working to create databases of theatrical materials (Theatre Finder, for example) or online environments replicating classical theatre spaces (Playhouses of 17th-Century Paris) or performance archives like Global Shakespeares, in the compression of analog to digital humanities, the distinctive history and contemporary practices of theatrical *making* can apparently be inferred from the data of literature, history, and media studies, from the practices of reading and writing, from the technologies of the camera and the screen.[33]

In this regard, Shakespeare and early modern drama studies is something of an anomaly in the humanities, as the recovery of the material conditions of the stage has been constitutive of the field at least since E. K. Chambers; Garrick, Kemble, Charles Kean, or Henry Irving notwithstanding, the very tenuous interpretive authority of performers in the field dates perhaps to Harley Granville Barker, inaugurating an intermittent ear for the insights of actors and directors that extends today to one corner of professional Shakespeare studies, and even to the *Tempest* for iPad app. In an important sense, though, digital humanities risks losing access to theatre by modeling it as absorbed by other modes of representation. In the rhetoric of digital humanities, theatre practice has little to contribute to fashioning new practices of "knowledge representation" or the campus politics they will require, and theatre studies more generally – understood as the study of a textually driven intermedium – can be, apparently, fully engaged by the research methods, protocols, and priorities of older (literary) and newer (media) fields.

Hamlet today appears to be both about and inseparable from the dialectical interpenetration of analog and digital performance technologies. The effort to conceive theatre in relation to the discourse of digital technologies is surely more productive than ignoring its distinctive practices and technologies or than maintaining an essentialized "opposition between live performance and the digital world," between live and mediated, mediated and theatrical conceptions of performance, as though the "specific communal nature of an event which will never be repeated stands in direct contrast to digital technology which confuses the issues of location, time and perhaps most dramatically of 'liveness'" (Carson, "eShakespeare" 283).[34] Theatre is, after all, all about *repetition*, rehearsal, re/stored behavior, a "liveness" mediated by both the conventions structuring the event and the changing interplay between its digital and analog instruments.

Bringing a sense of digital mediation to bear on theatre practice as it has been used to rethink print, we might describe a discrete performance as itself a kind of versioning in ways that underline this mediality: a singular event in a series, less like a printed edition than like the version of this essay now on my laptop screen, a single event in which the display is continuously reconfigured, an event that performs the "text" through another medium (here voltage differentials transmitted electronically), an event that is not only always simultaneously different from itself but will be a different (continuously changing) event after I save it and re-perform it tomorrow.[35] The dialectical encounter between digital humanities and theatre practice – revived every day, as iPads are deployed in rehearsals, scripts learned from training apps – is in this sense as much preempted by the absence of theatre from the digital research horizon as it is by the absence of a medial critique from the horizon of performance-making. As the authors of *Digital_Humanities* note, in "the era of personal broadcasting, the art of oratory must be *rediscovered*," insofar as "digital networks and media have brought orality back into the mainstream of argumentation after a half-millennium in which it was mostly cast in a supporting role vis-à-vis print" (11, my emphasis). Theatre is part of the contemporary landscape of digital media and performance; since one of the most powerful aspects of technological succession has to do with how new technologies both represent and are altered by the technologies they succeed, we should expect digital technologies not to displace theatre, nor merely to render new insights about its presumed identity with media studies and literature, but also to be inflected by its practices as well. "OK, you can play the tape."

The "tendency to elicit what is 'new' about new media by contrasting its radical mutability with the supposed material stolidity of older textual forms is a misplaced gesture" (Kirschenbaum, *Mechanisms* 166), not least because the mutability of digital media is, in Kirschenbaum's sense, only skin – or display screen – deep. Much as "Remediation makes the medium as such *visible*" (Guillory, "Genesis of the Media Concept" 324), digital media appear to model theatre according to the traditional disciplinary division between the analytical/critical/intellectual "work" of textualized media (books) and the play of performance, understood largely as a practice of embodied reproduction.[36] How is theatrical performance modeled, and so epistemologically constrained, in the digital humanities? "A digital text is like a music score or theater script: its written inscription is meant to be executed, either by the underlying code alone, or through a feedback loop that leads from the user to the underlying code to the display, and back to the user. Digital texts thus present the same contrast as the classic performing arts between the invariability of the script and the variability of its execution" (Marie-Laure Ryan, "Multivariant Narratives" 416). *Execution*, *feedback*, and *display*: as the *score* image implies, this way of modeling theatrical performance as an "Algorithm-driven operation" fails to account for the practical and ideological independence of performance practice from textual determination, its incommensurability with the principal professional activity of literary scholarship, textual "interpretation."[37] The regulatory dimension of this understanding of theatre is suggested by Stephen Ramsay's promotion of the power of an "algorithmic criticism" which, by adjudicating "questions about the properties of objects," would provide tools "that can adjudicate the hermeneutical parameters of human reading experiences – tools that can tell you whether an interpretation" – or a performance – "is permissible" (*Reading Machines* chapter 1). The multifarious relation of dramatic text to theatrical performance is often represented as a straightforward act of execution or reproduction; yet much as a single "text" is stored in multiple locations on a hard drive, and exists simultaneously in many different complete and incomplete versions (see Kirschenbaum, *Mechanisms* 50–53), texts in stage performance are never singular and in the early modern English theatre never were singular, as Tiffany Stern has shown (see *Documents in Performance*): "For this reason it would be more accurate to call an electronic text" – and a text in the theatre – "a *process* than an object" (Hayles, *My Mother* 101). Unlike the teleprompted news reading, theatrical performance does not execute a text, merely lend an analog display to the digital command: there's the promptbook, the director's book, the stage manager's book used to call the show, the actors' scripts (inscribed, highlighted, annotated, whether in hard copy or on screen), their notebooks and research, the costume designs, light plots, scene drawings and elevations, to say nothing of the various densely conventionalized practices – acting, directing, spectating – that structure the signification of the event. Any theatrical production is prodigiously inscribed, yet the "execution" of any one of those texts (actual or metaphorical) is difficult to model in digital terms, on/off.

At the same time, *Hamlet* today appears to its theatrical makers to provide a critical site of vantage *on* digital reproduction, much as the analysis of print enabled by digital media has reciprocally qualified assumptions about digital media. This perspective cannot be occupied if theatre – in practice, in history, in theory – is merely dropped from agency in the discussion of the digital humanities.[38] For despite its analog character, theatre today cannot escape both the instruments and ideology of digital culture. Much as we might understand most forms of software – such as JPEG – as "discarding ('losing') information that falls below the threshold of human vision," theatrical performance is inherently a "lossy" process only when modeled on the digital terms of textual transmission (Kirschenbaum, *Mechanisms* 192). Even the most "faithful" production is unlikely to be word perfect (the multitextuality of theatre practice suggests how misapplied, and tendentious, the notion of "word perfection" really is), precisely because the purpose of transmitting informational patterns in the noisy medium of embodiment is to enable distinctive forms of meaning to transpire. As Hayles suggests, "the combination of analog and digital" may well "prove far more powerful than either by itself [. . .] for each has properties that complement the other. [. . .] digital representations allow for precise error control, extreme fragmentation and recombination, whereas analog processes have the advantages of the continuum, including the ability to transmit informational patterns between differently embodied entities" (*My Mother* 29). In Almereyda's film, Hamlet gazes into the screen, his eye reflected by that other I, the memory encoded as digital archive. This relationship is, the film suggests, powerfully cybernetic, a process – like theatrical performance – in which analog means are rehearsed not for their ability to conform to a preexisting algorithm, but to bring about something new.

Shakespeare's plays marked and helped to define a medial interface between theatre and literature at the emergence of new technologies (print) and social formations (publishing, professional theatre); they "have never fitted neatly into successionist narratives of the wholesale transition from orality to literacy, or from manuscript to print to hypertext" or to digital media (Gayley and Siemens, "Introduction" 219). The disciplinary discourse of digital humanities makes a powerful argument for the ongoing, interminable transformission both of the objects and the practices of the humanities by new technologies. This body of work also evokes a shrewd skepticism toward simplistic narratives of succession and obsolescence. Given the marginality of theatre to traditional humanities and the relatively low profile of scholarship and critical instruction in those American theatre departments driven by studio work, it is not entirely surprising to see theatre absorbed by the digital humanities as a kind of skeuomorph of media studies and stepchild of literature. Nonetheless, insofar as digital humanities is constitutionally aware of the need "to ensure that data can be rendered or read in the future when the software they were written in and/or the hardware on which they were designed to run are obsolete and no longer supported at the point of use" (Smith, "Preservation" 578), for data and software to be capable of migrating forward to new platforms of operation, display, analysis, we might wonder at the consequences of rendering theatre – as a mode of production, creation, and critique – prematurely obsolete, especially since, like a radio from the 1920s or a copy of the First Folio, its technologies continue to function, develop, and innovate (Ernst, "Media Archaeology"). As productions like those of Ostermeier or the Wooster Group imply, theatre also adapts, not only absorbing other technologies as it has always done, but constantly reimagining – and staging – how technological and ideological change enable new affordances of performance.

Zoom in: Hamlet's screens

How does *Hamlet* perform theatre in the era of digital performance culture? Ethan Hawke's Hamlet illustrates the contemporary situation of much artistic work: the prince writes, records, edits, and produces it himself. And, as in much contemporary digital and media practice, the performance art form most visibly absent from his activities is theatre. At the same time, *Hamlet* also performs an archaeological critique of the place of theatre and of *Hamlet* in digital culture, in part by complicating the text–performance dialectic of traditional dramatic performance analysis.

In *Hamlet*, two scenes focus the relationship between media temporality and dramatic performance: the scene corresponding to 2.2., Hamlet's encounter with the Player and his "rogue and peasant slave" soliloquy, and the scene corresponding to 3.2, the film within the film, *The Mousetrap*. The "rogue and peasant slave" soliloquy (2.2.485–540) deftly allegorizes the film's location of drama in the history of its technological production. In all early versions of the play, the soliloquy closes a long scene, which proceeds from Hamlet's toying with Polonius, the "Words, words, words" business with the book, through the arrival of Rosencrantz and Guildenstern and Hamlet's metatheatricalized alienation from their badly acted espionage ("this goodly frame the earth seems to me a sterile promontory"), concluding with the arrival of the players. There is no outside to Hamlet's theatre, to actions that a man might play; even after he's dead he's borne to "the stage." In the written play, presumably in Shakespeare's theatre, and surely in most theatrical productions since, Hamlet's confrontation with the actor – his recitation and invitation to perform the Pyrrhus speech – is a means of developing a complex network of reflections. It is a bookish speech that Hamlet misremembers and then recalls again, smacking not so much of dramatic speech in 1600 as of the emphatic, Marlovian diction of a decade before. The Player's performance seems at once to galvanize Hamlet into comparable extroversion ("Who calls me villain") and to embarrass him with the unseemly promiscuity of performance ("Why, what an ass am I"). And for all the hesitations enforced by language and its enactment, by the playwright's and the actor's ways and means, Hamlet catches his image in the glass of acting: playing's the thing.

Almereyda's Hamlet is a filmmaker rather than a prince with a flair for writing a bit of dialogue now and then, and Almereyda's vision of Hamlet's *making* is now a convention of contemporary performance. Even while Lars Eidinger's Hamlet – eating the dirt that forms much of the playing area, scampering nearly naked over the seats in the audience ad-libbing all the while – foregrounds the physical immediacy, vulnerability, and availability of the actor's body as the sign of a specifically theatricalized, mediated presence, the Schaubühne performance opens with Eidinger taking his image on video, an image projected on a shimmering metallic upstage screen. *Hamlet* today – Scott Shepherd flanked by cameras and monitors, Richard Burton projected upstage behind him – is *about* a kind of intermedial conflict, dialecticizing theatre and recorded media through the performance of *Hamlet.*

The specificity of Almereyda's engagement with Hamlet's medium emerges more clearly, though, in contrast with another recent production staging Hamlet's camera, Gregory Doran's 2010 film based on his 2008 Royal Shakespeare Company production. In this *Hamlet*, David Tennant, conspicuously costumed in jeans and T-shirt, occupies a familiar landscape of electronic surveillance: the grainy black-and-white security camera is now apparently *de rigueur* for the Ghost's scenes, and for keeping an eye on Hamlet. Tennant's Hamlet also dabbles in home movies, recording *The Mousetrap* on an even more retro device than Hawke's Pixelvision toy camera: a vintage hand-held Super-8 camera. Yet, Almereyda's and Doran's films deploy their recording technologies with a difference, as Doran uses the technology of film in effect to "restore" the relations of theatre, and so not surprisingly to restore a relatively traditional subordination of performance to textual mimesis. Throughout his film, Doran's camera operates in familiar narrative terms, disclosing the space, the characters, their actions, moving from wide shot to close up in order to emphasize motive (Patrick Stewart fixing his glance on Hamlet and shaking his head "no" when leaving the *Mousetrap* scene), or to clarify details of the action (how Hamlet is wounded by Laertes). Brief sections of the action are often shown through video surveillance cameras: we see the guards parting for the (to the surveillance camera) invisible Ghost; we observe the "nunnery" scene through the mirrored wall with Polonius and Claudius, but also intermittently from the surveillance camera mounted in the chamber, the camera that Hamlet rips down from the wall at the "rogue and peasant slave" soliloquy. Doran's camera also sutures us into the perspective of an individual character, as it does to great effect in the opening scene, in which we don't see the Ghost on his first appearance but see Horatio and the guards cowering away from us, their agony of perceivedness calling Beckett's *Film* to mind.

Hawke's Hamlet does not address the film's audience: when we see his eye gazing back at us in the "rogue and peasant slave" scene, for instance, the camera occupies the perspective of the computer. We look back at Hamlet as his screen. Almereyda films the soliloquies as voice-over, inward monologue. Tennant's Hamlet, on the other hand, replicates a theatrical Hamlet's public availability to the audience by delivering the same lines directly to the camera. Tennant rips down the surveillance camera and first throws himself about the room during the soliloquy, before circling the camera 360 degrees. Doran's scene recalls theatrical direct address here, but remediating it as film alters the relations of theatre. Tennant's Hamlet no longer speaks from the sterile platform to the groundlings standing before him in the pit, nor does he speak across the footlights and proscenium to the darkened house. Here, circling the camera, Hamlet represents the viewer within his fictive scene, replicating the notion of an audience present both to the performers and to the characters, and rephrasing that presence in the characteristic discursive modes of modern film. Doran capitalizes on the camera's ability to represent a kind of multiperspective theatricality, acknowledging the spectators' performance in the interplay of subjects and subjectification.

Most *Hamlet* films eliminate this soliloquy (as Olivier did), or displace and truncate it (as Zeffirelli did); in this sense, Tennant's performance, more or less true to the Folio text and delivered as a version of "theatrical" address to a spectator represented, at least notionally, within the scene, instrumentalizes the text in ways that recall the relational terms of live performance: Hamlet seizes on the conventions of stage revenge, and Tennant's performance – like the Player's to Polonius – puts us on the receiving end of its complex, duplicitous, and perhaps ironically empty power. At the same time, drawing the spectator into the fictive space, Doran's camerawork reframes the alterity of the theatrical spectator within the totalizing realism of film representation.

Almereyda, on the other hand, differentiates performance technologies by framing them in an intermedial dialectic. For while Doran both preserves the players and encodes a kind of gesture toward the theatre, in Almereyda's film, there's little left of the long section of the scene preoccupied with the arrival of the players, their brief performance, and Hamlet's soliloquy. The film eliminates the players, and after Rosencrantz and Guildenstern "report" on the speaker phone to Gertrude and Claudius in bed, we see Hamlet, also on his bed, playing with the Pixelvision camera and a monitor (Almereyda rearranges much of *Hamlet*'s narrative sequence here; more on that below). Rather than a remediated experience of theatrical relationality, Almereyda implies that writing, acting, and recording are all now part of the archive, stored and replayable binary code: Almereyda's *Hamlet* engages in the critical use of new media. *Making* the "rogue and peasant slave" soliloquy sustains Hamlet's compositional encounter with recorded performances, performances of "acting" on stage and screen. These performances not only imply his forthcoming "film/video," *The Mousetrap*; they articulate the utility and function of theatre and recorded performance, of *Hamlet*, in digital culture.

Constantly cutting back and forth between Hamlet's face and the images on his video monitors and computer screen defines "reflection" in an internalized, psychological register, an aspect of the scene underscored (as it often is in *Hamlet* and throughout Shakespeare film) by having Hamlet's soliloquy presented as voice-over, interior monologue. But while Shakespeare's Hamlet is horrified by the "monstrous" *modus vivendi* of a living actor, Almereyda's Hamlet faces an image, an actor-in-character, an image that's almost purely image, the actor absorbed as "movie star" icon: James Dean, the rebel without a cause, shown here in a 1955 television film, "The Unlighted Road" for *Schlitz Playhouse of Stars*.[39] The film image provides Hamlet with a strikingly different choice than the Player's performance does, inviting him to contemplate the character rather than its performance, as though Pyrrhus could be staged without the simultaneously affecting, alienating histrionic aggression of the live actor. While the Player's performance must bring the dead language of Pyrrhus to life, enforcing and communicating a palpable horror through the grotesque process of taking it on (at least for Polonius: "Prithee no more!" 2.2.458), Hawke's Player – James Dean – registers the pastness of his drama in the register *of* the past, a discrete image, boxed on the screen, that Hamlet controls, starting and pausing the temporal process of performance. Moreover, while Pyrrhus is definitively a figure of restorable epic performance, James Dean is an icon of nostalgia: like Buddy Holly or

J.F.K., the image of James Dean inescapably evokes a regret for what can no longer come into being as action, a lost performative.

Almereyda's allegory of the functioning of drama in the technologies of contemporary performance opens with this confrontation: Hamlet's encounter with the Player is played to the music of nostalgia, sustained not merely by the image of the young, dead star, but also by the softly elegaic frame that black-and-white film, like photography, draws around the past. Granted, Almereyda's Hamlet writes no code, creates no new applications, is more an experimental user of available technologies than a creator of new instruments. Nonetheless, *Hamlet*'s recording remakes the past in the present under the technological sign of the archive, black and white, using "digital artifacts as theories," as "hermeneutical instruments" to interpret, understand, and remake "other phenomena" (Ramsay and Rockwell, "Developing Things" 79). While Shakespeare's stagey Player is a historical precursor to the lambent image of James Dean, the stage and the photograph articulate the living and the dead with a difference: Shakespeare's Hamlet is harrowed by the ways the absent, fictive ghosts of Pyrrhus and Hecuba possess, double, and degrade the actor's presence, and he attempts a similar act of shamanism, more visible perhaps in the Folio than in the Q2 text: "O vengeance!" (F 2.2.576). James Dean occupies the screen of the past, a visual field transmitted from the cultural archive of memory, in black and white, an icon of Roland Barthes' sense of photography as "a kind of primitive theater, a kind of *Tableau Vivant*, a figuration of the motionless and made-up face beneath which we see the dead" (*Camera Lucida* 32).[40] This player here appears as an object to be seized by reflection (Hamlet's eyes) rather than impersonation. While Shakespeare's Hamlet is a poet, like Shakespeare and his contemporaries well versed in making "additions" to older plays, Almereyda's Hamlet writes in the recorded materials of the archive. Shakespeare's Hamlet recites a speech from memory, watches the Player, promises to write him a few new lines, and imitates his quality; Almereyda's Hamlet records the film image displayed on the VCR monitor with his PXL 2000 camera, moving the camera in and out, rescaling the image, subjecting it to the special aesthetics of this technology, and – since the PXL camera converts analog to digital output – rendering his recorded Player, James Dean, as material for future creative work.

Hawke's Hamlet moves the perpetual crisis of dramatic performance – the interplay between acting and writing, analog and digital, between the actor's quality and the script of Pyrrhus that animates and hollows out his performance, rendering it as mere "acting" – into the realm of digital performance; it's encoded, but only indirectly displayable. Print identifies storage and display, at least insofar as *reading* is concerned. One of the challenges of modeling theatrical performance either on reading (imaginary audition) or on digital communications (information) is that texts are not algorithmic in relation to performance. Even if we understand the use of texts in a rehearsal within a kind of feedback loop, the purpose of the feedback is not to adequate the performance to the text, but to adjust its proximity toward a desired, often emergent, performance. In this regard, Hamlet's *making* here resembles rehearsal, both in the sense of toying around with James Dean's image to see what new, more refined performance might emerge, but also in the sense that Dean's performance functions as a text, subjected to an external logic and technology of production that determines how it will be enacted in a new performance-in-the-making.

Hamlet doesn't merely display or model the text; openly engaging the performance archive, his practice is, like the contemporary "practice of the humanities," thoroughly "integrated with the digital and is, at this point, impossible to separate from it" (Parry, "Digital Humanities" 432).[41] Hamlet lies on his bed watching Dean on a TV monitor overhead while he records and so digitizes the image on his PXL 2000 hand-held. The screen fills with Dean's image, but the camera then travels along the adjoining wall, and when it pulls back, Hamlet has now moved to his desk and we are behind his head, recalling the famous shot of the back of Olivier's head as he stares out from the beetling Elsinore cliffs to ask the question, "To be, or not to be." Almereyda's primal scene of contemporary "knowledge representation," though, isn't one of solitary contemplation, but takes place at the workstation: the computer screen to the left, flanked by an audio speaker; various photo-postcard portraits (print) of the dead tacked up on the wall center (manufactured images of Shakespeare, Nietzsche, and Mayakovsky now, later we see other rebels with a cause, Ché Guevara and Joe Orton) above a stack of books (also print), that instrument of inscription – the keyboard – in the foreground; TV monitor to the right. On this monitor, Dean has been replaced by a very different image, John Gielgud as Hamlet – in a velvety romantic-Renaissance "period" slashed doublet – speaking to Yorick's skull. Almereyda's scene both enacts and represents a moment of technological convergence. Gielgud's performance is a moment of remanence – the "residual physical representation of data that has been in some way erased" (Kirschenbaum, *Mechanisms* 26) – too, a clip taken from Humphrey Jennings's elegant black-and-white wartime propaganda film, *A Diary for Timothy*, documenting a moment from Gielgud's 1944/1945 production at the Haymarket Theatre in London (as far as I know, there is no other film footage of this performance – this *Hamlet* has always, only, been a citation, a clip; Jennings's film is now available on YouTube).[42] It's a canny image. Silently imaging Gielgud as Hamlet, Hawke's screen summons the memory of silent film (which will soon play a crucial part in Hamlet's *Mousetrap* film/video), deftly incorporating and displacing the theatrical tradition into the film archive, recalling the phases of its transformation, the process of the theatre's demise as the definitive technology of the drama, the moment of the invention of "liveness" by the possibility of recorded images, movement, and sound, anticipating in a sense the invention of the analog by the digital. Theatre, live acting still exists, of course; it can even be preserved, in a way, by film. Capturing a silent Gielgud underlines the moment when dramatic, Shakespearean acting marked the interface between two technologies of performance, as, perhaps, the early modern players simultaneously figured both Hamlet's past, fictional stage and Shakespeare's present, actual one. Hamlet's work is inseparable from the history of *Hamlet*, and so engages, however indirectly, with the play's inscription in the cultural legacy systems of speech and writing.

But of course Gielgud was not a silent star: what we remember Gielgud for is that voice, the audible echo of a bygone theatricality, a theatricality that – by controlling and emphasizing the vocal register of performance – asserted the stage as the site for the reproduction of verbal poetry. First educated at Lady Benson's Acting School, and the great nephew of Ellen Terry, Gielgud self-consciously occupied the fulcrum between the rhetorical traditions of the nineteenth-century stage and the practices of twentieth-century acting. A splendid Hamlet, a landmark Lear, alternating Romeo and Mercutio with Laurence Olivier, grooming younger actors (Richard Burton) and directors (Peter Brook), teaming with Ralph Richardson in the definitive performance of modern roles (Spooner and Hirst in Harold Pinter's *No Man's Land*), Gielgud's formative role in the modern London stage was complemented by his extensive career in film (Hitchcock's *The Secret Agent*, 1936) and television (*Brideshead Revisited*, 1981), culminating in the role that Peter Greenaway assigns him in *Prospero's Books* (1991), ventriloquizing – who else? – Shakespeare-as-Prospero, writing/reading/narrating very nearly the entire text of *The Tempest*, grounding the text's visible presence in the film in *that voice* (John Gielgud died in May, 2000, just as *Hamlet* was being released).

An icon of dramatic performance, silent Gielgud locates the theatre as a mode of production silenced by new technologies. Yet, while Gielgud's live performance is long dead, its recorded performance is now – as information – susceptible to transcoding.[43] Gielgud is rendered as information, recorded and transmitted in ways that dramatize the instability of the analog in information culture: despite the power of their interaction, the analog is precisely what digital display can represent only asymptotically, dithering between the pixels. The regression from Dean to Gielgud seems to document less the invention or obsolescence of "liveness" by recording than something else, a third process by which performance media – theatre, film, digital – engage in ongoing, reciprocal, interminable acts of intermediation, an exposure of "human actions and older, analog, informatics archives" to critical reperformance (Bianco, "This Digital Humanities" 108). The camera dwells on Gielgud, but then pans back to the left across Ché and Joe Orton, to the computer screen, the screen of digital composition. As the digital screen looks back, so to speak, across the books to the memorialized image of the actor, Almereyda seems to strike a note of caution: like squaring the circle, the digital can never fully capture the curve of the analog, and both performances speak above, outside, beyond the book. The digital archive is the repository of a material history it must encode, silence, and to some extent amputate, in order to render it as material for remaking.

Hamlet's confrontation with the Player-as-image, Dean and Gielgud, recalls the "old melodrama" typically provoked by "new media," that the "intimate contact with the material world" claimed for the old media has been infected, displaced, repudiated, undone by the slick new thing (Bill Brown, "Materiality" 53). Like *Hamlet*, we should be wary here of posing a neat alternative between old and new, live and recorded performance; as Rebecca Schneider notes, *Hamlet* itself "holds no such distinction," since the live *Murder of Gonzago* simultaneously replays an altered textual "recording" (its script), asserts a duplicitous dramatic "record" of Old Hamlet's murder, and frames a charge of regicide, all in the here-and-now of performance, "*in the meantime* of the live" (*Performing Remains* 89). Moreover in *Hamlet*, even the most intimate knowledge of the self is mediated, as perhaps it must be: the "tables" of Hamlet's "memory" were rewritable tablets, magic writing pads (see Stallybrass, Chartier, Mowery, and Wolfe, "Hamlet's Tables"); even in the early seventeenth century, memory was facilitated, created perhaps, at the intersection of the subject with "aesthetics, technology, and society" (Mitchell and Hansen, "Introduction" xvii). While it displays Gielgud's performance as past and receding into a deeper pastness, Hamlet's sly confrontation with the motive and cue of Gielgud's Hamlet also restages the temporal polychrony of theatre performance: in Shakespeare's play, an early modern English theatre company flees the Poets' War to land in medieval Elsinore, where they're well known to the prince.

Shakespeare's moment of urgent metatheatre is phrased in the terms of a contemporary technological double-time that places *Hamlet* in Hamlet's archive. Hamlet's uptake of the forms, moods, and shapes of conventional stage revenge is enacted here in a series of visual encounters drawn from the archive, first with the sultry icon of a previous era's adolescent rebellion and then with his own performance avatar, Gielgud's live-on-film Hamlet anticipating Hawke's Hamlet-gone-digital. Almereyda rewrites the play's analog awareness of theatrical citationality as a digital parable of *Hamlet*'s force, the play's force, in the cultural archive. Shakespeare can both quote and parody his writerly predecessors and contemporaries; at the same time, books (and dramatic performances, too) have a different logic than digital texts, in part because they "are discrete documents that operate with internal cohesion more than external linkages" (Vaidhyanathan, *Googlization of Everything* chapter 5). Nonetheless, nearly from their origin, printed books, even books of plays, have been recognized as commonplacable digests of detachable wisdom; the Q1 "bad" quarto was printed with its most sententious phrases set in quotation marks, *selected*, so to speak, for copying (see Lesser and Stallybrass, "First Literary *Hamlet*" and Erne, *Book Trade* 114–29). Recorded performance is, perhaps in ways akin to pointed *sententiae*, susceptible to reperformance in contexts that alter the significance of the clip, much as the irony of Corambis's advice to Leartes is typically lost in citation.

The most iconic visual image in western theatre, the memento mori of the Prince and the skull, here a clip cut from Jennings's film illustrating London bearing up in the war, a performance clearly staged only for the film camera, is for Hamlet, for Almereyda, and for us no longer intrinsically identified with and within the dramatic logic of Shakespeare's play or its theatrical performance, but as a distinct, conventional (both then and now) image, a citation, a trope, a meme. Hamlet's monitor suggests that digital technologies can emulate older platforms, while at the same time underlining the "lossiness" of the display: not only is Gielgud silenced, but since Almereyda cut the grave-digger scene (5.1) from his film, this cameo is our last and only glimpse of poor Yorick. As a parable of digital *poiesis*, Hamlet's soliloquy here rejects the false alternatives of either replaying or replacing the Player's complex theatrical "liveness." As Derrida recognized in his reading of Austin, for performative speech ("O vengeance!") to have force as action, it must be effectively indistinguishable from an "action that a man might play." Hamlet can reject the Player but cannot escape his medium; now, no *Hamlet* can escape the discrete events that compose *Hamlet,* the archive which any performance will re/decompose.

As the camera dollies around behind Hamlet's head, we lose sight of Gielgud, and, crossing over the postcards, attend finally to the dialogue between Hamlet's eyes and the computer screen. Acting is auratic, continuous, occupying the temporal and material duration of unique human bodies: acting is indivisible, and emphatically *analog*. Shakespeare's *Hamlet* oscillates between the technologies of writing and acting, as the Player brings a palpably literary text to histrionic "life," and Hamlet vows to "wipe away all trivial fond records" (1.5.99) in order to take on the Ghost's summons to action. Shakespeare's scene emphasizes the subtle monstrosity of acting, as discrete identities – actor, Player, Pyrrhus, Hecuba – blend into the analog performance of a single "individual." But acting, or even reciting, is not *this* Hamlet's medium; it is, in Marshall McLuhan's sense, perhaps, too *hot* for cool Hamlet. As Walter Benjamin recognized, film transfers the site of performance from the auratic presence of the live actor to the work of the camera, which denies the actor's performance as a "unified whole." Citing Pirandello's prescient sense that the film actor's "body has lost its substance, that he has been volatilized, stripped of his reality, his life, his voice, the noises he makes when moving about, and has been turned into a mute image that flickers for a moment on the screen," Benjamin notes that in the "Age of Technological Reproducibility," the audience's identification in the process of performance is not through the actor but through the work of the camera ("Work of Art" 261, 260). But *Hamlet* also shifts the terms of Benjamin's critique, occupied less with the loss of unique aura or presence in the movement to mechanical reproducibility than with the consequences of digital storage and manipulation. Hamlet neither takes on, replicates, reperforms, or restores the actor's analog performance, nor does he compose with the instrument of film, the camera. Hamlet composes with images. The mastering art of Almereyda's film is not writing, nor acting, nor filmmaking: it's *curating* the digital archive.

Digital encoding transforms images into data that can be manipulated in a much wider range of ways, in part by storing them in a medium finally disconnected from the scale of human time, perspective, or sequence. As we lose sight of both Dean and Gielgud, our attention is focused on the editing screen, as Hamlet uses its icons to begin making his film, a bricolage of sequences from the film archive. Almereyda emphasizes the emerging functions of digital technology as a metaphor for human consciousness, rapidly cutting now not between the computer and television screens, but from the computer screen – imaging the terrified visage of a woman from the 1963 Mexican horror film *La Maldición de la Llorona* – to a close-up of Hamlet's eyes, sustaining the functionalist sense that the computer, its strategies of archiving and displaying "information," has fully displaced both the stage (the theatre of the mind) and "the book and volume of [the] brain" (1.5.103) as the most dynamic – if inaccurate – contemporary metaphor for human thought (see Golumba, *Cultural Logic of Computation* chapter 3).[44] But *Hamlet* represents this encounter not in the terms of Shakespeare's book-and-volume, embedding "human cognition at the center of self-organizing systems that support it"; rather, continuously using his instruments as the means to experience, Hamlet performs a paradigm of the technological extension of cognition, imaging "the cognitive system as a whole and its enrollment of human cognition as a part of it" (Hayles, *How We Think* 93). And as Hamlet conceives catching the "conscience of the King," the screen goes black; the next image is the video box, *The Mouse Trap*, "A Film/Video by Hamlet," which turns out to be – like other media in Denmark – in Claudius's hand.

Much as Hamlet's encounter with the Player resonates throughout the play's meditation on acting and action, so Almereyda's allegory of performance technologies is concentrated in Hamlet's scene of editorial composition, an index of the film's own conceptual design and practice. When test audiences of the film thought the Shakespearean plot "felt flat" (begin with the sidekicks seeing the Ghost, bring in the stars in the second scene), Almereyda fashioned a more "urgent start" for the film by sitting down with Ethan Hawke, getting the "pixel camera," and working "out a new introduction, a video diary excerpt from one of our favourite speeches" – the "what a piece of work is a man" speech (2.2.269–276) – that had been dropped from the film (Almereyda, "Director's Notes" 135). Editing – not writing, acting, or even camerawork – is the presiding practice of Almereyda's *Hamlet*: even in the opening scene, the camera shows the sign of Hamlet's editorial agency, his hand working along the bottom of the frame. Ever since print's power of duplication unchained the manuscript book from its lectern, books and images have been portable. What digital technology has enabled is an exponential increase in the ease and power with which we can rework this data, transform it into something else. As a script for the theatre, *Hamlet* was always susceptible to additions, subtractions, reordering in performance, and as Tiffany Stern has argued, an early modern dramatic script was from the outset typically a "patchily" constructed network of variably authored documents (*Documents in Performance* 2). Locating *Hamlet* among other items in the digital archive, *Hamlet* dramatizes a sense of the play as digital hypertext, "information" susceptible to refunctioning in various visual structures of representation, capable of being interlinked in nonlinear ways, and of being combined readily with other data forms: a cartoon Godzilla, a stealth bomber, explosions, Gielgud and Yorick.

Hamlet pins Giotto, Nietzsche, Shakespeare, Mayakovsky, Joe Orton to his wall, memorializing the era of print, an era – in terms of printed drama – very nearly inaugurated by Shakespeare's plays. Digital editing is, though, often seen to alter the ideological contours of Benjamin's mechanical reproduction. In his fascinating account of the "craft" of digital design, Malcolm McCullough remarks that "Where a photographic print requires little more work to make many identical images, a computer image requires little more work to make many, no two of which are exactly alike" (*Abstracting Craft* 47). Mechanical technology has historically been sustained by an ideology of *reproduction*, as a single text, image, sound can be copied to an apparently stable medium that appears to enable exact duplication and massive dissemination. Digital technology is sustained by a rhetoric of *transformation*, as text, image, or sound are not copied to distinct stable media, but represented by a common electronic code, susceptible to being combined, exchanged, displayed, performed in ways that depart significantly from the material form of the data initially encoded, generating a sense of almost limitless fungibility. Indeed, as files, they are displayed only as the consequence of constant electronic updating, variation in the current enabling the transmission of the data. And yet, much as we have indeed come to recognize the ideological complexity of the rhetoric of reproduction – Random Clod's "transformission" ("Information on Information" 246) – the notion that digital records do not have the properties of materiality arises from a reciprocally misleading "screen essentialism," the sense that what we see on the screen relates directly to, or determines, the conceptual logic of the computer's processes of inscription and storage (Kirschenbaum, *Mechanisms* 43).

This dialectic in medial ideologies, between the apparent fixity, permanence, and authority of print and the – threatening, liberating – mobility of performance, should sound familiar, recapitulating as it does not only the history of antitheatrical prejudice but also the reciprocal disciplining of "performance" as a genre of Literature (in English), where it's located on Alan Liu's useful outline of digital resources, Voice of the Shuttle. Hamlet's editing of the performance archive, his editing of *Hamlet*, reverses the text-to-performance assumptions of literary drama. Clipping bits of performance, Hamlet recomposes them into a new work, more than the sum of individual quotations: performance remakes its texts. *Hamlet* also points to the limitations of this useful distinction between reproduction and transformation as an index to the transformission of performance, limitations rendered visible by the pressure that digital technologies have placed on our understanding of print. For even in print, *Hamlet* is not *one*: the Prince says "scullion" and "O vengeance!" in the 1623 Folio, but "stallion" in the 1604/5 second quarto, where he fails to mention "vengeance" at all. Gielgud isn't the only ghost in the archive: beyond Sam Shepard, there's another old *Hamlet* haunting Almereyda's film. For what makes Hamlet's editorial activity comprehensible in the "rogue and peasant slave" scene is the fact that he has already rented the movies he's watching, encoding, editing (we can see them stacked up on his monitor). The editing Prince has already been to Blockbuster, where he has already ruminated "To be, or not to be – that is the question." In both Q2 and F versions of *Hamlet*, Hamlet raises this question *after* his reflections on acting and revenge, but Almereyda's decision to reverse the order of these scenes – so that Hamlet shops "To be, or not to be" before deciding "The play's the thing" – has a longstanding, if (to some) unpalatable warrant "in the text." Almereyda's film invokes the narrative order of the maligned, and mysterious, 1603 "bad" quarto, a text long taken to overwhelm the authorial signal with the corrupting noise of the playhouse, the printshop, the unknown pirate.[45]

While Hamlet's activity reminds us of the fallacy of the textual determination of performance, it nonetheless transpires in a densely scripted milieu, the database. Encountering the Player, Hamlet summons the archive; *making* performance, Hamlet replicates the scene of the digital humanities, our scene, where digital technology functions as a "tool, study object, medium, laboratory, and activist venue" (Svensson, "Beyond the Big Tent" 41). As the authors of *Digital_Humanities* argue, digital storage and the possibility of migrating content "from platform to platform, to be used in a variety of outputs and for a range of readers and forums" creates alternative modes of authorship: "Authorship is multiplicative and dissemination happens across the Web as others add to, borrow, remix, and republish the work" (Burdick et al. 56). It is notable here that the agency for this activity is attributed not to individuals, nor even to the collaborative "team that merges their identities into a corporate subject" (110), but to an "ever-expanding space of design and curation" (56). In one sense, the performance of digital media reflects the performance of the stage: the team (though whether artistic teams ever really see their identities merged into that of a corporate structure seems open to question) remixes a range of activities (acting, design) and materials (text, cloth, lights) to produce an event that has no single author, warranted by the consensual rules – the social and artistic conventions of the ambient theatricality – operating in that cultural "space." In *Hamlet*, though, the "digital artifacts" providing the "hermeneutical instruments through which we can interpret other phenomena" include Shakespeare's *Hamlet* (Ramsay and Rockwell, "Developing Things"). As Hamlet goes to work, he suggests that *Hamlet* – like the computer, the camera, the pencil, the page – is an instrument in our contemporary system of extended cognition. If there is a "database logic of new media, in which textual and media objects can be created, combined, remixed, and reused" (Fitzpatrick, *Planned Obsolescence* chapter 3), *Hamlet* now participates in that logic, is accessible to and by it, and is performed – for many research, teaching, entertainment, and creative purposes (O, vengeance!) – within it as well.

The Mousetrap in the database

> the method of storage must not place its own restraints on the information (Tim Berners-Lee, "Information Management: A Proposal" 212)

Hamlet illustrates one of the fault lines running through contemporary digital humanities: like the abusive caricature of socially and technologically obsolete "individual scholars hunched over separately bound texts, each working individually," apparently indulging themselves in "the myth of individual genius, in which the great man produces noble ideas wholly from his own intellectual resources," Hamlet appears to embody the "planned obsolescence" of pre-networked scholarship (Fitzpatrick, *Planned Obsolescence* chapter 3). If *Hamlet* registers an anxiety about emerging technology, it may well arise here, at the intersection between Hamlet's *making* and the social transformission of *Hamlet*. Hamlet's editing enacts the dialectics of transformission in digital culture: dependent on the database, working in a culture of *curation* that redefines the materials of artistic and scholarly creation, and the process and value of that labor as well: "in the age of the network, the editorial or curatorial labor of bringing together texts and ideas might be worth as much as, perhaps even more than, the production of new texts" (Fitzpatrick, *Planned Obsolescence* chapter 2).[46] Writing is intertextual, but as the application of *curating* to contemporary art-making and scholarly production implies, working in the digital archive – and in a digital textual environment, which we do when we write – has summoned alternative models, practices, and values, which define both the act of *making* and the value attributed to what is made, *Hamlet*, for instance. *Curating* has a double valence: applied to, say, conference organizers or anthology editors, it honors their sometimes invisible work by recognizing it as the exertion of expertise; yet, by implicitly foregrounding the function of taste, *curation* perhaps overwrites or devalues the nuts-and-bolts labor signified by words like *organize*, *edit*, and *write*. Of course, neither connotation is entirely divorced from the attribution of the nobility of genius, which *curating* locates on the axis of socially moderated combination rather than that of individual invention – after all, in some circles "calling yourself a curator is the new power move" (Burdick et al., *Digital_Humanities* 10). Anticipating the complex identity of sampled video shared on social networking sites today, Hamlet's "film/video" performs its public intervention in the representation of Claudius's court through the distinctive means of digital technology, here the *curation* of the archive.

In Shakespeare's play, *The Murder of Gonzago* is stylistically bracketed within *Hamlet*: the static character of its action, its moral simplicity, the outmoded formality of its language are all set against the more complex, multiple, fluid, and ambiguous forms of Shakespeare's play, a fluidity dramatized by Hamlet's constant interruption of – and irruption into – the performance. Shakespeare's play "quotes" as passé a style of drama (and perhaps a style of performance) to mark the boundary, the (dis)continuity between *The Mousetrap* and its fictive host, a membrane Hamlet instantiates through his transgression of it. In Almereyda's film, *The Mousetrap* operates in a different temporality. Hamlet's film combines items from an unidentified cinematic past, dramatizing the situation of *Hamlet* in the performance of knowledge representation today, using "remix tools" in the practice of critical curation.[47] *The Mousetrap* dramatizes the situation of *Hamlet* in the performance of knowledge representation, as the movement of the "story [. . .] extant and written in very choice Italian" (3.2.255–256) from narrative to dramatic writing to stage performance in Shakespeare's play is replayed as a movement from drama to theatre to film to the recombinatory "logic" encoded in the social practice of digital media.[48] Much as the touring players are defined by their economic circumstances – they're in medieval Elsinore because the "late innovation" of children's companies in early modern London has made the road more profitable – Hamlet's film reminds us that the "essence of the economic model of the information society is that information is regarded as a commodity"

(Feather, "Theoretical Perspectives" 4), performing an avant-garde aesthetic within the corporate domain. From its opening moment, the film discloses the implication of its instrument – the editing suite – in the culture of the corporation: the title for *The Mousetrap. A Tragedy. By Hamlet Prince of Denmark* not only replicates the design of Almereyda's opening title, but clearly sets Hamlet in the lineage of the Denmark Corporation.

The Mousetrap's inscription in the instruments of corporate commodification is signaled by the digitally animated rose, blooming and dying, with which it opens; the image is strikingly generic, the kind of imagery that once came packaged with the editing software. The notion that "information wants to be free" is hedged by the fact that much of the available information is proprietary, not free and not remakable.[49] For Hamlet, as for other curators (and scholars), compositional work "is ultimately premised upon a simple, practical fact: it requires a digital object, either a born-digital object or an analog object that has been somehow scanned, photographed, mapped, or modeled in a digital environment" (Sample, "Unseen and Unremarked" 188). As Mark L. Sample observes, the ability to work with digital materials depends on access to the objects: copyrighted works – his example is the work of Don DeLillo – without a malleable digital identity are simply unworkable, uncuratable. And yet, as the travesty of Google Books demonstrates, the corporate production of the objects and instruments of the humanities is no guarantee of their utility (see Vaidhyanathan, *Googlization of Everything* chapter 5). Hamlet's art-making is precisely marked by the status of digital property, by property rights rendered visible in both films – Hamlet's and Almereyda's – that determine the performative identity and use value of the curated "past."

This dimension of curatorial *making* is registered by the films' credits, or – more accurately – by their absence. For although Hamlet's *Mousetrap* curates "found footage," at least some of that footage is used in ways that seem to render it even more lost. Hamlet's "childhood" is represented by two equally generic "home movies" – file footage that seems to represent the "home movie" rather than being actual home-movie film – drawn apparently from two different eras. In the first – in color, perhaps taken from advertising – a 1950s family sits happily before a large boxy television, dominating the lower right-hand corner of the screen; in the second, we see a family in what appears to be an earlier scene, perhaps the 1940s – patterned furniture, wallpaper, hooked rug, mother sewing, no TV in sight – and watch as the father follows the little boy to the bedroom, down a long, Olivier-like hallway. Time passes, signaled by an animated spinning globe (spinning the wrong direction) reminiscent of sci-fi films; it's hard to say whether this image is original to Almereyda's film (doubtful), taken from a sci-fi animation from the 1950s or 1960s, or is merely a "retro" refiguration in the mode of advertising imagery from Old Navy to Yahoo, and of contemporary TV soaps like *Mad Men*.[50] The film then attends to the poisoning, first registered by a cartoon poison bottle, then a manifestly retro-animation sequence of cells coagulating, a 1950s businessman relaxing in his recliner, and a drop of poison slipping into his ear, reminiscent of the *Rocky and Bullwinkle* style, though more directly recalling Terry Gilliam's animations for *Monty Python's Flying Circus*. Then, a series of silent clips – a man staggering, a shot of Cleopatra from Enrico Guazzoni's 1913 Italian silent *Antony and Cleopatra*, a line of men (military trainees?) falling like dominoes, an animated spiral (again recalling Hitchcock's *Vertigo*), the animated flower dying, the black-and-white little boy coming downstairs to "watch," apparently seeing Cleopatra again, and a short sex clip from *Deep Throat*. The film concludes – although Claudius interrupts, we see "The End" displayed on the screen – with a scene of applause, and the image of Solomon Mikhoels as King Lear in 1935 at the Moscow State Jewish Theatre.[51] The clip shows Mikhoels making up for the role and adjusting his crown, from a longer sequence documenting the stage production: *The Mousetrap* absorbs the history of Shakespearean theatre as its climactic gesture of exposure. As Mark Thornton Burnett notes, *Deep Throat* signifies in several registers, too, having sparked a censorship controversy that reached the US Supreme Court, and exemplifying the "cinematic terrorism" of the porn industry, "whose net effect was to oppress women's minds and bodies" ("'To hear and see the matter'" 60). Of course, "Deep Throat" is also famous in another sphere, as Bob Woodward and Carl Bernstein's nickname for the informant who led them to unearth the Watergate conspiracy, exposure that eventually drove President Richard Nixon from power. Much as *The Mousetrap*'s villainous "Lucianus, nephew to the king" collapses Claudius murdering Old Hamlet into Hamlet's stalking of his uncle, so *Deep Throat* images the court's visibly tawdry and exploitative sexual politics and also perhaps suggests Hamlet's critical effort to reveal such corruption.

Hamlet's encounter with Gielgud's Hamlet frames *Hamlet* as recursive: while live performance is richly and variously citational – think of the ways in which direction, scenography, tonality, costume, gesture can recall a previous performance – digital performance is archival, restoring that previous performance as a literal replaying. "Found footage" implies that the archive is conceptually random, but of course like any database it has a conceptual structure that determines the parameters of its use.[52] Mixing animation, silent and sound film, black-and-white and color film, scored to Tchaikovsky, Hamlet's anticipatory mash-up is conceptually dependent on the principle enshrined in UNIX programming as the "Rule of Modularity: Write simple parts connected by clean interfaces." Yet, as Tara McPherson has argued, while the technical function of "modularity" is to segregate the operation of one component of a complex program from another, enabling each phase to be developed and debugged separately ("Why are the Digital Humanities so White?" 145), "modularity" is a resonant paradigm of cultural transformission as well. For the "compartmentalizing" dimension of UNIX depends on the modular concealment of the "kernel from the shell": "The kernel loads into the computer's memory at start-up and is 'the heart' of UNIX (managing 'hardware memory, job execution, and time sharing'), although it remains hidden from the user" (148). As McPherson suggests, the sense in which the display conceals its productive structure is ideologically resonant, both with the structure of capital, and, more to the point here, with scholarly practice that assumes the neutrality of its instruments: "Just as the relational database works by normalizing data – that is, by stripping it of meaningful, idiosyncratic context, creating a system of interchangeable equivalencies – our own scholarly practices tend to exist in relatively hermetically sealed boxes or nodes" (154).

Hamlet's film dramatizes the consequences of modular curation, in which the boundaries between objects are marked while the principle of combination is not. *The Mousetrap* performs not the "obsolescence or disposability of information" but its "resuscitability," the "'undeadness' of information" (Chun, "Enduring Ephemeral"). Yet, the nature of Hamlet's database is obscure, both to the court and to us: *these* clips didn't come from Blockbuster. The modularity of the film's editing dramatizes the extent to which digital technologies, unlike printed books, distinguish the storage from the delivery function: items in the archive can be snipped, clipped together, stripped of their historical, aesthetic, functional, and rhetorical contexts. The short clips represent the ideological impact of the digitization of analog performance, transforming the curve of performance into distinct sequences of data, each segment susceptible to conveying "information" in a different system of representation. Imported, digitized, anonymized, and recombined, neither the Gielgud clip nor any of the clips used in *The Mousetrap* are credited in either Almereyda's or Hamlet's film.

Most stage productions of the *Mousetrap* scene emphasize the Prince's by-play with Ophelia and chattering with "Lucianus, nephew to the king," constantly eliding the already blurred boundary between onstage and offstage in *The Mousetrap*, much as his many asides and soliloquies have created the opportunity for by-play with the audience in the theatre. In Almereyda's film, however, Hamlet processes analog film into digital code, using the archive to speak for him, a database represented as random uncitable collection rather than as a structured canon. In *Hamlet*, Shakespeare – *Antony and Cleopatra*, *King Lear*, *Hamlet* – is always already part of media history, digital objects curatorially and culturally interchangeable with other objects, pornography, advertising, animation. No Hamlet, now, can escape *Hamlet*, escape Shakespeare, if it was ever possible to perform Shakespeare's play without being haunted by Hamlets past. Hamlet's digitized bricolage is even scored to Shakespeare, Tchaikovsky's 1888 *Hamlet Fantasy*, the single credited avatar, witnessing the corporate power of the recording industry in Almereyda's film if not in Hamlet's. For while Almereyda's film credits two versions of Tchaikovsky's fantasy (by the Polish National Orchestra and by the London Symphony Orchestra), the Liszt "Hamlet Symphonic Poem No. 8" (performed by the Gerwandhausorchester Leipzig), *Crow II: City of Angels*, and "The Unlighted Road," other screen images, including both Gielgud's scene and the clips featured in *The Mousetrap* are credited merely as "STOCK FOOTAGE" from various providers. EMI, CBS, Naxos provide proprietary data, tracking the makers of knowledge work – the London Symphony Orchestra, etc. – into Almereyda's film; Shakespeare's plays and, significantly, their stage and film performances lack the corporate protection that identifies them as property, as works whose metadata is critical to their historical, cultural, and instrumental identity, and essential to their transformission. Gielgud and his Hamlet, Mikhoels and his Lear are lost in being "found," merely the unidentified data of pastness.

Shakespearean drama has, historically, marked moments of changing performance technology (professional companies, women onstage, moveable scenery, naturalistic illusionism, silent film, sound film, digital film, digitally animated film). Shakespeare performance appears in Hamlet's film, and in Almereyda's, through the atomized and decontextualized rhetoric of the database, which suppresses the logic of its structure to enable the illusion of unconstrained searchability. As a figure of knowledge work, then, *Hamlet* seems at once to acknowledge the complexity of the textual tradition (adapting the narrative of Q1, Almereyda contests the notion of performance merely "executing" the design of the software text), while at the same time understanding digitized performance as a kind of text, stored in discrete, unrelated, locations on the hard disk and in cultural memory, susceptible to being searched and recomposed, and to being curated for an audience for whom metadata – including the script's provenance in Q1, Q2, and/or F – are often insignificant, and for whom the corporate ownership of the materials and instruments of research is increasingly the condition of knowledge work. Remember Google Books.[53]

Altering the sequence of the play's action, cutting and pasting soliloquy to voice over visually extended scenes, moving between different "texts" of the play's plot structure, thematizing the representation of *Hamlet* as corporate property, Almereyda's film locates a moment of technological change of which we are still a part, a moment in which changing media technologies alter the users' understanding of themselves, of culture and history, and of performance in and of the humanities. As the final moments of the film flip back and forth between dying Hamlet's eye and his "thoughts" and "memories" – represented here as the digital output of the PXL 2000 camera – *Hamlet* seems to verge on a cybernetic sense that "these recursive feedback loops between culture and computation create a coevolutionary dynamics in which computational media and humans mutually modify, influence, and help to constitute one another" (Hayles, "Cybernetics" 154). There is no "outside" information technologies in *Hamlet*, either within the mystified depths of the subject or an economic/political order determining their use and function. Like the figure of the theatre in Shakespeare's play, digital information technologies are not the tragedy of contemporary *Hamlet*, only its condition. Here, Almereyda's film avoids the familiar dichotomies hamstringing the critique of dramatic performance, implying instead their mutually constitutive relations: text/performance; information/noise; the archive/the repertoire; writing/speech; digital/analog. This is the moment in which Almereyda's film reaches beyond the terms of Shakespeare and Performance Studies, locating *Hamlet* in a wider consensus about the inseparability of media and experience – Kittler's famous "Media determine our situation" comes to mind (*Gramophone, Film, Typewriter* xxxix).

What does it mean to use Shakespearean drama as Hamlet does? Remembering theatre, we might recall one of the animating gestures of modern naturalistic theatricality, the sense that the image enacts its most powerful, coercive work when it conceals, displaces, or denies its means of production, when it operates in a "modular" way, evoking a kind of display essentialism. Sherry Turkle anatomized a stunning transformation in the ideology of computer culture in the final decades of the last millennium, perhaps best captured by the shifting meaning of the word "transparency":

> In 1980, most computer users who spoke of transparency were referring to a transparency analogous to that of traditional machines, an ability to "open the hood" and poke around. But when, in the mid-1980s, users of the Macintosh began to talk about transparency, they were talking about seeing their documents and programs represented by attractive and easy-to-interpret icons. [. . .] This was, somewhat paradoxically, a kind of transparency enabled by complexity and opacity. (*Life on the Screen* 42)

Almereyda's Hamlet uses a version of Microsoft Windows, which once required a DOS command to load but which now emulates the superficial character of the Macintosh "desktop," a transparency now ubiquitous as mobile apps. The power of Almereyda's film arises from this double perspective, and it is notable that in composing *The Mousetrap*, Hamlet deploys Brecht's favorite filmic device, the montage that spoke to him most vividly about technology's ability to disembed images from the "transparency" machine of ideological seduction. For Brecht, the "discovery" enabled by epic theatre can be "accomplished by means of the interruption of sequences," an interruption that "here has the character not of a stimulant but of an organizing function." Recognizing that montage is often deployed as a merely stimulating "modish procedure," Brecht nonetheless models the theatrical *gestus* on "the method of montage decisive in radio and film," which should compel the spectator "to adopt an attitude vis-à-vis the process, the actor vis-à-vis his [*sic*] role" (Benjamin, "Author as Producer" 778). At the same time that his montage renders the culpability of the court transparent, Hamlet's editing renders the database, its organization, its metadata, transparent only in the display-oriented, "Macintosh" sense.

Hamlet's dying eye reflected in an unseen screen, the film sharpens the point of digital technologies and knowledge representation in contemporary culture: "Can something still be called a medium when it is the foundation for physical reality, continuously generating the world and everything we know through its computations" (Hayles, "Cybernetics" 153)? Shakespeare's play represents an undecidable continuity between the world and the stage, that hollowing out of the nontheatrical innate to the medium of theatrical performance. Almereyda's film, though it represents the theatre as closed and silent, nearly inaccessible, nonetheless replicates a sense of the play's representation of theatricality. Rather than seeing the theatre as an alternative antitechnology that might "help to humanize and contextualize the changes of the digital world" (Carson, "eShakespeare"

272), *Hamlet* implies the continuity of theatre with the electronic technologies now essential to human performance. The dialogue between technology and embodiment – the dialogue of dramatic performance – illustrates one aspect of contemporary extended cognition, perhaps familiar to everyone who has ever reached into a pocket for a lost cellphone, the sense of "a body whose embodiment is realized, *and can only be realized*, in conjunction with technics" (Hansen, *Bodies in Code* 20). In Shakespeare's play, many of those *actants* are inscribed objects, the book, the poem, the letters that drive the plot; and one of those technics is the technique of *acting*, embodied by a human *actant*, the Player. Almereyda's film recognizes the more radical conception pointed out by Hayles, in which objects and technics – like Latour's *actants* – gain "agential capacities to act outside the human's mobilization of its stimuli" (*Electronic Literature* 109), not only to make the lifeworld, but to reconfigure the human as well.[54]

Poised at a moment of technological change, a moment allegorized in the film itself, Almereyda's *Hamlet* implicates *Hamlet* in this discourse of technological change, a discourse of remaking, remediation, and obsolescence, the terms that have perennially defined the dramatic theatre, perhaps always threatened by its palpable potential to out-Herod Herod. Rather than conceiving Hamlet's database *making* as distinct from the practices of Shakespeare's play, Almereyda's film enables us to see Hamlet's activity, the technologies of and in *Hamlet*, as "the instruments of humanism at large, dynamically engaged within and as part of the socially realized protocols that define sites of communication and sources of meaning," part of the ongoing history of "material cultures of knowledge and information" (Gittelman, *Always Already New* "Epilogue"). Hamlet's *making* promotes a distinction with the legacy systems of writing and acting, a distinction with the theatre that has always been a distinctive preoccupation of theatre: "the complexity of Shakespeare's texts" – and of Shakeseparean performance, dramatic performance – prompts "us continually to rethink concepts like *content, medium, record,* and *performance*" (Gayley and Siemens, "Introduction" 218). For although we can still read *Hamlet* in a book (most of which today began their lives as digital files), and see a staged production with no cellphones or cameras or monitors in sight, the contemporary conception of human action is inseparable from the role of digital culture and its instruments, much as it is inseparable from speech, writing, clothing, sexual mores, variable technologies for making the human.[55] It is partly for this reason that the absence of theatre, of dramatic performance, from the theoretical reach of digital humanities' knowledge representation is important: theatre is an ongoing practice, not merely a residual medium consigned before its time – like manuscript, radio, black-and-white film, television, print – to the past.

Shakespeare performance frames the problem of transformission now, not only in the era of digital technologies but in an era in which digital technologies both complicate and erase distinctions between media, and are in the process of transforming the objects of culture, the instruments of our access to and understanding of the humanities, our means of representing knowledge, and so the knowledge we can represent. How has the performance of encoding, storing, representing, and displaying altered the work – and the works – of digital humanities? What is *Hamlet* now? Reordering the arrangement of scenes, staging a silent Gielgud, Almereyda's film – like *Hamlet* in the contemporary theatre – marks a slippage between the legacy systems of writing and speech, the digital and the analog, both in the practice of theatre and in the claims of digital media (writing, film, video) to store the "information" of performance. Both on stage and in digital media, *Hamlet* represents knowledge work and suggests, especially for those living in the places where stage performance continues to provide a vehicle of critical artistic discourse, not simply the displacement of analog by digital means, but an ongoing, mutual engagement and definition of the materials, means, and practices of performance. Staging a constantly variable interaction between digital and analog, a changing understanding and practice of the relation between writing and acting across the horizon of contemporary performance, *Hamlet* today witnesses the slow, interminably turning narrative of the media of making dramatic performance.

Intermediated between manuscripts, performances, printed texts, radio broadcasts, films, digital productions, *Hamlet* has always already been about the instruments of its making. When Jan Kott remarked in his essay, "Hamlet of the Mid-century," that "*Hamlet* is like a sponge. Unless it is produced in a stylized or antiquarian fashion, it immediately absorbs all the problems of our time," he had a specific, mediagenic Hamlet avatar in mind, one who had never played Hamlet: "I prefer the youth, deeply involved in politics, rid of illusions, sarcastic, passionate and brutal. A young rebel who has about him something of the charm of James Dean" (64, 62). Separated from us, now, by half a century, Dean has emerged as the icon less of political rebellion than of bitter ennui, an irritable, disengaged, undirected angst trapped within regimented 1950s America; fittingly enough – and nothing marks the distance from James Dean to Ethan Hawke as much as their personal information devices – the Cracow Hamlet of "late autumn, 1956, read only newspapers," and the Warsaw Hamlet of the following year could be visualized "in black sweater and blue jeans. The book he is holding is not by Montaigne, but by Sartre, Camus or Kafka" (68, 69). Our understanding of ourselves, and of how dramatic action represents us, speaks to and for us, is necessarily changed by the media "in which it is accomplished."[56] Much as we have come to understand the impact of the technological transformation separating Hamlet's stagey Player from James Dean, we're just beginning to recognize the impact of the transformation separating Dean from Ethan Hawke or other Hamlets immersed in technology, Scott Shepherd or Lars Eidinger, whose performances perhaps just touch on what Hayles calls a "third-order cybernetics," which "redraws the boundary once again to locate both the observer and the system within complex, networked, adaptive, and coevolving environments through which information and data are pervasively flowing," a system that recalls another site of multiple exchange between digital and analog representation: the modern theatre ("Cybernetics" 149). And, of course, we are only beginning to suspect the effects of a constant exposure to digital media, the constant performance of digital media, on our investment in theatrical performance.

One of the discoveries of contemporary performance is that we have always been there in the theatre; however much it may claim merely to transmit the work of literature, theatre is always a postdramatic event, a recognition obscured only as long as we conceive dramatic theatre as a design for interpreting textual information to an audience of absent readerly interpreters. While digital technologies have massively reordered the practices of visual, verbal, and inscribed communications, they also alert us to enduring conceptual instabilities. *Hamlet*'s account of dramatic writing – it's hypertextual, capable of being reordered, inseparable from a gestural archive, unable to determine performance, always lost and recreated by intermedial transformission – implies that dramatic performance is, and has always been, transformative, altering both the material and instruments of its making, and reshaping the archive as well. As a kind of cultural Turing machine, performance perhaps illustrates the principle that there is no algorithm for demonstrating the "provability" of all expressions arising from the text.[57] Dramatic writing provides "equipment for living," but in the theatre that equipment is hardly virtual: it is one instrument for playing our part – as actors, characters, spectators – in the event, for rendering sensible, so to speak, the disposition of the theatre. *Hamlet*, the Nature Theater of Oklahoma *Romeo and Juliet*, *Sleep No More*, and many other performances explore the uses of Shakespeare in the purposes that bring us together in the here and now, to act at the intersection between "acting" and the acts it represents, to perform in the event of dramatic performance.

Notes

1 SHAKESPEARE PERFORMANCE STUDIES

1 More recently, Lehmann has noted that the theatre "practices of the 18th and 19th centuries put more emphasis on aspects of theatrical illusion and the predominance of literary value" (Lehmann, Jürs-Munby, and Fuchs, "Lost in Translation" 16), implying that "dramatic theatre" arises at the confluence of competing modes of authority, the spectacular forms of theatre, and the increasingly authoritative genres of print literature.

2 A recent student handbook series is a case in point: "The Shakespeare Handbooks are student-friendly introductory guides which offer a new approach to understanding Shakespeare's plays in performance. The commentary at the heart of each volume explores the play's theatrical potential, providing an experience as close as possible to seeing it in the theatre." By providing close commentary on the script, the commentaries "enable a reader to envisage the words of a text unfurling in performance"; the "aim is to *present* the plays in the environment for which they were written," exploring each "play's theatrical potential" (Brown, "General Editor's Preface" vi, my emphasis). The initial comment above is taken from the series description on the flyleaf of the book.

3 References to *Hamlet*, unless otherwise noted, are to the Q2 edition edited by Ann Thompson and Neil Taylor; references to Q1 and F are to the separate edition edited by Thompson and Taylor.

4 Though Kivy doesn't discuss stage performance at length, he does perhaps recall Lehmann's understanding of "dramatic theatre" in his suggestion that an actor like Julie Harris reading aloud from *Jane Eyre* performs much the same activity she would perform in an onstage dramatization of the novel: "she read the simple narration with great expression; and when she came to reciting the speeches of the dramatis personae, she declaimed them as an actor or actress would have if performing in a play" (*Performance of Reading* 46).

5 In *Shakespeare and the Power of Performance*, Robert Weimann and Douglas Bruster have, justly noting the limitations of my sense that performance should not be understood as merely interpreting a text, suggested that "questions arise which so far have not received satisfying answers," especially, "What kind of practice, what type of staged action and delivery do we actually mean when talking about performance in its own right – that is, as an independent, even

sovereign force in Shakespeare's theatre?" (7). They intend to show how "the performed interpretation goes hand in hand with something larger than itself," which I would call something like the ideological structure embedded in the performance conventions of a given form of theatre and theatricality. To my mind, though, while Weimann and Bruster frequently capture the suggestive variety of ways Shakespeare's roles imagine the uses of writing, their own use of "interpretation" gestures toward textual determination: not only are actors involved in "delivery," but the effort to seize "from where and by what means does the actor's practice reach beyond the ministerial delivery of the text" points to "the exceptional difficulties in fixing what is, in fact, a radically fleeting borderline between textually sanctioned interpretation and what is more than such interpretation" (8). The practice by which a performance can be understood as "textually sanctioned" not only lies outside the performance but also outside the text; it would arise in the productive, often regulatory, and typically incommensurable discursive structures of literary critique, acting practice and training, and so on.

6 Although the rehearsal process often involves the "interpretation" of the text (What does this word mean? Does Hamlet intend to destroy Ophelia in the "nunnery" scene?), as a process, what rehearsals "interpret" is the rehearsed performance itself, and what that performance is measured against is not the text, but a sense of what the participants (director, dramaturg, designers, actors) want the final performance to be and to do.

7 I have in mind here, of course, J. L. Austin's famous hesitation with regard to the way "performatives" do and don't do their ordinary work in the theatre; *How To Do Things With Words* lecture 2.

8 Rancière's understanding of *mimesis*, though, depends on a complex genealogy of successive ways of locating art in the "distribution of the sensible": for a useful summary of his distinction between the *ethical* regime ("in which the poem's images provide the spectators, both children and adult citizens, with a certain education and fit in with the distribution of the city's occupations"), the *representative* regime ("a pragmatic principle that isolates, within the general domain of the arts (ways of doing and making), certain particular forms of art that produce specific entities called imitations"), and the *aesthetic* regime (which "asserts the absolute singularity of art, and, at the same time, destroys any pragmatic criterion for isolating this singularity") see *Politics of Aesthetics* 21–23.

9 My thanks to Daniel Larlham and his fine work on the history of acting for the notion of *mimetizing* as a principle of acting.

10 Rancière's comment on Appia and Craig is worth quoting at length here: "The two great renovators of theatre carried the logic of renovation to the extreme point where it signalled the death of spectacle performed on stage by actors for spectators. The realization of a true essence of theatre thus led to its suppression. Yet it was at the juncture of these impossible realizations – at the meeting point between the fusion of parasite bodies in the space of the stage made absolute and the over-presence of bodies denying the artifice of the stage – that

the modern art of *mise en scène* would find its principles and its strategies" (*Aisthesis* ch. 10).

2 INTOXICATING RHYTHMS: SHAKESPEARE, LITERATURE, AND PERFORMANCE

1 Although plays had been published for some time, the cultural status of contemporary plays in print was still unsettled in the England of the 1590s. Drama may have been "understood to play itself out in two arenas – on the stage and on the page," but much of this current controversy concerns the cultural status of those pages (Peters, *Theatre of the Book* 8, quoted in Erne, *Literary Dramatist* 7). I refer throughout to the first edition of *Shakespeare as Literary Dramatist*; references to the "Preface to the Second Edition" are noted as "Preface."

2 As Erne points out in *Shakespeare and the Book Trade*, the "fraction of the book trade's output accounted for by playbooks" fluctuated between the mid-sixteenth century and the 1620s, sometimes exceeding "6 per cent of the total number of speculative titles." Playbooks were often reprinted, though no other playwright's plays "sold as well as Shakespeare's" (20–21).

3 Kastan rightly suggests, though, that for some time printed drama may have remained in "a category of its own, competing in the marketplace with other recognizable categories of reading material like literature, religion, and history" ("'To think these trifles'" 45).

4 Authors were on many occasions involved in proofing, and Laurie E. Maguire reminds us that John Marston apologized that his "'enforced absence' from the printing house obliged him to 'rely upon the printer's discretion' in the first quarto of *The Malcontent* (1604)" ("Craft of Printing" 443). Richard Knowles notes that "Shakespeare could not have been unaware of his growing marketability or indifferent to his growing literary (not just theatrical) reputation" (Review 546), and Erne points out, echoing James Shapiro, that Shakespeare must have been habituated to the climate of the London bookshops (*Book Trade* 22–23).

5 On the plays' representation of writing and performance, see Cheney, *Literary Authorship*; Scott, *Shakespeare and the Idea of the Book*; Weimann and Bruster, *Power of Performance*; Worthen, *Drama*.

6 As Jeffrey Knapp observes, it was possible to write plays whose only – and very successful – life was in print: Samuel Daniel's *Cleopatra*, published in 1594, was reissued in eight editions in the next eighteen years (*Shakespeare Only* 8).

7 Tiffany Stern notes, "Advertisements for books consisted of title-pages separately printed and hung up on the posts of the city" (*Documents in Performance* 55).

8 On the economics of publishing plays in quarto, see Blayney, "Alleged Popularity" and "Publication of Playbooks" as well as Farmer and Lesser, "Popularity of Playbooks."

9 In the second edition of *Shakespeare as Literary Dramatist*, Erne notes that the question of whether Shakespeare "is of the stage or of the page, should we watch

him or read him?" poses "false dichotomies, but the realization that they are false does not mean we can easily escape them, and surveying responses to *Shakespeare as Literary Dramatist* makes me realize that some have seen these dichotomies affirmed in it" ("Preface" 3).

10 Jeffrey Knapp, however, carefully documents Jonson's effort to arrogate prestige simultaneously to actors and the author, by listing the names of his players in the 1616 *Works* (*Shakespeare Only* 65).

11 Dutton suggests elsewhere that while it "has been usual throughout the twentieth century to pay lip service to the idea of Shakespeare as a 'man of the theatre,'" "editorial judgments" (and, I would say, critical judgments) have relied on "essentially aesthetic rather than theatrical grounds," in ways that have finally favored "the 'writerly' Shakespeare, who remains the dominant voice in the English-speaking world's construction of its definitive author" (*Licensing, Censorship and Authorship* 112). Yet as David Bevington asks, "In what sense was Shakespeare a man of the theater? He wrote plays for the acting company to which he belonged and took part in the performance of many of those plays, and yet to succeeding generations of students and readers his reputation has often been primarily that of a great poet, a profound thinker, and a perceptive observer of the human condition" (*Wide and Universal Theater* 1).

12 Tiffany Stern puts this question somewhat differently, based on her reading of the patchwork of documents used in early modern performance: "whether surviving playbooks are ever fully representative of plays as they were performed ('performance texts') and whether playbooks are ever fully stripped of the theatre to become plays in an ideal literary form ('literary texts')" (*Documents in Performance* 254).

13 I have slightly altered Knapp's wording here, though not, I think, the sense that Shakespeare's achievement is to incorporate the contributions of actors and audiences into his writing, rather than merely providing actors material for their own labor – "the decisive effect of his audience and fellow actors on his dramaturgy" are Knapp's exact words (*Shakespeare Only* 123).

14 While I don't agree with all of Erne's assessment of "performance criticism," I do share much of his sense of its shortcomings, and am grateful for his very productive engagement with my work.

15 This sense of the social and political consequences of the displacement of embodied by inscribed forms of knowledge pervades Performance Studies of the 1990s; see, for instance, Roach, *Cities of the Dead*, and Worthen, "Disciplines/Sites."

16 A sense of the limitations of Taylor's dichotomy here is gained from Weimann and Bruster's account of *King Lear*: "The rendering of characters alone includes a full, bewildering assortment of acting styles and affects of the personal, from allegorical figuration and iconographic portraiture to the improvised personation and 'deep' characterization" (*Power of Performance* 199).

17 On Brooks and Heilman, and on Taylor's *archive* and *repertoire*, see Worthen, *Drama* ch. 1. It might also be noted that a dialectic between the intellectual

"difficulty" associated with masculinized literary studies, and a parallel lack of rigor assigned to practices of embodied arts has long structured the relationship between literature and theatre in the American academy; see Jackson, *Professing Performance*.

18 Michael J. Hirrel suggests that both before the mid 1590s and after, when the starting time of performance was moved from around 2 in the afternoon to around 4, the "Elizabethan theatrical event [. . .] was a flexible vehicle that probably could accommodate full performances of Shakespeare's longer plays" ("Duration of Performances" 159); he marshals considerable evidence here, especially noting that cuts in the few existing scripts we have are "seldom substantial" and do not "significantly narrow the range of script lengths" (172). In his "Preface to the Second Edition" of *Shakespeare as Literary Dramatist*, Erne stringently disputes both Hirrel's evidence and his interpretation of it ("Preface" 14–17).

19 On the use of sides, and their impact on both stage directions and revisions, see Palfrey and Stern, *Shakespeare in Parts*.

20 On the many late nineteenth- and early twentieth-century productions staging Cleopatra's barge, see Margaret Lamb, *Antony and Cleopatra*.

21 On the signifying dimension of typographic design in modern drama, see Worthen, *Print and the Poetics of Modern Drama* 73–84; on Katherina's exit, see Hodgdon, ed., *The Taming of the Shrew*, 306–308.

22 Taking a rather different perspective, Stern notes that the appearance of prologue and chorus – typically written, she argues, to accompany the first performances – in the Folio text implies an early date for that text, preceding the date of the Q text which drops them out, in part due to the "time-specific references in one chorus." In this perspective, then, the F text is longer because it includes materials that have a directly theatrical provenance (see Stern, *Documents in Performance* 108–109).

23 Citing Barbara Mowat's account of Sir Richard Cholmeley's men performing *King Lear* and *Pericles* from quartos in Gothwaite, Yorkshire in 1609, Weimann and Bruster suggest that print "tended to multiply all sorts of performance options – gestural, verbal, semantic, characterizing – and thereby could enhance the performer's range of 'self-generative' action" (*Power of Performance* 25). See Mowat, "Theatre and Literary Culture" 213–215. Moreover, as Stern argues, even the copy approved by the Master of the Revels provided little constraint on the performance script; "plays were regularly altered, particularly after first performances," regularly receiving "'new additions' for revival; in neither of these instances does the Master of the Revels seem to have been asked habitually to approve the 'new passages'" (*Documents in Performance* 235). She also suggests evidence showing "actors learning their parts before the book has been officially approved (and changes made to it) if not before it has been fully written (237).

24 Gary Taylor's claim that the working practices of the theatre are best understood as "an unwritten paratext which always accompanied" the dramatic manuscript, "an invisible life-support system of stage directions, which

Shakespeare could either expect his first readers to supply, or which those first readers would expect Shakespeare himself to supply orally" ("General Introduction" 2) provides the editorial warrant for the Oxford's expanded stage directions, in effect supplying a scripted version of this "paratext."

25 In this conflict, I have played, admittedly, a perhaps unduly polarizing part; see also Robert Weimann, *Author's Pen and Actor's Voice.* For the record, I'm not "against" texts, textual critique, or indeed "literary" modes of critique that stand apart either from the history of Shakespeare in performance, or from a conception of the texts as intentionally or institutionally involved in performance. But much as I would, along with Erne, repudiate the notion that the "written for performance" vision of Shakespeare's plays disables non-performance-oriented forms of critique, I would also resist the notion that Shakespeare performance streamlines and simplifies a more complex hermeneusis promised to readers of the plays, or that Shakespeare performance should be evaluated in terms of its apparent restatement or interpretation of "the text." That is, both versions of the "written for" – for actors, for readers – dynamic strike me as artificial, simply false to the rich variety of ways in which Shakespeare's writing has been made to speak, and so to have cultural significance.

26 Not surprisingly, given the care with which this argument is framed, Weimann and Bruster immediately warn us that "such neat juxtapositions (here designed, again, as a summary introduction) can be dangerous as soon as they threaten to obscure the full range of engagements between dramatic language and histrionic bodies," and the argument of *Shakespeare and the Power of Performance* does indeed explore these engagements with a rich sense of their variety. For instance: "Put simply, the making of Shakespeare's *dramatis personae* can be traced on a wide spectrum bracketed by two extreme ways of figuration. One is where writing, in shaping dramatic speech and action of imaginary agents, provides given, more or less authoritative contours for staging images of artificial persons. The other sees the strength of the performative, the material act of staged counterfeiting, as pervasive enough to assert itself in its own right and to affect by its own authority the imaginary figuration of a person even before it comes to be staged" (139).

27 Berger's model is also invoked by Cheney, *Literary Authorship* 9 note 16.

28 Nonetheless, for Berger, "Plays, then, like other texts, appear to be intended for interpretation, which includes performances in various media; and like other texts, their apparent 'intentions' are dissociated from those of their authors and subject to continual critical revision" (*Imaginary Audition* 24).

29 For a rewarding reading of Berger's career, see Margreta de Grazia, "Harry Berger Jr." She remarks that Berger's reading strategies involve a "transferral of agency from individual characters to social discourses," in effect responding to a searching "deconstruction of personal identity and the language that gives it voice" (548, 549). On Berger's role in the development of "performance criticism" in the 1970s and 1980s, see Worthen, *Shakespeare and the Authority of Performance* ch. 4.

30 As Anthony Dawson notes, Berger takes Shakespeare to stage "the inadequacy and relative superficiality of theatrical meanings" (Dawson and Yachnin, *Culture of Playgoing* 35 note 52).

31 Although approaches to theatre from a "cognitive science" perspective have, as we will see, a long way to go in demonstrating many of their reflexively antitheoretical claims about the stage, it seems clear that from a physiological as well as a phenomenological and philosophical vantage, spectating is hardly passive.

32 See also Robert Weimann's remarks on a "dated reading of (neo)Aristotelian versions of mimesis" that ignores the fact "that the thrust of early forms of mimesis was not exclusively towards imitation, but was also marked by strong links to dance and song" ("Performance in Shakespeare's Theatre" 8).

33 The program for the June 2013 performance notes that "approximately 30 people were asked to tell the story from beginning to end," which resulted in much more material than could actually be used onstage. Of these conversations, eight sources were edited down for the final set of performance monologues.

34 According to Kelly Copper, the eight monologues represent eight different interview subjects, though one of the monologues is devised from material taken at two separate interviews. The final scene between Anne and Bobby was the result of one of the participants calling Pavol Liska back with some additional thoughts about love after the initial phone interview about *Romeo and Juliet*. The interview subject here was Anne Gridley's mother (Copper, Message, 6 July 2010). My thanks to Kelly Copper and to the Nature Theater of Oklahoma for providing me with a script of the play and with a recording filmed at The Kitchen in New York on 27 December 2009, and for answering my many questions about the production and the process of its devising. I saw this production several days later, in early January 2010, and again in Berlin in June 2013. I cite here from *Nature Theater of Oklahoma's Romeo and Juliet*, as published in *Theater* in 2010, which occasionally differs – sometimes in small ways, sometimes more extensively – from the words performed on the DVD, or in any stage performance. I'm also grateful to Kelly Copper and Pavol Liska for taking the time to let me see the performance ledger, and for answering many questions about the genesis and production of *Romeo and Juliet* and about their more current work.

35 In transcribing the conversations, Copper is especially careful to note coughs and to transcribe as accurately as possible the various nonverbal sounds the interview subjects use – the various kinds of "um," "ah," and so on (Message, 6 July 2010).

36 This volume is part of the Teacher's Toolkit available free from the Shakespeare in American Communities website; it contains the *Teacher's Guide*, the DVD, and other materials.

37 In this sense, both the translations and contemporary performance illustrate what Michael Bristol identifies as a fear of the "encroachment of vulgar popular or mass culture into the institutional reproduction of Shakespeare"

that threatens to transform "the classical body of the authoritative text into something weak, flattering, and ultimately meretricious," a view that has historically taken in both the theatre as an institution, and a theatrical, performance-oriented critique of Shakespearean drama as well (Bristol, *Shakespeare's America* 35).

38 For an account of the complex ways YouTube now provides an important instrument of vernacular performance in pedagogical and nonpedagogical contexts, see Ayanna Thompson, "Unmooring the Moor," and her wider treatment of Shakespeare "Reform" in *Passing Strange*, ch. 6. Todd Landon Barnes presents a detailed analysis of the uses of Shakespeare across a range of contemporary entertainment, political, and pedagogical platforms in "Immanent Shakespearing." My sincere thanks to Professor Thompson for providing me with an advance copy of her book manuscript, and to Professor Barnes for a copy of his as yet unpublished dissertation.

39 Published in the 1980s, the *Shakespeare Made Easy Romeo and Juliet* locates its purposes within a life-long Shakespeare curriculum: "Generations of students have complained that 'Shakespeare was ruined for me at school.' Usually a fuller appreciation of Shakespeare's plays comes in later life. Often the desire to read Shakespeare for pleasure and enrichment follows from a visit to the theater, where excellence of acting and production can bring to life qualities which sometimes lie dormant on the printed page" (6). By evoking a "visit to the theater," the rhetoric of "enrichment" and "appreciation," and even by naming an editor ("edited and rendered into modern English by Alan Durband"), though, *Shakespeare Made Easy* plays the music of another era. In the case of *Romeo and Juliet*, *Side by Sides* and *Shakespeare Made Easy* tend to incorporate as much of the original wording as possible into the translation on the facing page; *No Fear Shakespeare: Romeo & Juliet* and its companion *No Fear Shakespeare Graphic Novels: Romeo & Juliet* more assiduously rewrite the dialogue into a contemporary American idiom.

40 *Side by Sides*, however, undoes the status issue by having Gregory make a distinction that doesn't seem much of a difference – they're not "mere servants." These issues run through the scene – the "maidenheads" joke, "poor-john" and (rather surprisingly) the bawdry involving tool, standing, and so on – and are addressed with considerable difficulty.

41 I don't mean to imply that the translations are always warranted, or even accurate. The gnat wagoner of Mercutio's "Queen Mab" speech becomes a mere "bug" in *No Fear*, which also seems a little inattentive to other aspects of the speech, translating the parson's dream of another benefice into "dreams of a large donation" (*Side by Sides* has him dreaming of "another gift").

42 *No Fear* addresses a palpable market of "Shakespeare-phobic" parents, whose "inability to comprehend the language 20-plus years ago" makes the books attractive (Customer Reviews for *No Fear Shakespeare: Romeo & Juliet*), as well as a mixture of regret and irritation with regard to the project of secondary-school Shakespeare ("If your child needs to endure Shakespeare, this book is

invaluable ... Why wasn't this available when I was a kid????" [Customer Reviews for *Side by Sides*]).

43 Some reviews misidentify this as a "mock-Elizabethan style" and generalize it to "the traditional manner of bad Shakespearean acting the world over" (Isherwood "Just the Gist"), "high-falutin' pronunciations," "fruity voices and grandiose gestures" (Soloski, "Verona").

44 The performance ledger notes a number of TASKS: HYPER-ARTICULATION, SOUTHERN ACCENT, BRITISH ACCENT, BEGINNINGS OF WORDS, ENDS OF WORDS, AMERICAN R'S, which suggest the performance's constant focus on the quality and detail of the speaking. The "southern accent" derives, according to Kelly Copper, from Robert Johanson's Virginia background.

45 Keithley notes that "Most of the performance parameters for *Romeo and Juliet* emerged from the mid-nineteenth-century traveling Shakespearean theater," using what Kelly Copper described to her as "acting techniques employed (or imagined to be employed) by great Shakespearean actors" ("Uncreative Writing" 70). Copper also notes being inspired by curtains from a collection posted at Curtains Without Borders (Copper, Message, 6 July 2010).

46 As Todd Landon Barnes notes, after the election of George W. Bush in 2000, the budget of the NEA "rebounded 28 percent (a nearly 27 million dollar increase)," in which nearly "all this new funding was reserved for Gioia's 'favorite' program: *Shakespeare in American Communities*" ("Bush's 'Three Shakespeares'" 6). He also notes the "*million*-dollar" contribution by the Department of Defense (7). On his side, Gioia's recourse to Shakespeare, and its successor American Masterpieces, is often regarded as having spared the NEA from defunding.

47 As part of a longer-range study of the Shakespeare in American Communities initiative, Ashley Duncan Derr's work tracks both the goals and the practices of implementing and selling the initiative; see "Making Shakespeare" and "Changing the Conversation."

48 Giguere also remarks that the United States became involved in wars justified as the assertion of democracy in Iraq and Afghanistan just as the NEA initiated "a program that returns America to its heyday of the nineteenth century [...] when Shakespeare plays were popular forms of entertainment for everyone" (*Shakespeare in American Communities* 49).

49 Although Frost's poem was published in 1947, on his 1963 visit to Amherst College to honor Frost, President Kennedy delivered a speech "recognized by the NEA as a precursor to its own formation" (Barnes, ("Bush's 'Three Shakespeares'" 14).

50 "The earliest known staging of his [Shakespeare's] plays in the colonies" was not in 1750, as the *Teacher's Guide* informs us [13], but in 1730; see Wilmeth and Curley, "Timeline" 33.

51 Barnes cites James G. Macmanaway to suggest the unlikelihood that "many copies of Shakespeare were to be found" among the books of the colonists ("Immanent Shakespearing" 131); he also notes the extent to which the performance of British drama, including Shakespeare, in the years leading up to

the Revolution, was regarded as "'suited to extravagant royalist tastes,'" suggesting that the tensions between patriots and royalists that led to the closing of the theatres during the Revolution merely resurfaced during the Astor Place Riot. Kim C. Sturgess also notes the uses of Shakespeare in both rebel and royalist rhetoric (*American Nation* 58).

52 The film *Why Shakespeare?*, distributed by the NEA as part of the educational materials, takes a contemporary perspective on the relationship between Shakespeare and cultural, ethnic, and racial diversity: the professional actors and middle- and secondary-school students who discuss and perform Shakespeare evince a principle of multicultural casting. As in the *Teacher's Guide*, however, the issue of race remains implicit and is not addressed directly.

53 See, for example, Levine's discussion of Charles Matthews's travesty of the "Nigger's (or Negroe's) theatre" during his visit to New York in 1822 (*Highbrow/Lowbrow* 14), and Roach, "Emergence of the American Actor."

54 As Ayanna Thompson notes, "The deeper critical engagement about which Tina Packer speaks (helping to 'define the aesthetic and ethical standards of a culture') does not seem to be part of the process" (*Passing Strange* 134).

55 On decontextualization, see Giguere, *Shakespeare in American Communities* 59, 62; on the nationalist implications of oratorical training, see Barnes, "Immanent Shakespearing" 136. Audrey Carmeli, Director of Development of Classic Stage Company in New York, notes that when the CSC Young Company applied for support to join the initiative, they were required to perform an entire beginning-to-end version of a Shakespeare play, even if that production could last only 90 minutes, and that they brought their own teaching materials into the schools. Their brief handbook contains a twelve-page overview of Elizabethan English culture, Shakespeare's theatre and *Romeo and Juliet*, materials considerably richer and more detailed than those supplied to instructors by the NEA. In preparation for their visit, the materials invite teachers to assign two exercises. In the first, the double-sonnet speech is printed out as prose and students are asked to lineate; in the second, they are presented with a group of photographs and asked to cast various roles in *Romeo and Juliet* from headshots (Carmeli, telephone interview, 13 January 2011; Young Company, "Study Guide"). My thanks to Audrey Carmeli for making the time to discuss the project, and for supplying me with the guide.

56 The selections are weighted toward the secondary-school canon – four from *Romeo and Juliet*, four from *A Midsummer Night's Dream*, three from *Hamlet*, two each from *Henry V*, *As You Like It*, and *The Tempest*, with one each from *Macbeth*, *Twelfth Night*, *Othello*, *Richard III*, *Julius Caesar*, *2 Henry IV*, *Merchant of Venice*, *Cymbeline*, *Antony and Cleopatra*, and *Taming of the Shrew*.

57 For example: "Earl of Essex: You are a nobleman, of noble birth and title, and one of Queen Elizabeth's favorites. You have been friends with the Queen since you were children. Some gossip that you have had a romantic relationship with the Queen. Nevertheless, you are plotting her overthrow. You are gathering the support of other nobles before attempting a coup and riot on the

streets of London. You are one of the wealthiest men in England and have many servants to attend your every need. You attend The Globe and sometimes have been known to hire Shakespeare's company to play 'politically incorrect' plays, including Richard II, to stir up trouble with the people and the Crown. Your line is: 'Have you seen the Queen?'" (*Teacher's Guide* 21).

58 The Nature Theater of Oklahoma in fact represents the "American theatrical tradition of touring" much more literally than some of the companies funded by the NEA: the company has extensively toured (and devised work in) Europe precisely because it received financial funding and performance opportunities abroad.

59 The Nature Theater production is not about the work of race in nineteenth-century Shakespeare theatre, either; while there was not a wide range of ethnic or racial diversity among the interview subjects for *Romeo and Juliet*, though, there was an interesting range of age and gender: five of eight subjects were mothers, and ages ranged from 17 to 70 (Copper, Message, 21 February 2011).

60 In the talkback with the Berlin audience after a June 2013 performance, one person – the same British woman who remarked "I've never heard it in American before" – asked "Does Shakespeare win the competition?" It's perhaps a mark of the challenge of this kind of performance inquiry that Liska's answer, "No, Shakespeare doesn't win for me," was more or less rejected by the interlocutor, who remarked, to the apparent approval of the audience, "Shakespeare always wins."

61 Kelly Copper reports that the final moments of the performance are in effect to mirror "what we were doing when we began – taking ordinary language and theatricalizing turns into taking theatrical language and rendering it private, intimate, etc." Indeed, the "actors have had nights where the Shakespeare really gets to them and they are in tears as well as the audience, so it does have an emotional charge, but they're not on emotional display" (Copper, Message, 21 February 2011).

3 "THE WRITTEN TROUBLES OF THE BRAIN": WRITING, CHARACTER, AND THE COGNITION OF PERFORMANCE

1 References to *Macbeth* are to the Norton edition, ed. Stephen Greenblatt et al.

2 On the soundscape, see Als, "Shadow and Act." Readers interested in glimpses of *Sleep No More* should consult *Gossip Girls* Season 5, Episode 5: www.cwtv.com/cw-video/gossip-girl/the-big-sleep-no-more/?play=f4ab59d4-f920-416f-8658-f5d7a9aec4af.

3 Over the first several months of the run, *Sleep No More* also became a popular subject for tweets, Facebook commentary, and even celebrity blogging (see Cumming, "Sleep No More").

4 The souvenir program that began to be sold sometime between May and September 2011 lists several narrative structures: *Macbeth* (Duncan, Malcolm, Banquo, Macbeth, Lady Macbeth, Macduff, Lady Macduff); "The

Supernatural" (Hecate, Agnes Naismith ["has come to Gallow Green to look for her sisters"], the Speakeasy Bartender ["Hecate's familiar"], and Witches ["three supernatural beings"]); "Townspeople of Gallow Green" (Mr. Bargarran ["the taxidermist in Gallow Green"], J. Fulton ["the tailor in Gallow Green"]); the King James Sanitorium (Nurse Christian Shaw, The Matron, Orderly); the McKittrick Hotel (Catherine Campbell ["Innkeeper"], The Porter, The Bellhop). See *Emursive Presents* n.p. [18–19]. Several of the names – Catherine Campbell, Mr. Bargarran – are taken from a seventeenth-century account of witch trials in Paisley, Scotland. See Metcalfe, *History of the County of Renfrew.*

5 For the enthusiastic response of the interior design press, see Sekules, "Thane of Chelsea."

6 As Carol Chillington Rutter notes, "Knights didn't see *Macbeth*'s child-imagery as one of those 'imaginative constructions mediated through the poetry' that shaped dramatic meaning. And he certainly wasn't interested in the play in performance, though just as he was graduating from Cambridge, Barry Jackson's Birmingham Rep *Macbeth* was making news by putting the play in modern dress and restoring the onstage murder of Macduff's boy – killed over a cup of afternoon tea by assassins who climbed in through a casement window" (*Child's Play* 168).

7 Yachnin and Slights describe the poststructuralist critique of character as having "two major strains. The first *theoretical* challenge argues for the impossibility of inward, agential personhood altogether on the grounds that subjects are merely the effects of the social, linguistic, and ideological determinations of individual identity. The second *historical* challenge argues that inwardness as we understand and experience it did not exist in the early modern period. On both of these accounts, readings of Shakespeare that presuppose an inward, agential personhood are certainly anachronistic and probably also politically retrograde" ("Introduction" 3). On the "aesthetic reflection of the eternally true, the unchanging human condition" as a feature of character criticism, see Dollimore, *Radical Tragedy* 58; on the sense of early modern interiority as "a loose and varied collection of assumptions, intuitions, and practices that do not at all logically entail one another," however unified they may appear, see Maus, *Inwardness and Theater* 29.

8 Edward Burns, for instance, asks, "Does the character deal in transferable properties, or personal identity?" (*Character* 124), and Yachnin and Selkirk describe character as "a set of dynamic relationships" ("Metatheater" 148). I take "transactional" here from Burns, who notes that "one could speak of a 'substantive' and a 'transactional'" concept of character (*Character* 6).

9 For Belsey, of course, the "scenic theatre unfolds as an object of sight for a subject who is held in place by the spectacle" (*Subject of Tragedy* 25); on the simultaneous positioning and erasure of the spectator in the discourse of realistic theatre, see Worthen, *Modern Drama* ch. 1. While realistic theatre, which Tobin Nellhaus terms "artistic realism" cannot provide a positivist sense of "knowledge," its rhetorical structure manifestly participates in this fantasy (*Theatre, Communication* 24).

10 In both design and psychology, "affordance" refers to the interplay between the intended and perceived uses of an object. For instance, if you are trying to open a can of paint, a screwdriver – not designed for that purpose – will do the trick; if you're caught without your Swiss Army knife, you'll have to improvise, in effect create that "affordance" in another object: your house key, the ear piece of your eyeglasses, and so on. Affordance is elaborated in psychological terms by J. J. Gibson, *Senses Considered* 285: "I have coined this word as a substitute for *values*, a term which carries an old burden of philosophical meaning. I mean simply what things furnish, for good or ill. What they *afford* the observer, after all, depends on their properties." At the same time, how we conceive the properties themselves, and relate them to systems of action or technology, is not entirely a function of the object itself, but a function of "*situated interaction* within a given ecology," as Teemu Paavolainen puts it ("Theatre/Ecology/Cognition" 46).

11 Amy Cook notes that one prominent "cognitive" critic was sidelined by a "literary department . . . disinterested [*sic*] in his questions and answers" (Cook, *Shakespearean Neuroplay* 15). See also Jonathan Kramnick's fine discussion, "Against Literary Darwinism" 315–16.

12 McConachie notes that an anthology of film criticism that featured "a few articles that advanced a cognitive approach," nonetheless "provoked a vicious counterattack from psychoanalytic critics who feared that cognitive science would delegitimize their ascientific epistemology and method" (*Engaging Audiences* 15). Whether or not "Post-structuralism has indeed run aground" (Nellhaus, *Theatre, Communication* 3), attributing motive, a feature of McConachie's argument throughout *Engaging Audiences*, does of course raise the question of empirical evidence: it is rather difficult to believe that Slavoj Žižek, the author of the "counterattack," is really fearful that his epistemology or method are illegitimate.

13 McConachie has suggested a way to define "cultural models" as a means to account for the different expressions of innate schemata: "Cultural models are cognitive and social, composed of complex mental schemas and elaborated social beliefs and practices. Built from a wide range of cognitive concepts that develop in an infant's mind, these schemas are shaped by local cultural experiences, such as language, ritual, and other events, and memories that occur throughout life" ("Toward a Cognitive Cultural Hegemony").

14 As Ellen Spolsky puts it, "The general shape of my claim is that nothing could be more adaptationist, more Darwinian, than deconstruction and post-structuralism since both understand structuration – the production of structures (and this is the same thing as the production of theories of structures, ad infinitum) – as an activity that happens within and in response to a specific environment [. . .] Darwinism is appealing as a theory of mind and meaning because it is a theory of survival that depends on adaptation (troping, reinterpretation, rerepresentation) by recategorization" ("Darwin and Derrida").

15 On extended and distributed cognition, see Clark, *Supersizing the Mind*; Hutchins, *Cognition in the Wild*; Tribble, *Cognition in the Globe*; and

Paavolainen, "Theatre/Ecology/Cognition"; Paavolainen's fine dissertation has been published as a book of the same title. On image schemata, see Lakoff and Johnson, *Metaphors We Live By* and *Philosophy in the Flesh*; Crane, *Shakespeare's Brain*; Freeman "'Catch[ing] the nearest way'"; and Nellhaus, "Performance Strategies." For more evolutionary and deterministic perspectives, see the essays in Gotschall and Wilson, *Literary Animal*; McConachie, *Engaging Audiences*.

16 The polarities here are striking, and worth noting. Crane, for instance, building on Antonio Damasio's work, notes that cognition is dependent on neural networks, rather than a single organizing "self," however much it may develop a consistent perspective for organizing experience (see *Shakespeare's Brain* 21); evolutionary perspectives tend to be more deterministic, envisioning "the mind as consisting almost exclusively of 'domain-specific' cognitive mechanisms, that is 'cognitive modules' that have evolved specifically for the purpose of solving adaptive problems within a Paleolithic environment. And that ancient environment is itself conceived as a set of statistically stable physical and social conditions, the environment of evolutionary adaptedness" (Carroll, "Human Nature" 79). This evolutionary perspective informs McConachie's imagination of audiences at several points in *Engaging Audiences*: "We are social animals. Because evolution has equipped our species with more sensitivity to the needs and emotions of others than is evident in other mammals, we carry these cognitive capabilities with us into theatrical viewing" (65); "emotions, which evolved earlier than many cognitive operations, continually exert regulating and energizing influences on cognitive processing" (93); "As spectators, we want emotional engagement and the chemical changes it brings to our brains; empathy often provides the means for a direct jolt" (95–96); "Historical context matters, but the basic operations of moral understanding have not changed all that much since the initial performance of *Twelfth Night*" (151). In their discussion of cognitive blending, Fauconnier and Turner note, "Around 50,000 years ago, this level of blending was achieved, presumably through neurological evolution" (*Way We Think* 389). A sense of the "evolutionary" perspective can be gained more directly from Merlin Donald, "Art and Cognitive Evolution" 19.

17 As Kramnick notes, "literary Darwinism tacitly presupposes the strong form of psychological nativism provided by evolutionary psychology. All minds enter the world with a common structure and set of tools. This structure and set of tools are part of the genetic endowment and develop independently of environment or learning. The particular culture in which an individual matures merely fills in content or turns the switches in one direction or the other. Each feature of the innate mind, moreover, is present in us now because it solved an adaptive problem in the past" ("Against Literary Darwinism" 334). Kramnick discusses the "Pleistocene" argument 325–327.

18 I am clearly avoiding the term "naturalism" here, which I reserve for specific use: to refer to the late nineteenth-century movement associated with Émile Zola and others to align theatre practice with an objectivist epistemology, a

sense of theatre as experiment that is in many ways absorbed by the masters who interrogate and transcend its conventions and rhetoric – Ibsen, Strindberg, and Chekhov. The transfer of a "scientific" ethics to the practice of art is a manifestly ideological move in the period; at the same time, it helped to install a notion of theatrical propriety – the proper role of the text in performance, effective practices of acting, the conceptual positioning of the spectator – that has remained active long after the particular concerns and some of the stage practices of "naturalism" have waned. This conceptual field is here termed *realism* or *stage realism*. In his original draft preface to *An Actor Prepares*, Stanislavsky welcomes "rigorous criticism both scientific and non-scientific" which he imagines his systematic approach to acting will engender (Stanislavski, *Actor's Work* xxiv).

19 Tobin Nellhaus, in *Theatre, Communication, Critical Realism*, sees the transformation of communications media – writing, print, digital media – in dialogue with changing elements of theatre, and attempts to locate changing dramatic, theatrical, and writing technologies in a generally "cognitive" paradigm. Several of the respondents to Kramnick's "Against Literary Darwinism" also note the implied "realist" or "mimetic" orientation of this line of interpretation; see Vanessa Ryan, "Living in Duplicate" 413; and G. Gabrielle Star, "Evolved Reading" 420–421.

20 Nellhaus's discussion of critical realism distinguishes between these perspectives usefully here, *Theatre, Communication* 20–23. The emphasis on truth and knowledge tends to situate Nellhaus's effort to balance the positivist and constructivist perspectives – which in his own practice are closely associated with a valorization of historical over literary methods – toward positive claims of truth.

21 N. Katherine Hayles, "Materiality of Informatics," quoted in Crane, *Shakespeare's Brain* 220 note 99. Crane remarks that different image schemas "might carry quite different emotional valences depending on historical or cultural positioning."

22 Tribble's approach to distributed cognition in the early modern Globe, for instance, is predicated on a sense that the typical text of early modern drama posed such steep cognitive challenges that the material and social practices of the theatre company were implicitly devised to resolve them; see her discussion *Cognition in the Globe* 31–32. The distinctive cognitive burden ascribed to this theatre – having to perform long plays, from memory, in repertory – leads Tribble to assert the principle of "cognitive thrift" (32) as driving the distributive cognitive means engrained in early modern theatrical practice. This account of theatre as distributed cognition is text-based; whether memorization by practiced professionals is in fact the determining cognitive burden – especially in an era in which there was little expectation of a performance being word-perfect, a print notion – could use fuller exploration; see her discussion of *King Lear* (38–39) for an instance of how "cognitive thrift" is at once used to assert the practical superiority of a specific pattern of blocking, as well as to maintain a realistic "set" for the stage geography – in effect implicating the audience in the performers' cognitive process.

23 A very different approach to this problem has recently been undertaken by Franco Moretti, who approaches the "character networks" of different plays: the "protagonist" of *Hamlet* is, in this sense, important for the way in which he stabilizes the network of character relations. See "Networks, Plots."

24 Of course, the "falsifiable" or "empirical" character of much of the discussion of cognitive blending is far in the background; in the foreground is the practice of metaphorical interpretation, and here "cognitive" interpretation seems to have no greater or more authoritative purchase than other modes of formalist critique.

25 Despite McConachie's commonsensical approach, there's no "strong neurophysiological evidence, say from PET scans or functional MRI results, that the same neural mechanisms used in perception and movement are also used in abstract reasoning" (Lakoff and Johnson, *Philosophy in the Flesh* 38). They continue: "What we do have is an existence proof that this is possible and good reasons to believe that it is plausible."

26 McConachie alludes to what "works" several times in *Engaging Audiences*, notably finding that what "works" today can be harnessed as a means of understanding "how a play has worked" for earlier audiences (17).

27 Discussing nonwestern performance modes like *kathakali*, McConachie notes that the division of actor from narrator would require a synchronizing of verbal and gestural delivery that conforms to research suggesting that verbal and gestural expression arises from the same area of the brain. Perhaps, but "Whatever the style of theatre, performers in all cultures try to ensure that the articulatory and manual gestures are mutually reinforcing," apparently regardless of the nature of those gestures, which are assumed to operate more or less as they do outside the theatre (*Engaging Audiences* 89).

28 McConachie suggests that "In the theatre, after the spectator 'gets to know' the stage person, s/he may mentally shift gears from empathizing to sympathizing. Spectators can shift back again to empathy, and often do, but the two are separate cognitive operations. Rather than stepping into an actor/character's shoes, sympathy involves the spectator in projecting her or his own beliefs and feelings onto the stage figure" (*Engaging Audiences* 99). Tania Singer and Susanne Leiberg define the terms of conscious empathy precisely: "(1) the presence of an affective state in ourselves, (2) isomorphism between our own and another person's affective state, (3) elicitation of our affective state upon observation or imagination of another person's affective state, and (4) knowledge that the other person's affective state is the source of our own affective state" ("Sharing the Emotions" 974).

29 One sign of the difficulty of thinking outside realism is precisely the challenge of inscribing rational or intellectual work into the acting process, at least as far as American acting is concerned. In this sense, the "cognitive" critique of acting seems surprisingly to distinguish emotion and intellect, reinforcing conventional attitudes toward the inadvisability of "head work" in rehearsal, and the inability of "heady" acting to be theatrically effective, to "work." Attempting in some respects to modify this dichotomy, John Lutterbie reports that actors "associate intellectuality with a sharply focused attention" and "a softer focus to be placing trust in the emotional, suggesting ways of behaving

that are not immediately obvious in the initial context" ("Neuroscience and Creativity" 164). The dialectic here is revealing, reinscribing in many respects a romantic rhetoric of creativity that fully suffuses American acting traditions. What is more surprising, though, is that "cognitive" analysis, which depends on seeing empathy and judgment as mutually defining and sustaining activities, persistently distinguishes them in the analysis of acting, avoiding the notion that rational activity has a central role in actor training, in effective performance, or in the spectator's response.

30 On Stanislavsky's engagement with nineteenth-century philosophy and Romantic mysticism, see Daniel Larlham's superb account, "The Meaning in Mimesis." As Sharon Marie Carnicke points out in her fine discussion of the negotiation of Stanislavsky's writings under Soviet censorship, the terms "realism," "truth," and "theatricality" had specific, changing, and potentially dangerous resonances during the 1930s, when Stanislavsky was completing *An Actor's Work*. She suggests that despite a politically necessary emphasis on "realism" in his writings, Stanislavsky may have understood "truth" less in terms of realistic *mimesis* than as a foregrounding of "technique" (*Stanislavsky* 106).

31 Karin S. Coddon's "'Unreal Mockery'" provides a fine instance of how *Macbeth* is engaged by ideological critique: "Macbeth, then, is not the victim so much as the *effect* of a disorder that manifestly precedes and, I would suggest, produces him" (490).

32 Crane cautiously and persuasively situates Shakespearean texts among what she takes to be more or less essential systems of perception and cognition and early modern regimes for engaging, assessing, and understanding those processes, contextualizing a reading strategy in which "traces of cognitive as well as ideological processes" can be found in Shakespeare's texts: "the plays represent what it is like to conceive of oneself as an embodied mind, along with all of the problems and dilemmas that condition entails" (*Shakespeare's Brain* 4).

33 The metaphorical character of these "spaces" is not lost on many cognitive cultural critics; my thanks here to Amy Cook for pointing out the sense in which these "spaces" could be understood as "categories." Yet it strikes me that the rhetorical power of "spaces" in cognitive theatre studies has much to do with their topographical implication, which appears, however inaccurately, to lend them a material character. Burke considers the "paradox of substance" throughout his discussion in *Rhetoric of Motives* 20–27.

34 I am grateful to Robert Shaughnessy for sharing his paper "Immersive Shakespeare and the 'Emancipated Spectator,'" in the Shakespearean Performance Research Group of the American Society for Theatre Research meeting in Montreal, November 2011.

35 Burns, too, notes that "Most actresses playing the role would still be likely to ask – had she children? What happened to them? Did she expect to have any more? (What kind of marriage was it? How long had they been married? . . . and so on)" (*Character* 221).

36 Berger's comment is useful here as well: "Performance helps this project forward by assimilating the unseen world to those *visibilia* so that the status

of the referents of imagery may be equated with that of the embodied speakers: one is as fictive or as real as the other; both inhabit a single 'world'" ("Text Against Performance" 123).

37 I have seen this scene several times; sometime between May and September 2011 the headpiece was changed – the September version was considerably less detailed, less scary; I had the chance to examine it more closely before the scene, finding it stored beneath the bar.

38 Here, I describe a sequence I last saw in 2011; in 2013 this lip-synching was (also?) assigned to a different (male) performer at a different point in the evening, who sang in the hotel lobby.

39 The production rearranges the players in several different castings, and like all productions continues to change: when I saw it roughly six months after my first visit, I saw someone else taken by the Nurse for this scene. This time she left the door open, and several of us peered in.

40 In the various commentaries posted on the *Sleep No More* NYC Facebook site, there have been occasional complaints of the audience being too involved with their cellphones to participate in the "immersion."

41 How should we respond to the hair collection in the doctor's office, each lock meticulously pinned to a card, a typewritten "Patient No." along the top followed by a handwritten specimen number? Reminding me and others of the piles of hair, eyeglasses, shoes in the Third Reich's concentration camps, and of the Nazis' obsessive documentation, this chilling association rhymes with other elements of *Sleep No More*, and coordinates the structure of realist space with other forms of oppressive totalizing representation.

42 My thanks to my colleague in New York and Berlin Niky Wolcz for bringing the Büchner reference to my attention.

43 Berger continues, "These traces tease us by suggesting the presence of a loophole, or peephole, through which we may target the triumphant fiction our applause ratified" ("Text Against Performance" 125).

44 Anthony B. Dawson suggests something of the force of this perspective in his comments about acting, text, and conventional acting: "Hence I do not see any value in abandoning the search for conveying meaningful and interesting persons to an audience, at least not in regard to the production of Shakespeare – for him, the person is a key element of theatrical pleasure. Nevertheless, training actors to recognize contingency, to understand textual and psychological indeterminacy as a way of encountering some of the fixed strategies of Stanislavskian methodology, could open them up to new ways of approaching character, new meanings, new pleasures" ("Continuity and Contradiction" 95).

4 RETROTECH: WRITING, THEATRE, AND TECHNOLOGIES OF PERFORMANCE

1 N. Katherine Hayles productively distinguishes between remediation, which appears to locate "the starting point for the cycles in a particular locality and

medium, whereas 'intermediation' is more faithful to the spirit of multiple causality in emphasizing interactions among media" (*My Mother* 33).

2 Shakespeare's plays were part of Project Gutenberg (1971), and the later Complete Moby Shakespeare (1993), which were available before more fully edited sites like Internet Shakespeare Editions.

3 Although I could joke at the 2004 conference at which I first discussed the film about having *Hamlet* on my Palm Pilot, there was no iPhone (2007) or iPad (2010), to say nothing of YouTube (2005). The moment of that essay is perhaps best marked by its inspiration, Jane McGonigal's remark, "You know, I don't really have to remember things, since anything I really need to know is online," and her incisive dissertation on immersive and pervasive gaming; Jane McGonigal is now best known as the author of *Reality is Broken*, and designer of a range of alternative reality games, including *SuperBetter*. My reading of technological temporality in Almereyda's *Hamlet* intersects in some respects with Thomas Cartelli and Katherine Rowe's sense of the film as "an extended meditation on the resources film and digital video" bring to the problem of remediation (*New Wave Shakespeare* 49), though as I hope this chapter makes clear I'm particularly interested here in the the way *Hamlet* figures the fortunes of performance in contemporary digital humanities as it has developed over the past decade.

4 On skeuomorphs, "details that were previously functional but have lost their functionality in a new technical ensemble," like the "stitching" impressed into the vinyl of an automobile seat or dashboard, see Hayles, *How We Think* 89.

5 Burnett ascribes this resonance to Rosencrantz and Guildenstern, who seem more louche than politically oriented in their portrayal; see "'To hear and see the matter'" 62.

6 I have in mind Philip Auslander's familiar remark, "historically, the live is actually an effect of mediatization, not the other way around. It was the development of recording technologies that made it possible to perceive existing representations as 'live'" (*Liveness* 51); see also Birgit Wiens' notion of contemporary intermedial performance confirming "the definition of theatre as a *hypermedium*" ("Hamlet and the Virtual Stage" 235); and Ralf Remshardt's sense that one consequence of theatre's combination of media is to render "its putative *immediacy* visible as theatricality" ("Actor as Intermedialist" 41).

7 On device culture, see Chiel Kattenbelt's discussion, "Theatre as the Art" 33–34.

8 I have discussed this production at length in *Drama* 123–138. As of the time of writing, both the Wooster Group and Ostermeier productions are still in the repertoire of the companies. When I saw the Wooster Group *Hamlet* again in the autumn of 2012, however, I noted that the live editing of the Burton film had changed considerably: it is much more "erased" in performance now than previously.

9 Despite its familiarity, Shannon's famous phrasing is worth recalling precisely: "The fundamental problem of communication is that of reproducing at one point either exactly or approximately a message selected at another point.

Frequently the messages have *meaning*; that is they refer to or are correlated according to some system with certain physical or conceptual entities. These semantic aspects of communication are irrelevant to the engineering problem. The significant aspect is that the actual message is one *selected from a set* of possible messages" (Shannon, "Mathematical Theory of Communication" 3).

10 Hayles makes a similar point, noting that Peter Shillingsburg's understanding of texts seeks "to protect the 'work' from the noisiness of an embodied world – but this very noise may be the froth from which artistic effects emerge" (*My Mother* 94). She also comments on "Shannon's distinction between signal and noise" articulating "a conservative bias that privileges stasis over change" (*How We Became Posthuman* 63). For Mark C. Taylor, "Noise and information, in other words, are thoroughly relative; what is noise at one level or in one location is information in another moment or in another location" (*Moment of Complexity* 110). See also Jussi Parikka, "Mapping Noise." On various uses of the word *performance*, see McKenzie, *Perform or Else* 9–12.

11 On Shannon's influence on Jakobson and on linguistic, cultural, and literary theory, see Guillory, "Genesis of the Media Concept" 351–352; Geohegan, "Information Theory to French Theory" 111–121. In this regard, the noisiness of dramatic performance illustrates what Alan Gayley describes as a "major blind spot in Shannon and Weaver's communications model," insofar as it mistakes "where complexity lies, not just in signal and noise but especially in encoding and decoding" ("Networks of Deep Impression" 307).

12 "**Experiencer**. In the context of contemporary arts and media, experiencer serves where audience or even 'spect-actor' (Boal) prove inadequate. It suggests a more immersive engagement in which the principles of composition of the piece create an environment designed to elicit a broadly visceral, sensual encounter, as distinct from conventional theatrical, concert or art gallery architectures which are constructed to draw primarily upon one of the sense organs – eyes (spectator) or ears (audience)" ("Experiencer").

13 In "Editing the Interface," Matthew Kirschenbaum also points out that Fredson Bowers's *Principles of Bibliographical Description* and Claude Shannon and Warren Weaver's *The Mathematical Theory of Communication* were both published in 1949: "Though this is plainly nothing more than happenstance on one level, it reminds us that for both textual scholars and information theorists the immediate post-war years were a period dedicated to codifying their respective disciplinary methodologies" (19 note 12), methodologies which, like Charlton Hinman's famous collator, ultimately derived from wartime intelligence work. See also Geohegan, "From Information Theory." Alan Liu points out that the notion of "information" unaffected by the medium of its transmission and realization is reinforced by the corporate, privatized instrumentation of digital culture, a distinctively "postindustrial" understanding of technology as a mediator of cultural history: the sense "that there are no fundamental differences between the past and the present, only technical differences like the contrast between black-and-white film and today's high-sensory, special-effects cinema" (*Laws of Cool* 302).

14 I refer here to Kirschenbaum, "Digital Humanities As/Is a Tactical Term," which provides a useful overview of the disciplinary self-reflection in the field of digital humanities, describing the move toward "knowledge representation" as a means of defining a theoretical and disciplinary field, rather than the construction of a service practice for other fields. Hayles dates the term "digital humanities" to the late 1990s at the University of Virginia (*How We Think* 24).

15 In their pendant chapter, Cartelli and Rowe suggestively describe the "historically *composite* nature of the specific technologies through which individuals and cultures remember" and, as we shall see, perform (*New Wave Shakespeare* 51).

16 The distinctive look and somewhat hazy images of the PXL 2000, the screen shading into black toward the edges of the frame, is a function of its remarkable technological specifications. Designed to record both sound and images on chromium-oxide audio cassette tapes (the camera ran the tapes at high speed, a 90-minute tape producing 5 minutes of video), some cameras also came with a hand-held viewer that could be adapted to battery power (as Hamlet has evidently done in the film). Built to record in very low light, the camera refreshed the screen at half the rate of a standard NTSC video camera (as Michael O'Reilly explains, "Standard NTSC video is 30 fps [frames per second], 2 fields per frame, for a screen refresh rate of 60 times per second. This [the PXL 2000] only refreshes the screen 15 times per second"); it accomplished this feat by gathering a significantly narrower data stream, providing roughly 100 lines of resolution to the standard NTSC camera's 500. O'Reilly explains that the PXL 2000 achieves its characteristic ghostly shimmering through the subpixel "dithering" that occurs between the pixels (akin to the effect that sometimes occurs when film, with its greater resolution, is transferred to videotape). While we might regard this "dithering" as a negative feature of the PXL 2000, "this dithering has a counter-intuitive effect. It is the same effect that anti-aliasing has on fonts on a computer screen. The fonts look best (and are perceived to be sharper or of higher quality) when there is a small amount of blurring that takes place, instead of seeing the jagged edge of each pixel that makes up the letter . . . Events and imaging of a sub-pixel nature are of paramount importance to making video look less like video and as a by-product more like film." This "sub-pixellist viewpoint," combined with the unusually wide depth-of-field are perhaps responsible for the camera's typical use, both by Hawke's Hamlet, and by directors like Benning and Almereyda: all those extreme low-light close-ups of Ophelia, the face-in-the-camera confessional. For a useful summary of the camera and its popularity, see "Dead Medium." Michael O'Reilly's excellent "Pixelvision" is apparently no longer online; nor is "The Pixelvision Home Page." For a detailed summary of the camera's development and use by video artists, see Peter Donaldson's superb essay, "Hamlet Among the Pixelvisionaries."

17 That is, Hamlet's retrotech aesthetic is, in Alan Liu's terms, "cool" rather than "uncool"; he's not an "anti- or last-generation tech, anti-media, traditionalist" despite his tools of choice (*Laws of Cool* 287).

18 On surveillance in *Hamlet* as a function of the film's visual design, see Burnett, "'To hear and see the matter'" 52. It is important to recognize that Hamlet's camera is both "*the* technology of interiority" in the film and more than that; see Cartelli and Rowe, *New Wave Shakespeare* 59. Alastair Black dates the interaction between technologies and cultures of surveillance to the nineteenth century; see "Information Society" 32–33.

19 As Peter Boenisch remarks, "Once upon a time, not too long ago, the division of medial labour appeared to be in perfect order. Film was one thing, clearly, theatre was another and a newspaper was something completely different" ("Aesthetic Art" 103).

20 Bernhard Rieder and Theo Röhle also note "the strong current of universalism running through discourses on the merits of computation," a universalism derived from "the notion of *mathesis universalis*, the ideal of a universal mathematical science" that can be traced through "the history of Western thought" ("Digital Methods" 78).

21 For a useful discussion of the ways the emerging telephone industry resisted what we now take to be the principal use of the telephone – personal communications – and also for the uneven distribution of telephone use among different regions and classes in the United States, see Fischer, *America Calling*, especially chapters 3 and 4.

22 Carolyn Jess notes the likeness of the Denmark Corporation logo to a camera shutter in "Promethean Apparatus" 93; Samuel Crowl remarks that "Kyle McLachlan's Claudius is conceived as the CEO of a multimedia corporate giant" (*Shakespeare at the Cineplex* 191).

23 In 1999 DVDs were available in the US, but VHS remained the dominant format for home video; DVD sales surpassed sales of VHS in 2003 ("DVD").

24 Providing a rich list of Almereyda's quotations of other *Hamlet* films, Elsie Walker identifies the marquee from its "best musical of the year" tag, noting that *The Lion King* also derives from *Hamlet* ("'Harsh World'" 324). Patrick J. Cook notes that *The Lion King* played at the New Amsterdam Theatre, and suggests that this citation recalls Michael Eisner's struggle for power at Disney "following the death of the previous CEO" (*Cinematic Hamlet* 197, 199).

25 Although Burnett suggests the "tragedy of Hamlet and Ophelia, as the film elaborates it, is that the lovers are caught between, and frustrated by, competing older and emergent technological disciplines," it strikes me that the polychrony of technology is the condition rather than the cause of the drama ("'To hear and see the matter'" 57).

26 As Frierich Kittler might note, "ghosts, a. k. a. media, cannot die at all. Where one stops, another somewhere begins" (*Gramophone, Film, Typewriter* 130): after discontinuing its instant film cameras, Polaroid now markets an instant digital camera.

27 On the ideographic understanding of writing essential to its transformation to digital "information," see Lydia Liu, *Freudian Robot*. As Cary Wolfe notes, Gregory Bateson argued that language is "not an *analogue* system of

communication and representation, in which real 'magnitudes' of physical properties have a direct and causal link to the signs used to express them," but rather a "*digital* system" in which "signs have no 'correspondence of magnitude' with what they stand for" ("Language" 235). Paul DeMarinis notes that "Practitioners with unconsciously techno-futurist thought habits commonly err when they refer to analogue as 'old' and digital as 'new.' They furthermore imagine the 'real' world to be analogue in nature, instead of merely material" ("Erased Dots").

28 Kirschenbaum notes that when signals are read from the hard drive's platter, patterns of magnetic fields, "actually patterns of magnetic resistance" are "received as analog signals, are interpreted by the head's detection circuitry as a voltage spike, which is then converted into a binary digital representation (a one or a zero) by the drive's firmware. The relevant points are that writing and reading to and from the disk are ultimately a form of digital to analog or analog to digital signal processing" (*Mechanisms* 89–90).

29 See Moretti, "Networks, Plots," and Mueller, "Digital Shakespeare."

30 Theatre has very little presence on Liu's Voice of the Shuttle website: while Art (Modern and Contemporary), Dance, Media Studies, Music, and Photography are located among the many fields listed in the Contents menu, "Drama, Theater, & Performance Art Studies (Including Screenwriting)" can be found only as one of a long list of subheadings to "English Literature by Genre," which can be found – again, among a long list of subheadings – under the Literature (in English) Contents heading. The architecture of the database openly "models the way the humanities are organized for research and teaching as well as the way they are adapting to social, cultural, and technological changes" (Voice of the Shuttle): "Drama, Theater, & Performance Studies," then, is modeled as a single field, and as a sub-subfield of literary studies.

31 William Pannapacker's concern, expressed in his blog from the 2011 Modern Language Association convention, for the shape of digital humanities as a field expresses a more general anxiety with regard to disciplinary formations: "But the field, as a whole, seems to be developing an in-group, out-group dynamic that threatens to replicate the culture of Big Theory back in the 80s and 90s, which was alienating to so many people. It's perceptible in the universe of Twitter: we read it, but we do not participate. It's the cool kids' table" ("Digital Humanities" 233). See also Scheinfeldt, "Sunset for Ideology."

32 The emerging institutional and disciplinary structure of the digital humanities as a distinctive field of research has been the subject of considerable reflection, and even, perhaps, a certain degree of regulatory discourse as well, recalling some of the issues – who's in, who's out – animating the formation of Performance Studies in the 1990s (see Worthen, "Disciplines/Sites"). Matthew K. Gold's collection *Debates in the Digital Humanities* offers a valuable overview of new perspectives and some now-classic – and combative – statements.

33 Stephen Ramsay provocatively urges, "If you are not making anything, you are not [. . .] a digital humanist. You might be something else that is good and

worthy – maybe you're a scholar of new media, or maybe a game theorist, or maybe a classicist with a blog (the latter being a very good thing indeed) – but if you aren't building you are not engaged in the 'methodologization' of the humanities" ("Who's In and Who's Out"). It should also be noted that there are a number of projects underway working to render historical theatres as digital environments; what's important to me here is the absence of theatre as part of the disciplinary definition of the practice and theory of digital humanities.

34 Gayley and Siemens remark that Shakespeare studies, and by extension Shakespeare "admits none of the straight lines and unidirectional arrows implied by the conjunction *to* in a phrase like *manuscript to print to hypertext*" ("Introduction" 219).

35 These efforts were anticipated by Brenda Laurel's imaginative effort to model a reciprocity between the practice of theatrical and digital representation in *Computers as Theatre*. It's worth remembering, as Random Clod does, that any early modern printed text also typically illustrated the principle of "non-identity with itself" ("Information on Information" 246).

36 As Alan Liu notes, "design theory and practice," alongside "science and technology studies," understands "design as a principle of knowledge discovery and generation rather than (more typical in the digital humanities) as an after-the-fact rendering of data in scatter plots, social-network graphs, and other stale visualizations or, equally tired, book-like or blog-like publication interfaces" ("Meaning of the Digital Humanities" 416).

37 Gayley and Siemens's understanding of modeling is apposite: "The strongest analogy for this ethos," the ethos of *thinking through making*, "in the Shakespeare world may be performance: just as theatre practitioners model Shakespeare's plays by staging them, so do digital humanists stage their knowledge representations like productions of plays, some better than others but none finally definitive – each another's audience outside the limits of the page" ("Introduction" 220). This is a shrewd formulation, consistent with their imaginative sense of the function of Shakespeare and performance in digital research; at the same time, I think this image still suggests that performance's success is measured against the design of the script.

38 Kirschenbaum suggests the paradigmatic relationship between digital and print textuality: we can "consider what electronic textual artifacts have to tell us about the nature of textual transmission writ large, and conversely what textual studies has to teach about the textual condition of electronic objects" (*Mechanisms* 164).

39 The film is available in three segments on YouTube, "James Dean on TV"; as Patrick J. Cook notes, the scene is frequently misidentified as taken either from *Rebel Without A Cause* or *East of Eden* (*Cinematic Hamlet* 237 note 36).

40 This moment also implies Rebecca Schneider's critique of "the model of death-as-loss romanced by Barthes," to the extent that the tableau vivant also implies process, what's before and after, what's outside the field of vision (*Performing Remains* 144).

41 Without disputing Parry's point here, it's nonetheless possible to note that the means of thinking is difficult to distinguish from the thinking itself: jotting notes in the margin (pencil humanism at work) is one kind of thinking and memory practice that digital technologies – PDF readers on the iPad, for instance – have worked to replicate. Noting a conversation in which Richard Feynman refused to understand the paper on which he works as merely a record of the work – "'It's not a *record*, not really. It's *working*. You have to work on paper and this is the paper'" – Hayles notes, "the process of writing down was an integral part of his thinking, and the paper and pencil were as much a part of his cognitive system as the neurons firing in his brain" (Hayles, *How We Think* 93).

42 I'm grateful to Luke McKernan of the British Universities Film and Video Council for drawing me to Jennings and *A Diary for Timothy*, and for several other invaluable pointers. I am also thankful to Olwen Terriss, formerly of the British Film Institute film and television archives, who also assisted me in efforts to identify elements of Hamlet's film archive in the era before YouTube.

43 Unlike remediation, to which it is related, "transcoding" implies that the object has already been encoded in some form of representation: transcoding "refers to the conversion of data from one (digital) format into another. Facilitated by shared structural principles of data organisation and processing (such as numeric coding, modular organisation, and automation) it allows digital media to copy, convert, blend, store and reproduce any kind of contents and information, whether textual, visual, acoustic, or other" ("Transcoding"). My thanks here to Alan Gayley, who notes that my question whether "drama is 'assimilable to information'" is mistaken: "the question is how and why that assimilation takes place anyway – both in digital Shakespeare projects and in the cultural imagination – and what to do about it" ("Networks of Deep Impression" 309).

44 Patrick J. Cook identifies this film, and suggests a provocative engagement between the myth of La Llorona, Ophelia, and Gertrude (*Cinematic Hamlet* 190). He also notes that the pattern on the cover of Hamlet's film/video *The Mousetrap* recalls the spiral running throughout Hitchcock's *Vertigo*.

45 Although there is a glimpse of Hamlet back at the Blockbuster after the "nunnery" scene – the beep of Ophelia's answering machine bleeding into the beep of the light pencil recording his videos – it seems logical that in that scene Hamlet is returning the videos he has already used, rather than buying new videos, since Claudius has already received the *Mousetrap* film/video. Almereyda's editing of the scenic order here approximates Q1 in moving the "To be" soliloquy earlier, though his arrangement of the scenes here is more complex: "fishmonger"; Polonius, Claudius, Gertrude – revealing Hamlet's poem; "To be"; Rosencrantz and Guildenstern arrive; Rosencrantz and Guildenstern report to Claudius (3.1); "Rogue and peasant slave"; "nunnery"; *The Mousetrap*. In other words, Almereyda follows the Q1 order in placing "To be" before the arrival of the players, "Dunghill idiot slave," and the play. At the

same time, he places the "nunnery" scene – which follows from "To be" in all three versions – just before *The Mousetrap*, where it appears in Q2 and F. He has, of course, reordered other elements of this sequence as well, notably moving the "fishmonger" sequence prior to Polonius's meeting with Claudius and Gertrude regarding Hamlet's poem to Ophelia. I depart here from Melissa Croteau's suggestion that the "To be" scene at Blockbuster is "placed in the traditional sequence of the play (i.e., in 3.1 [cf. Q2 and F])," even though it does appear "after Polonius's conversation with Claudius and Gertrude" ("Celluloid Revelations" 120).

46 Without entering the contentious discussion of the value-added quotient of peer review and of scholarly print publishing, it's important to recognize the extent to which digital communications and online publishing have altered some of the mechanics of publication; see, for instance, Fitzpatrick, *Planned Obsolescence*; Cohen, "Social Contract"; Davidson, "Humanities 2.0"; and McGann, "Information Technology." The modeling of scholarly writing in the digital community as an act of "curating" is widespread; see Cohen, "Social Contract." Daniel J. Cohen's most intemperate assertion is that the process of scholarly editing and publishing adds only marginal value – assuring correct spelling, tidy grammar, a consistent layout, all of which lend a merely cosmetic authority to the published book. In this regard, if the publisher no longer performs this work on texts distributed electronically, then "*Curation* becomes more important than publication once publication ceases to be limited" (321). Digital instruments also pose special problems to scholarship-as-curation; as Matthew K. Gold puts it, "Few attempts have been made to collect and curate the debates in a more deliberate fashion, with the result that some conversations, especially those on Twitter – a platform used extensively by digital humanists – are hopelessly dispersed and sometimes even impossible to reconstitute only a few months after they have taken place" ("Digital Humanities Moment" xi).

47 Fitzpatrick remarks of the possibility of the use of publications placed in the public domain of sites like Academic Commons: "Such a platform, for instance, might fruitfully allow authors to create complex publications by drawing together multiple preexisting texts along with original commentary, thus giving authors access to the remix tools that can help foster curation as a sophisticated digital scholarly practice" (*Planned Obsolescence* ch. 3).

48 Almereyda had originally planned to situate the "To be" scene both at Blockbuster and at the Whitney Museum's Bill Viola retrospective, setting up, as Peter Donaldson observes, a dialogue between *Hamlet* and Viola's "Slowly Turning Narrative" that would have placed *Hamlet* between popular video and the "potentially powerful presence of video as fine art" now absent from the film. Yet the "metastory of Hamlet as a video artist" is not fully compromised, as Hamlet's "film/video" articulates the tipping point between video art and a coming technology, digital media curation ("Hamlet among the Pixelvisionaries" 229).

49 See Alan Liu's excellent discussion of the interplay of political and corporate agendas, *Laws of Cool* ch. 7.

50 Fredric Jameson's well-known discussion of postmodern *pastiche* appeared in several essays published in the 1980s, and again in the 1991 *Postmodernism; or, The Cultural Logic of Late Capitalism.*

51 See "MIKHOELS playing King Lear 1935" on YouTube.

52 As Lev Manovich argues, the database has come "to function as a cultural form in its own right. It offers a particular model of the world and of human experience. It also affects how the user conceives the data it contains" (*Language of New Media* 37). On "database logic," see *Language of New Media* 218–236. On Manovich's "What is Digital Cinema?," see Wanda Strauven, "Observer's Dilemma."

53 Elsie Walker notes both Almereyda's rich and ironic texture of allusion to earlier Shakespeare films, and also points to the "fragmentary style and rapid rhythm of the film, the disjointed editing and the eclectic musical choices which draw attention to its construction, the way many of the key speeches are interrupted and/or separated from their bodily sources, the cacophony of surround-sound, and the dominance of advertising signs (visual and verbal)" ("'Harsh World'" 333).

54 I also have in mind here Bruno Latour's discussion of the various levels of interaction between social and technical relations, so that at some levels of his model, "*what has been learned from nonhumans is reimported so as to reconfigure people*" (*Pandora's Hope* 208).

55 Dave Parry's remarks are worth reading at length: the notion that there is "a nondigital humanities – a humanities unaffected by the digital [. . .] comes to be a rather problematic claim when we realize that the digital has so altered the academic culture that there are relatively few scholarly activities that are not already significantly altered by the digital. Almost all scholars at this point use computers rather than typewriters and use e-mail to converse with colleagues dispersed around the globe. Library card catalogs have been replaced by computer searches, and journal articles are often available only by electronic means. The practice of the humanities, of the academy as a whole (certainly within the American and European contexts), is thoroughly integrated with the digital and is, at this point, impossible to separate from it" ("Digital Humanities" 232).

56 I have in mind here Walter Benjamin's observation, "Just as the entire mode of existence of human collectives changes over long historical periods, so too does their mode of perception," change that also includes both the "way in which human perception is organized" and "the medium in which it occurs" ("Work of Art" 255).

57 George Dyson's description of Turing's demonstration is worth quoting at length: "Turing was able to construct, by a method similar to Gödel's, functions that could be given a finite description but could not be computed by finite means. One of these was the halting function: given the number of a Turing machine and the number of an input tape, it returns either the value 0 or the value 1 depending on whether the computation will ever come to a halt. Turing called the configurations that halt 'circular' and the configurations

that keep going indefinitely 'circle free,' and demonstrated that the unsolvability of the halting problem implies the unsolvability of a broad class of similar problems, including the *Entscheidungsproblem.* Contrary to Hilbert's expectations, no mechanical procedure can be counted on to determine the provability of any given mathematical statement in a finite number of steps" (*Turing's Cathedral* ch. 13).

Works cited

Albanese, Denise. *Extramural Shakespeare*. Houndmills: Palgrave Macmillan, 2010. Print.

Almereyda, Michael. "Director's Notes." *William Shakespeare's Hamlet, Adapted by Michael Almereyda*. London: Faber & Faber, 2000. 135–143. Print.

"Preface." *William Shakespeare's Hamlet, Adapted by Michael Almereyda*. London: Faber & Faber, 2000. vii–xii. Print.

Almereyda, Michael, dir. *Hamlet*. Miramax, 2000. Buena Vista, n.d. DVD.

Als, Hilton. "Shadow and Act." *New Yorker* 2 May 2011: 86–87. Web. Accessed 7 October 2012.

Anderson-Rabern, Rachel. "The Nature Theater of Oklahoma's Aesthetics of Fun." *TDR: The Drama Review – The Journal of Performance Studies* 54.4 (T-208, Winter 2010): 81–98. Project MUSE. Web. Accessed 7 October 2012.

Aristotle. *Poetics*. Trans. M. E. Hubbard. *Classical Literary Criticism*. Ed. D. A. Russell and Michael Winterbottom. Oxford University Press, 1993. Print.

Auslander, Philip. *Liveness: Performance in a Mediatized Culture*. London: Routledge, 1999. Print.

Austin, J. L. *How to Do Things with Words*. Ed. J. O. Urmson and Marina Sbisà. 2nd edn. Cambridge, MA: Harvard University Press, 1977. Print.

Barker, Francis. *The Tremulous Private Body: Essays on Subjection*. 2nd edn. Ann Arbor: University of Michigan Press, 1995. Print.

Barnes, Todd Landon. Message to the author. 2 August 2011. E-mail.

"George W. Bush's 'Three Shakespeares': *Macbeth, Macbush*, and the Theater of War." *Shakespeare Bulletin* 26.3 (2008): 1–29. Print.

"Immanent Shakespearing: Politics, Performance, Pedagogy." Ph.D. dissertation. University of California, Berkeley. 2010. PDF file.

Barrett, Felix, and Maxine Doyle. "An Interview." "Emursive Presents Punchdrunk's Sleep No More." Program. 5 September 2011. Print.

Barthes, Roland. *Camera Lucida: Reflections on Photography*. Trans. Richard Howard. New York: Hill & Wang, 1981. Print.

Bay-Cheng, Sarah, Chiel Kattenbelt, Andy Lavender, and Robin Nelson, eds. *Mapping Intermediality in Performance*. Amsterdam University Press, 2010. Print.

Beckett, Samuel. *The Complete Dramatic Works*. London: Faber & Faber, 1983. Print.

Endgame. Complete Dramatic Works 89–134.

Belsey, Catherine. *The Subject of Tragedy: Identity and Difference in Renaissance Drama*. London: Methuen, 1985. Print.

Benjamin, Walter. "The Author as Producer: Address at the Institute for the Study of Fascism, Paris, April 27, 1934." *Walter Benjamin: Selected Writings.* Volume II, Part 2, *1931–1934*. Trans. Rodney Livingstone et al. Ed. Michael W. Jennings, Howard Eiland, and Gary Smith. Cambridge, MA: Harvard University Press, 2005. 768–782. Print.

"The Medium through which Works of Art Continue to Influence Later Ages." Trans. Rodney Livingstone. *Walter Benjamin: Selected Writings.* Volume I, *1933–1926*. Ed. Marcus Bullock and Michael W. Jennings. Cambridge, MA: Harvard University Press, 2004. 235. Print.

"The Work of Art in the Age of its Technological Reproducibility. Third Version." *Walter Benjamin: Selected Writings.* Volume IV, *1938–1940*. Trans. Edmund Jephcott et al. Ed. Howard Eiland and Michael W. Jennings. Cambridge, MA: Harvard University Press, 2006. 251–283. Print.

Bennett, Benjamin. *All Theater is Revolutionary Theater*. Ithaca, NY: Cornell University Press, 2005. Print.

Berg, James. "The Properties of Character in King Lear." Yachnin and Slights, *Shakespeare and Character* 98–116.

Berger, Harry, Jr. *Imaginary Audition: Shakespeare on Stage and Page*. Berkeley: University of California Press, 1989. Print.

"Text Against Performance: The Example of 'Macbeth.'" 1982. *Making Trifles of Terrors: Redistributing Complicities in Shakespeare*. Ed. Peter Erickson. Stanford University Press, 1997. 98–125. Print.

Berners-Lee, Tim. "Information Management: A Proposal." Randall Packer and Ken Jordan, eds., *Multimedia from Wagner to Virtual Reality*. New York: W. W. Norton, 2001. 208–224. Print.

Berry, David M. *Understanding Digital Humanities*. Houndmills: Palgrave Macmillan, 2012. Print.

Bevington, David. *This Wide and Universal Theater: Shakespeare in Performance Then and Now*. University of Chicago Press, 2007. Print.

Bianco, Jamie "Skye." "This Digital Humanities Which Is Not One." Gold, *Debates in the Digital Humanities* 96–113.

Black, Alastair. "The Information Society: A Secular View." *Challenge and Change in the Information Society*. Ed. Susan Hornby and Zoë Clarke. London: Facet, 2003. 18–41. Print.

Blair, Rhonda. *The Actor, Image, and Action: Acting and Cognitive Neuroscience*. London: Routledge, 2008. Print.

Blayney, Peter M. "The Alleged Popularity of Playbooks." *Shakespeare Quarterly* 56 (2005): 33–50. Print.

"The Publication of Playbooks." *A New History of Early English Drama*. Ed. John D. Cox and David Scott Kastan. New York: Columbia University Press, 1997. 383–342. Print.

Bloom, Harold. *Shakespeare: The Invention of the Human*. New York: Riverhead, 1998. Print.

Boenisch, Peter M. "Aesthetic Art to Aisthetic Act: Theatre, Media, Intermedial Performance." Chapple and Kattenbelt, *Intermediality* 103–116.

Bradley, A. C. *Shakespearean Tragedy*. 1904. 2nd edn. London: Macmillan, 1926. Print.

Brantley, Ben. "Shakespeare Slept Here, Albeit Fitfully." *New York Times* 14 April 2011: C1, C5. Web. Accessed 7 October 2012.

Bristol, Michael D. "Confusing Shakespeare's Characters with Real People: Reflections on Reading in Four Questions." Yachnin and Slights, *Shakespeare and Character* 21–40.

Shakespeare's America, America's Shakespeare. London: Routledge, 1990. Print.

Brooks, Cleanth. "The Naked Babe and the Cloak of Manliness." 1947. *Modern Shakespearean Criticism: Essays on Style, Dramaturgy, and the Major Plays*. Ed. Alvin B. Kernan. New York: Harcourt, Brace & World, 1970. 385–403. Print.

Brooks, Cleanth, and Robert Heilman. *Understanding Drama: Eight Plays*. New York: Henry Holt, 1945. Print.

Brown, Bill. "Materiality." Mitchell and Hansen, *Critical Terms for Media Studies* 49–63.

Brown, John Russell. "General Editor's Preface." *The Shakespeare Handbooks: King Lear*. Houndmills: Palgrave Macmillan, 2009. Print.

Burdick, Anne, Johanna Drucker, Peter Lunenfeld, Todd Presner, and Jeffrey Schnapp. *Digital_Humanities*. Cambridge, MA: MIT Press, 2012. Print.

Burke, Kenneth. "Literature as Equipment for Living." *The Philosophy of Literary Form: Studies in Symbolic Action*. 1941. 3rd edn. Berkeley: University of California Press, 1973. 293–304. Print.

A Rhetoric of Motives. Berkeley: University of California Press, 1969.

Burnett, Mark Thornton. "'To hear and see the matter': Communicating Technology in Michael Almereyda's *Hamlet* (2000)." *Cinema Journal* 42.3 (Spring 2003): 48–69. ProQuest. Web. Accessed 7 October 2012.

Burns, Edward. *Character: Acting and Being on the Pre-Modern Stage*. Houndmills: Palgrave Macmillan, 1990. Print.

Burrow, Colin. Review of *Shakespeare as Literary Dramatist*, by Lukas Erne. *Shakespeare Quarterly* 55 (2004): 322–325. Project MUSE. Web. Accessed 7 October 2012.

Buttner, Emily. "Restoration versus Reality: Punchdrunk's *Sleep No More*." May 2011. PDF file.

Carmeli, Audrey. Telephone interview with author. 13 January 2011.

Carnicke, Sharon Marie. *Stanislavsky in Focus: An Acting Master for the Twenty-first Century*. 2nd edn. London: Routledge, 2009. Print.

Carroll, Joseph. "Human Nature and Literary Meaning: A Theoretical Model Illustrated with a Critique of *Pride and Prejudice*." Gotschall and Wilson, *Literary Animal* 76–106.

Carson, Christie. "eShakespeare and Performance." *Shakespeare* 4.3 (2008): 270–286. EBSCO Host International Bibliography of Theatre and Dance. Web. 7 October 2012.

Cartelli, Thomas. "Doing it Slant: Reconceiving Shakespeare in the Shakespeare Aftermath." *Shakespeare Studies* 38 (2010): 26–36. ProQuest. Web. 7 October 2012.

Cartelli, Thomas, and Katherine Rowe. *New Wave Shakespeare on Screen*. Cambridge: Polity, 2007. Print.

Chapple, Freda, and Chiel Kattenbelt, eds. *Intermediality in Theatre and Performance*. Amsterdam: Rodopi, 2006. Print.

Cheney, Patrick. "Introduction." *Shakespeare Studies* 36 (2008): 19–25. ProQuest. Web. Accessed 7 October 2012.

Shakespeare's Literary Authorship. Cambridge University Press, 2008. Print.

Chun, Wendy Hui Kyong. "The Enduring Ephemeral, or, The Future is a Memory." Huhtamo and Parikka, *Media Archaeology*.

Clark, Andy. *Supersizing the Mind: Embodiment, Action, and Cognitive Extension*. Oxford University Press, 2008. Print.

Clarke, Bruce. "Communication." Mitchell and Hansen, *Critical Terms for Media Studies* 131–144.

"Information." Mitchell and Hansen, *Critical Terms for Media Studies* 157–171.

Clod, Random [Randall McLeod]. "Information on Information." *Text* 5 (1991): 241–281. Print.

Coddon, Karin S. "'Unreal Mockery': Unreason and the Problem of Spectacle in *Macbeth*." *ELH* 56.1 (1989): 485–501. JSTOR. Web. Accessed 7 October 2012.

Cohen, Daniel J. "The Social Contract of Scholarly Publishing." Gold, *Debates in the Digital Humanities* 319–321.

Complete Moby Shakespeare. http://Shakespeare.mit.edu. Web. Accessed 7 October 2012.

Cook, Amy. *Shakespearean Neuroplay: Reinvigorating the Study of Dramatic Texts and Performance through Cognitive Science*. Houndmills: Palgrave Macmillan, 2010. Print.

Cook, Patrick J. *Cinematic Hamlet: The Films of Olivier, Zeffirelli, Branagh, and Almereyda*. Athens: Ohio University Press, 2011. Print.

Copper, Kelly. Message to the author. 6 July 2010. E-mail.

Message to the author. 21 February 2011. E-mail.

Crane, Mary Thomas. *Shakespeare's Brain: Reading with Cognitive Theory*. Princeton University Press, 2001. Print.

Croteau, Melissa. "Celluloid Revelations: Millennial Culture and Dialogic 'Pastiche' in Michael Almereyda's Hamlet (2000)." *Apocalyptic Shakespeare: Essays on Visions of Chaos and Revelation in Recent Film Adaptations*. Ed. Melissa Croteau, Carolyn Jess-Cooke. Jefferson, NC: McFarland, 2009. 110–131. Print.

Crowl, Samuel. *Shakespeare at the Cineplex*. Athens: Ohio University Press, 2003. Print.

Csikszentmihalyi, Mihaly. *Beyond Boredom and Anxiety: Experiencing Flow in Work and Play*. San Francisco: Jossey-Bass, 1975. Print.

Cumming, Alan. "Sleep No More at Midnight in Paris." 13 August 2011. Blog. Web. Accessed 7 October 2012.

Curtains Without Borders. www.curtainswithoutborders.org. Web. Accessed 7 October 2012.

Customer Reviews, Amazon. *No Fear Shakespeare: Romeo & Juliet*. Web. Accessed 7 October 2012.

Sides By Sides: Romeo and Juliet. Web. Accessed 7 October 2012.

Damasio, Antonio. *Descartes' Error: Emotion, Reason, and the Human Brain*. Harmondsworth: Penguin, 1994. Print.

Davidson, Cathy N. "Humanities 2.0: Promise, Perils, Predictions." Gold, *Debates in the Digital Humanities* 476–489.

Dawson, Anthony B. "Continuity and Contradiction: University Actors Meet the Universal Bard." *Canadian Shakespeare*. Ed. Susan Knutson. Toronto: Playwrights Canada Press, 2010. 85–100. Print.

Dawson, Anthony B., and Paul Yachnin. *The Culture of Playgoing in Shakespeare's England: A Collaborative Debate*. Cambridge University Press, 2001. Print.

de Grazia, Margreta. *Hamlet Without Hamlet*. Cambridge University Press, 2007. Print.

"Harry Berger Jr. and the Tree of Acknowledgment." *Shakespeare Quarterly* 62 (2011): 541–554. Project MUSE. Web. Assessed 7 October 2012.

"Dead Medium: The Fisher-Price Pixelvision." Dead Media Project, Working Notes 35:7. Web. Accessed 7 October 2012.

DeMarinis, Paul. "Erased Dots and Rotten Dashes, or How to Wire Your Head for Preservation." Huhtamo and Parikka, *Media Archaeology*.

Derr, Ashley Duncan. "Changing the Conversation: The Branding of the NEA's *Shakespeare in American Communities* Initiative." Shakespearean Performance Research Group, American Society for Theatre Research, November 2012. PDF file.

"Making Shakespeare Work for Students: The Shakespeare for a New Generation Initiative." Shakespearean Performance Research Group, American Society for Theatre Research, November 2010. PDF file.

Deuze, Mark, Peter Blank, and Laura Speers. "A Life Lived in Media." *Digital Humanities Quarterly* 6.1 (2012). Web. Accessed 7 October 2012.

Diehl, Huston. "Horrid Image, Sorry Sight, Fatal Vision: The Visual Rhetoric of *Macbeth*." *Shakespeare Studies* 16 (1983): 191–203. ProQuest. Web. Accessed 7 October 2012.

Dillon, Janette. "Is there a Performance in this Text?" *Shakespeare Quarterly* 45 (1994): 74–86. Project MUSE. Web. Accessed 7 October 2012.

Dodd, William. "Character as Dynamic Identity: From Fictional Interaction Script to Performance." Yachnin and Slights, *Shakespeare and Character* 62–79.

Dollimore, Jonathan. *Radical Tragedy: Religion, Ideology and Power in the Drama of Shakespeare and his Contemporaries*. Reissued 3rd edn. Houndmills: Palgrave Macmillan, 2010. Print.

Donald, Merlin. "Art and Cognitive Evolution." *The Artful Mind: Cognitive Science and the Riddle of Human Creativity*. Ed. Mark Turner. Oxford University Press, 2006. 3–20. Print.

Donaldson, Peter S. "Hamlet Among the Pixelvisionaries: Video Art, Authenticity, and 'Wisdom' in Michael Almereyda's Hamlet." *Shakespeare on Screen*. Ed. Diana Henderson. Oxford: Blackwell, 2005. 216–237. Print.

Donnellan, Declan, dir. *Macbeth*, by William Shakespeare. Brooklyn Academy of Music Harvey Theatre. 12 April 2011. Performance.

Doran, Gregory, dir. *Hamlet*, by William Shakespeare. 2 entertain Video Limited, 2010. DVD.

Dutton, Richard. *Licensing, Censorship and Authorship in Early Modern England: Buggeswords*. Houndmills: Palgrave Macmillan, 2000. Print.

"'Not one clear item but an indefinite thing which is in parts of uncertain authenticity.'" *Shakespeare Studies* 36 (2008): 114–121. ProQuest. Web. Accessed 7 October 2012.

Review of *Shakespeare, National Poet-Playwright*, by Patrick Cheney. *Shakespeare Quarterly* 56 (2005): 371–374. Project MUSE. Web. Accessed 7 October 2012.

"DVD." Wikipedia. Web. Accessed 7 October 2012.

Dyson, George. *Turing's Cathedral: The Origins of the Digital Universe*. New York: Pantheon Books, 2012. Kindle.

Early English Books Online. Web. Accessed 7 October 2012.

Eglinton, Andrew. "Reflections on a Decade of Punchdrunk Theatre." *TheatreForum* (2010): 46–55. Print.

"*Emursive Presents Punchdrunk's Sleep No More*." Punchdrunk Theatre Company. Program. 5 September 2011. Print.

Erne, Lukas. "Preface to the Second Edition." *Shakespeare as Literary Dramatist*. Cambridge University Press, 2013. 1–25. Print.

"Reconsidering Shakespearean Authorship." *Shakespeare Studies* 36 (2008): 26–36. ProQuest. Web. Accessed 7 October 2012.

Shakespeare and the Book Trade. Cambridge University Press, 2013. Print.

Shakespeare as Literary Dramatist. Cambridge University Press, 2003. Print.

Ernst, Wolfgang. "Media Archaeology: Method and Machine Versus History and Narrative of Media." Huhtamo and Parikka, *Media Archaeology*.

"Experiencer." Bay-Cheng et al., *Mapping Intermediality* 45.

Eyes Wide Shut. Dir. Stanley Kubrick. 1999. Warner Home Video, 2007. DVD.

Farmer, Alan B., and Zachary Lesser. "The Popularity of Playbooks Revisited." *Shakespeare Quarterly* 56 (2005): 1–32. Project MUSE. Web. Accessed 7 October 2012.

Fauconnier, Gilles, and Mark Turner. *The Way We Think: Conceptual Blending and the Mind's Hidden Complexities*. New York: Basic Books, 2003. Print.

Feather, John. "Theoretical Perspectives on the Information Society." *Challenge and Change in the Information Society*. Ed. Susan Hornby and Zoë Clarke. London: Facet, 2003. 3–17. Print.

Fischer, Claude S. *America Calling: A Social History of the Telephone to 1940*. Berkeley: University of California Press, 1992. Print.

Fischer-Lichte, Erika. *Theatre, Sacrifice, Ritual: Exploring Forms of Political Theatre*. New York: Routledge, 2005. Print.

The Transformative Power of Performance: A New Aesthetics. Trans. Saskya Iris Jain. New York: Routledge, 2008. Print.

Fitzpatrick, Kathleen. "The Humanities, Done Digitally." In Gold, *Debates in the Digital Humanities* 12–15.

Planned Obsolescence: Publishing, Technology, and the Future of the Academy. New York University Press, 2011. Kindle.

Fletcher, Angus. *Evolving Hamlet: Seventeenth-Century English Tragedy and the Ethics of Natural Selection*. New York: Palgrave Macmillan, 2011. Print.

Foster, Susan Leigh. *Choreographing Empathy: Kinesthesia in Performance*. London: Routledge, 2011. Kindle.

Foucault, Michel. "Of Other Spaces." Trans. Jay Miskowiec. *Diacritics* 16.1 (Spring 1986): 22–27. Print.

Freeman, Donald C. "'Catch[ing] the nearest way': *Macbeth* and Cognitive Metaphor." *Journal of Pragmatics* 24 (1995): 689–708. Science Direct. Web. Accessed 7 October 2012.

Frost, Robert. "Directive." *Poems*. Ed. Louis Untermeyer. New York: St. Martin's, 1971. 266–268. Print.

"Gannet Company." Wikipedia. Web. Accessed 7 October 2012.

Gayley, Alan. "Networks of Deep Impression: Shakespeare and the History of Information." *Shakespeare Quarterly* 61 (2010): 289–312. Print.

Gayley, Alan, and Ray Siemens. "Introduction: Reinventing Shakespeare in the Digital Humanities." *Shakespeare* 4.3 (September 2008): 217–223. EBSCO Host International Bibliography of Theatre and Dance. Web. Accessed 7 October 2012.

Geohegan, Bernard Dionysus. "From Information Theory to French Theory: Jakobson, Lévi-Strauss, and the Cybernetic Apparatus." *Critical Inquiry* 38.1 (Autumn 2011): 96–126. JSTOR. Web. Accessed 7 October 2012.

Gibson, J. J. *The Senses Considered as Perceptual Systems*. Westport, CT: Greenwood Press, 1966. Print.

Giguere, Amanda. *Shakespeare in American Communities: Conservative Politics, Appropriation, and the NEA*. Saarbrücken: VDM Verlag Dr. Müller Aktiengesellschaft, 2010. Print.

Gioia, Dana. "Chairman's Message." "Shakespeare in American Communities," by the National Endowment for the Arts. Brochure 1. Web. Accessed 7 October 2012.

Gittelman, Lisa. *Always Already New: Media, History, and the Data of Culture*. Cambridge, MA: MIT Press, 2006. Kindle.

Global Shakespeares. Web. Accessed 7 October 2012.

Goehr, Lydia. *The Imaginary Museum of Musical Works: An Essay in the Philosophy of Music*. Revised edn. Oxford University Press, 2007. Print.

Gold, Matthew K., ed. *Debates in the Digital Humanities*. Minneapolis: University of Minnesota Press, 2102. Print.

"The Digital Humanities Moment." Gold, *Debates in the Digital Humanities* ix–xvi.

Golumba, David. *The Cultural Logic of Computation*. Cambridge, MA: Harvard University Press, 2009. Kindle.

Goodman, Wendy. "First Look: An Unnerving Night at the Theater." *New York Magazine* 1 March 2011. nymag.com. 22 March 2011. Web. Accessed 7 October 2012.

Gosson, Stephen. *The Schoole of Abuse. Markets of Bawdrie: The Dramatic Criticism of Stephen Gosson*. Ed. Arthur F. Kinney. Salzburg Studies in English Literature: Elizabethan Studies 4. Salzburg: Institut für Englische Sprache und Literatur, 1974. Print.

Gotschall, Jonathan, and David Sloan Wilson, eds. *The Literary Animal: Evolution and the Nature of Narrative*. Evanston, IL: Northwestern University Press, 2005. Print.

Guillory, John. "Genesis of the Media Concept." *Critical Inquiry* 36.2 (Winter 2010): 321–362. JSTOR. Web. Accessed 7 October 2012.

Hagendoorn, Ivar. "Some Speculative Hypotheses About the Nature and Perception of Dance and Choreography." *Journal of Consciousness Studies* 11.2/3 (2004). Web. Accessed 7 October 2012.

Hansen, Mark B. N. *Bodies in Code: Interfaces with Digital Media*. London and New York: Routledge, 2006. Print.

Hart, F. Elizabeth. "The Epistemology of Cognitive Literary Studies." *Philosophy and Literature* 25 (2001): 314–334. ProQuest. Web. Accessed 7 October 2012.

"Performance, Phenomenology, and the Cognitive Turn." McConachie and Hart, *Performance and Cognition* 29–51.

Hartley, Andrew James. "Page and Stage Again: Rethinking Renaissance Character Phenomenologically." *New Directions in Renaissance Drama and Performance Studies*. Ed. Sarah Werner. Houndmills: Palgrave Macmillan, 2010. 77–93. Print.

Hayles, N. Katherine. "Cybernetics." Mitchell and Hansen, *Critical Terms for Media Studies* 145–155.

Electronic Literature: New Horizons for the Literary. University of Notre Dame Press, 2008. Print.

How We Became Posthuman: Virtual Bodies in Cybernetics, Literature, and Informatics. University of Chicago Press, 1999. Print.

How We Think: Digital Media and Contemporary Technogenesis. University of Chicago Press, 2012. Print.

My Mother was a Computer: Digital Subjects and Literary Texts. University of Chicago Press, 2005. Print.

Healy, Patrick. "Care for Caviar and Cocktails with that Musical?" *New York Times* 23 June 2013. Web. Accessed 7 October 2012.

"A London Troupe Thrives with Ambitious Free-Range Theater." *New York Times* 7 August 2013. Web. Accessed 7 October 2012.

Hershock, Peter D. *Reinventing the Wheel: A Buddhist Response to the Information Age*. Albany: State University of New York Press, 1999. Print.

Hirrel, Michael J. "Duration of Performances and Lengths of Plays: How Shall We Beguile the Lazy Time?" *Shakespeare Quarterly* 61 (2010): 159–182. Project MUSE. Web. Accessed 7 October 2012.

Hodgdon, Barbara, ed. *The Taming of the Shrew*. London: Arden Shakespeare, 2010. Print.

Hodgdon, Barbara, and W. B. Worthen, eds. *A Companion to Shakespeare and Performance*. Oxford: Blackwell, 2005. Print.

Huang, Alexander. "Global Shakespeare 2.0 and the Task of the Performance Archive." *Shakespeare Survey* 64 (2011): 38–51. ProQuest. Web. Accessed 7 October 2012.

Huhtamo, Erkki, and Jussi Parikka. "Introduction: An Archaeology of Media Archaeology." Huhtamo and Parikka, *Media Archaeology*.

eds. *Media Archaeology: Approaches, Applications, and Implications*. Berkeley: University of California Press, 2011. Kindle.

Hutchins, Edwin. *Cognition in the Wild*. Cambridge, MA: MIT Press, 1995. Print.

Internet Shakespeare Editions. Web. Accessed 7 October 2012.

Isherwood, Charles. "Just the Gist of a Star-Cross'd Tale." *New York Times* 21 December 2009. Web. Accessed 7 October 2012.

Jackson, Shannon. *Professing Performance: Theatre in the Academy from Philology to Performativity*. Cambridge University Press, 2004. Print.

"James Dean on TV." YouTube. Web. Accessed 7 October 2012.

Jameson, Fredric. *Postmodernism; or, The Cultural Logic of Late Capitalism*. Durham, NC: Duke University Press, 1991. Print.

Jenkins, Henry. *Convergence Culture: Where Old and New Media Collide*. New York University Press, 2006. Print.

Jennings, Humphrey, dir. *A Diary for Timothy*, by E. M. Forster. Crown Film Unit, 1944/1945. DVD Image Entertainment, 2002. DVD.

Jess, Carolyn. "The Promethean Apparatus: Michael Almereyda's *Hamlet* as Cinematic Allegory." *Literature/Film Quarterly* 32.2 (2004): 90–96. ProQuest. Web. Accessed 7 October 2012.

Jowett, John. "Editing Shakespeare's Plays in the Twentieth Century." *Shakespeare Survey* 56 (2006): 1–19. Print.

Kastan, David Scott. *Shakespeare and the Book*. Cambridge University Press, 2001. Print.

"'To think these trifles some-thing': Shakespearean Playbooks and the Claims of Authorship." *Shakespeare Studies* 36 (2008): 37–48. ProQuest. Web. Accessed 7 October 2012.

Kattenbelt, Chiel. "Theatre as the Art of the Performer and the Stage of Intermediality." Chapple and Kattenbelt, *Intermediality* 29–39.

Keithley, Karinne. "Uncreative Writing: Nature Theater of Oklahoma's Romeo and Juliet." *Theater* 40:2 (2010): 67–73. EBSCO Host International Bibliography of Theatre and Dance. Web. Accessed 7 October 2012.

Kennedy, Mark. "UK Theater Company Finds Success in Jaded New York." *Associated Press* 15 July 2011. Web. Accessed 7 October 2012.

Kernan, Alvin B. *Printing Technology, Letters, and Samuel Johnson*. Princeton University Press, 1987. Print.

Kidnie, Margaret Jane. "Where is *Hamlet*? Text, Performance, and Adaptation." Hodgdon and Worthen, *Companion to Shakespeare and Performance* 101–120.

Kimball, Roger. "Farewell Mapplethorpe, Hello Shakespeare: The NEA, the W. way." *National Review Online* 29 January 2004. Web. Accessed 7 October 2012.

Kirschenbaum, Matthew G. "Digital Humanities As/Is a Tactical Term." Gold, *Debates in the Digital Humanities* 415–428.

"Editing the Interface: Textual Studies and First Generation Electronic Objects." *Text* 14 (2002): 15–51. JSTOR. Web. Accessed 7 October 2012.

Mechanisms: New Media and the Forensic Imagination. Cambridge, MA: MIT Press, 2012. Print.

"'So the colors cover the wires': Interface, Aesthetics, and Usability." Schreibman, Siemens, and Unsworth, *Companion to Digital Humanities* 523–542.

Kittler, Friedrich A. *Gramophone, Film, Typewriter*. Trans. and intro. Geoffrey Winthrop-Young and Michael Wutz. Stanford University Press, 1999. Print.

Optical Media: Berlin Lectures 1999. Trans. Anthony Enns. Cambridge: Polity, 2002. Print.

Kivy, Peter. *The Performance of Reading: An Essay in the Philosophy of Literature*. Oxford: Blackwell, 2009. Print.

Knapp, Jeffrey. *Shakespeare Only*. University of Chicago Press, 2009. Print.

Knapp, Robert S. *Shakespeare – The Theater and the Book*. Princeton University Press, 1989. Print.

Knowles, Richard. Review of *Shakespeare as Literary Dramatist*, by Lukas Erne. *Modern Philology* 103 (2006): 545–551. JSTOR. Web. Accessed 7 October 2012.

Knights, L. C. "How Many Children had Lady Macbeth?" 1933. *Modern Shakespearean Criticism: Essays on Style, Dramaturgy, and the Major Plays*. Ed. Alvin B. Kernan. New York: Harcourt, Brace & World, 1970. 46–76. Print.

Kott, Jan. "Hamlet of the Mid-Century." *Shakespeare Our Contemporary*. Trans. Boleslaw Taborski. New York: W. W. Norton, 1974. 57–73. Print.

Kramnick, Jonathan. "Against Literary Darwinism." *Critical Inquiry* 37 (Winter 2011): 315–347. JSTOR. Web. Accessed 7 October 2012.

"Literary Studies and Science: A Reply to My Critics." *Critical Inquiry* 38 (Winter 2012): 431–460. JSTOR. Web. Accessed 7 October 2012.

Lakoff, George, and Mark Johnson. *Metaphors We Live By*. University of Chicago Press, 1980. Print.

Philosophy in the Flesh: The Embodied Mind and Its Challenge to Western Thought. New York: Basic Books, 1999. Print.

Lamb, Charles. "On the Tragedies of Shakespeare, Considered with Reference to their Fitness for Stage Representation." Charles Lamb and Mary Lamb, *Works in Prose and Verse*. Ed. Thomas Hutchinson. London: Henry Frowde for Oxford University Press, n.d. [1908]. Print.

Lamb, Margaret. *Antony and Cleopatra on the English Stage*. Rutherford, NC: Fairleigh Dickinson University Press, 1980. Print.

Larlham, Daniel. "The Meaning in Mimesis: A Study in the Philosophy of Acting." Ph.D. dissertation, Columbia University, 2012. PDF file.

Latour, Bruno. *Pandora's Hope: Essays on the Reality of Science Studies*. Cambridge, MA: Harvard University Press, 1999. Print.

Laurel, Brenda. *Computers as Theatre*. Rev. edn. Reading, MA: Addison-Wesley, 1993. Print.

Lee, Young Jean. "Nature Theater of Oklahoma." *Bomb* 108 (summer 2009). Web. Accessed 7 October 2012.

Lehmann, Courtney. *Shakespeare Remains: Theater to Film, Early Modern to Postmodern*. Ithaca, NY: Cornell University Press, 2002. Print.

Lehmann, Hans-Thies. *Postdramatic Theatre*. Trans. Karen Jürs-Munby. London: Routledge, 2006. Print.

Lehmann, Hans-Thies, Karen Jürs-Munby, and Elinor Fuchs. "Lost in Translation." *TDR: The Drama Review – The Journal of Performance Studies* 52.4 (T-200, winter 2008): 13–20. Project MUSE. Web. Accessed 7 October 2012.

Leiblein, Leanore. "Embodied Intersubjectivity and the Creation of Early Modern Character." Yachnin and Slights, *Shakespeare and Character* 117–135.

Lesser, Zachary, and Peter Stallybrass. "The First Literary *Hamlet* and the Commonplacing of Professional Plays." *Shakespeare Quarterly* 59 (2008): 371–420. Project MUSE. Web. Accessed 7 October 2012.

Levine, Lawrence W. *Highbrow/Lowbrow: The Emergence of Cultural Hierarchy in America*. Cambridge, MA: Harvard University Press, 1988. Print.

Liu, Alan. *The Laws of Cool: Knowledge Work and the Culture of Information*. University of Chicago Press, 2004. Print.

"The Meaning of the Digital Humanities." *PMLA* 128 (2013): 409–423. Print.

Liu, Lydia H. *The Freudian Robot: Digital Media and the Future of the Unconscious*. University of Chicago Press, 2010. Print.

Luhrmann, Baz, dir. *William Shakespeare's Romeo + Juliet*. Twentieth Century Fox Home Entertainment, 2002. DVD.

Lutterbie, John. "Neuroscience and Creativity in the Rehearsal Process." McConachie and Hart, *Performance and Cognition* 149–166.

McCarthy, Willard. "A Telescope for the Mind?" Gold, *Debates in the Digital Humanities* 113–23.

McConachie, Bruce A. "Cognitive Studies and Epistemic Competence in Cultural History: Moving Beyond Freud and Lacan." McConachie and Hart, *Performance and Cognition* 52–75.

Engaging Audiences: A Cognitive Approach to Spectating in the Theatre. Houndmills: Palgrave Macmillan, 2008. Print.

"Preface." McConachie and Hart, *Performance and Cognition* ix–xv.

"Toward a Cognitive Cultural Hegemony." Zunshine, *Introduction to Cognitive Cultural Studies*.

McConachie, Bruce A., and F. Elizabeth Hart. "Introduction." McConachie and Hart, *Performance and Cognition* 1–25.

McConachie, Bruce A., and F. Elizabeth Hart, eds. *Performance and Cognition: Theatre Studies and the Cognitive Turn*. London: Routledge, 2006. Print.

McCullough, Malcolm. *Abstracting Craft: The Practical Digital Hand*. Cambridge, MA: MIT Press, 1996. Print.

McGann, Jerome. "Information Technology and the Troubled Humanities." *TEXT Technology* 2 (2005): 105–121. http://texttechnology.mcmaster.ca/pdf/vol14_2/mcgann14–2.pdf. Web. Accessed 7 October 2012.

Radiant Textuality: Literature after the World Wide Web. Houndmills: Palgrave Macmillan, 2001. Print.

The Textual Condition. Princeton University Press, 1991. Print.

McGonigal, Jane. *Reality is Broken; Why Games Make Us Better and How They Can Change the World*. Harmondsworth: Penguin, 2011. Print.

SuperBetter. Web. Accessed 7 October 2012.

McKenzie, Jon. *Perform or Else: From Discipline to Performance*. London and New York: Routledge, 2001. Print.

McMillin, Scott. "Professional Playwrighting." *A Companion to Shakespeare*. Ed. David Scott Kastan. Oxford: Blackwell, 1999. 225–238. Print.

McPherson, Tara. "Why are the Digital Humanities so White? Or Thinking the Histories of Race and Computation." Gold, *Debates in the Digital Humanities* 139–160.

Maguire, Laurie E. "The Craft of Printing (1600)." *A Companion to Shakespeare*. Ed. David Scott Kastan. Oxford: Blackwell, 1999. 434–449. Print.

Manovich, Lev. *The Language of New Media*. Cambridge, MA: MIT Press, 2001. Print.

"What is Digital Cinema?" www.manovich.net/TEXT/digital-cinema.html. Web. Accessed 7 October 2012.

Maus, Katharine Eisaman. *Inwardness and Theater in the English Renaissance*. University of Chicago Press, 1995. Print.

Meres, Francis. *Palladis Tamia, Wits Treasury*. London, 1598. Internet Shakespeare Editions. Web. Accessed 10 August 2010.

Metcalfe, William Musham. *A History of the County of Renfrew from the Earliest Times*. Paisley: Alexander Gardner, 1905. Google Books. Web. Accessed 7 October 2012.

"MIKHOELS Playing King Lear 1935." YouTube. Web. Accessed 7 October 2012.

Mitchell, W. J. T., and Mark B. N. Hansen, eds. *Critical Terms for Media Studies*. University of Chicago Press, 2010. Print.

"Introduction." Mitchell and Hansen, *Critical Terms for Media Studies* vii–xxii.

Moretti, Franco. "Networks, Plots." *New Left Review*. 2nd series 68 (March/April 2011): 80–102. Print.

Morgann, Maurice. *An Essay on the Dramatic Character of Sir John Falstaff*. London: T. Davies, 1777. Print.

Mowat, Barbara A. "The Theatre and Literary Culture." *A New History of Early English Drama*. Ed. John D. Cox and David Scott Kastan. New York: Columbia University Press, 1997. 213–230. Print.

Mr. William Shakespeares Comedies, Histories, & Tragedies. A Facsimile of the First Folio, 1623. Introduction by Doug Moston. London and New York: Routledge, 1998. Print.

Mueller, Martin. "Digital Shakespeare, or Towards a Literary Informatics." *Shakespeare* 4.3 (September 2008): 300–317. EBSCO Host International Bibliography of Theatre and Dance. Web. Accessed 7 October 2012.

National Endowment for the Arts. "Shakespeare in American Communities." Brochure. www.nea.gov/pub/SIAC4.pdf. PDF file. Accessed 7 October 2012.

Shakespeare in American Communities: Recitation Contest. Washington, DC: National Endowment for the Arts, n.d. Print.

Shakespeare in American Communities: Teacher's Guide. Washington, DC: National Endowment for the Arts, n.d. Print.

Shakespeare in American Communities: Why Shakespeare?, dir. Lawrence Bridges. Washington, DC: National Endowment for the Arts, n.d. VHS.

Nature Theater of Oklahoma. Web. Accessed 14 June 2013.

"Nature Theater of Oklahoma's *Romeo and Juliet*." *Theater* 40: 2 (2010): 75–113. EBSCO Host International Bibliography of Theatre and Dance. Web. Accessed 7 October 2012.

"Pentameter [excerpt]." *TDR: The Drama Review – The Journal of Performance Studies* 54.2 (T-206, Summer 2010): 2–3. Project MUSE. Accessed 7 October 2012.

Romeo and Juliet. Dir. Kelly Copper and Pavol Liska. The Kitchen, New York. January 2010. Performance.

Romeo and Juliet. Dir. Kelly Copper and Pavol Liska. Hebbel am Ufer, Berlin. 30 June 2013. Performance.

"*Romeo and Juliet*," dir. Kelly Copper and Pavol Liska. Hebbel am Ufer, Berlin, 30 June 2013. Program.

Romeo and Juliet. Dir. Kelly Copper and Pavol Liska. DVD.

"*Romeo and Juliet*." Performance ledger, 15 December 2010. Manuscript.

Talkback, with Elisabeth Conner, Kelly Copper, Anne Gridley, Pavol Liska, Robert M. Johanson, moderated by Annemie Vanackere. Hebbel am Ufer, Berlin, 30 June 2013. Performance.

Nellhaus, Tobin. *Theatre, Communication, Critical Realism*. Houndmills: Palgrave Macmillan, 2010. Print.

"Performance Strategies, Image Schemas, and Communication Frameworks." McConachie and Hart, *Performance and Cognition* 76–94.

Nelson, Alan H. "Shakespeare and the Bibliophiles: From the Earliest Years to 1616." *Owners, Annotators, and the Signs of Reading*. Ed. Robin Myers, Michael Harris, and Giles Mandelbrote. New Castle, DE, and London: British Library, 2005. 49–73. Print.

No Fear Shakespeare: Romeo & Juliet. New York: Spark Publishing, 2003. Print.

No Fear Shakespeare Graphic Novels: Romeo & Juliet. Illus. Matt Wiegle. New York: Spark Publishing, 2008. Print.

Noë, Alva. *Out of Our Heads: Why You are not Your Brain, and Other Lessons from the Biology of Consciousness*. New York: Hill & Wang, 2009. Print.

Norman, Donald A. *The Design of Everyday Things*. New York: Basic Books, 2002. Print.

O'Reilly, Michael. "Pixelvision." www.michaeloreilly.com/pixelpage.html. Web. Accessed 10 November 2004.

Orgel, Stephen. "What is a Character?" *The Authentic Shakespeare and Other Problems of the Early Modern Stage*. New York: Routledge, 2002. 7–13. Print.

Ostermeier, Thomas, dir. *Hamlet*, by William Shakespeare. Schaubühne, Berlin. 2008. 14 August 2013. Performance.

Othello, by William Shakespeare. Schaubühne, Berlin. 2009. June 2011. Performance.

Paavolainen, Teemu. "Theatre/Ecology/Cognition: Theorizing Performer–Object Interaction in Grotowski, Kantor, and Meyerhold." Ph.D. dissertation, School of Communication, Media and Theatre, University of Tampere, 2011. PDF file.

Theatre/Ecology/Cognition: Theorizing Performer–Object Interaction in Grotowski, Kantor, and Meyerhold. Houndmills: Palgrave Macmillan, 2012. Print.

Palfrey, Simon, and Tiffany Stern. *Shakespeare in Parts*. Oxford University Press, 2007. Print.

Pannapacker, William. "Digital Humanities Triumphant?" Gold, *Debates in the Digital Humanities* 233–234.

Parikka, Jussi. "Mapping Noise: Techniques and Tactics of Irregularities, Interception, and Disturbance." Huhtamo and Parikka, *Media Archaeology*.

Parks, Suzan-Lori. *The America Play, and Other Works*. New York: Theatre Communications Group, 1995. Print.

Parry, Dave. "The Digital Humanities or a Digital Humanism." Gold, *Debates in the Digital Humanities* 429–437.

Peters, Julie Stone. *Theatre of the Book 1480–1880: Print, Text, and Performance in Europe*. Oxford University Press, 2000. Print.

Piepenburg, Erik. "'Sleep No More' Finds Room in Chelsea." *New York Times* 12 January 2011. Web. Accessed 7 October 2012.

"The Pixelvision Home Page." http://elvis.rowan.edu/~cassidy/pixel/. Web. Accessed 10 November 2004.

Playhouses of 17th-Century Paris. Web. Accessed 7 October 2012.

Ponech, Trevor. "The Reality of Fictive Cinematic Characters." Yachnin and Slights, *Shakespeare and Character* 41–61.

Project Gutenberg. Web. Accessed 7 October 2012.

Puchner, Martin. "Entanglements: The Histories of *TDR*." *TDR: The Drama Review – The Journal of Performance Studies* 50.1 (T-189, Spring 2006): 13–27. Project MUSE. Web. Assessed 7 October 2012.

Quayle, Catherine. "Excuse Me, I'm Having a Macbeth Moment." *Need to Know on PBS* 13 July 2011. Web. Accessed 7 October 2012.

Ramsay, Stephen. *Reading Machines: Toward an Algorithmic Criticism*. Urbana: University of Illinois Press, 2011. Kindle.

"Who's In and Who's Out." stephenramsay.us 8 January 2011. Web. Accessed 14 December 2013.

Ramsay, Stephen, and Geoffrey Rockwell. "Developing Things: Notes Toward an Epistemology of Building in the Digital Humanities." Gold, *Debates in the Digital Humanities* 75–84.

Rancière, Jacques. *Aesthetics and its Discontents*. Trans. Steven Corcoran. Cambridge: Polity, 2009. Print.

Aisthesis: Scenes from the Aesthetic Regime of Art. Trans. Zakir Paul. London: Verso, 2013. Kindle.

The Emancipated Spectator. Trans. Gregory Elliott. London: Verso, 2009. Print.

The Politics of Aesthetics: The Distribution of the Sensible. Trans. Gabriel Rockhill. London: Continuum, 2005. Print.

Rebecca. Dir. Alfred Hitchcock. 1940. Anchor Bay Entertainment, 1999. DVD.

Remshardt, Ralf. "The Actor as Intermedialist: Remediation, Appropriation, Adaptation." Chapple and Kattenbelt, *Intermediality* 41–53.

"Review: Tips on Enjoying Punchdrunk's Sleep No More in NYC." *C + C Culture Factory: Life in London* 23 March 2011. Web. Accessed 7 October 2012.

Rieder, Berhnard, and Theo Röhle. "Digital Methods: Five Challenges." Berry, *Understanding Digital Humanities* 67–84.

Rizzolatti, Giacomo, Leonardo Fogassi, and Vittorio Gallese. "The Mirror-Neuron System: A Motor-Based Mechanism for Action and Intention Understanding." *The Cognitive Neurosciences*. Gen. ed. Michael S. Gazzaniga. 4th edn. Cambridge, MA: MIT Press, 2009. 625–640. Print.

Roach, Joseph. *Cities of the Dead: Circum-Atlantic Performance*. New York: Columbia University Press, 1996. Print.

"The Emergence of the American Actor." Wilmeth and Bigsby, *Cambridge History* 338–372.

Rokem, Freddie. *Philosphers and Thespians: Thinking Performance*. Stanford University Press, 2010. Print.

Rowe, Katherine. "'Remember me': Technologies of Memory in Michael Almereyda's Hamlet." *Shakespeare, the Movie, II: Popularizing the Plays on Film, TV, Video, and DVD*. Ed. Richard Burt and Lynda Boose. London and New York: Routledge, 2003. 37–55. Print.

Rutter, Carol Chillington. *Shakespeare and Child's Play: Performing Lost Boys on Stage and Screen*. London and New York: Routledge, 2007. Print.

Ryan, Marie-Laure. "Multivariant Narratives." Screibman, Siemens, and Unsworth, *Companion to Digital Humanities* 415–430.

Ryan, Vanessa. "Living in Duplicate: Victorian Science and Literature Today." *Critical Inquiry* 38 (Winter 2012): 411–417. JSTOR. Web. Accessed 7 October 2012.

Saltz, David Z. "Performing Arts." Schreibman, Siemens, and Unsworth, *Companion to Digital Humanities* 121–131.

"What Theatrical Performance Is (Not): The Interpretation Fallacy." *Journal of Aesthetics and Art Criticism* 59.3 (2001): 299–306. Wiley Online Library. Web. Accessed 7 October 2012.

Sample, Mark L. "Unseen and Unremarked On: Don DeLillo and the Failure of the Digital Humanities." Gold, *Debates in the Digital Humanities* 187–201.

Schalkwyk, David. "Text and Performance, Reiterated: A Reproof Valiant or Lie Direct?" *Shakespearean International Yearbook* 10 (2010): 47–75. Print.

Schechner, Richard. "Collective Reflexivity: Restoration of Behavior." *A Crack in the Mirror: Reflexive Perspectives in Anthropology*. Ed. Jay Ruby. Philadelphia: University of Pennsylvania Press, 1982. 39–81. Print.

Scheinfeldt, Tom. "Sunset for Ideology, Sunrise for Methodology?" Gold, *Debates in the Digital Humanities* 124–126.

Schneider, Rebecca. *Performing Remains: Art and War in Times of Theatrical Reenactment*. London and New York: Routledge, 2011. Print.

Schoch, Richard W. *Not Shakespeare: Bardolatry and Burlesque in the Nineteenth Century*. Cambridge University Press, 2002. Print.

Schreibman, Susan, Ray Siemens, and John Unsworth, eds. *A Companion to Digital Humanities*. Malden, MA: Blackwell Publishing, 2004. Print.

"The Digital Humanities and Humanities Computing: An Introduction." Schreibman, Siemens, and Unworth, *Companion to Digital Humanities* xxiii–xxvii.

Scott, Charlotte. *Shakespeare and the Idea of the Book*. Oxford University Press, 2007. Print.

Sekules, Kate. "The Thane of Chelsea. *Interior Design* 82.11 (September 2011). Web. Accessed 7 October 2012.

Sellars, Peter, dir. *Othello*, by William Shakespeare. Skirball Center, New York. September 2009. Performance.

Shakespeare Made Easy: Romeo and Juliet. Ed. and rendered into modern English by Alan Durband. Happauge, NY: Barrons, 1985. Print.

Shakespeare, William. *Antony and Cleopatra*. Ed. M. R. Ridley. Arden Shakespeare. London: Methuen, 1977. Print.

Hamlet. Ed. Ann Thompson and Neil Taylor. London: Arden Shakespeare, 2006. Print.

Hamlet: The Texts of 1603 and 1623. Ed. Ann Thompson and Neil Taylor. London: Arden Shakespeare, 2007. Print.

Macbeth. The Norton Shakespeare, Based on the Oxford Edition. Ed. Stephen Greenblatt et al. New York: W. W. Norton, 1997. Print.

Romeo and Juliet. The Norton Shakespeare, Based on the Oxford Edition. Ed. Stephen Greenblatt et al. New York: W. W. Norton, 1997. Print.

Shannon, Claude. "The Mathematical Theory of Communication." Shannon and Weaver, *Mathematical Theory of Communication* 3–91.

Shannon, Claude, and Warren Weaver. *The Mathematical Theory of Communication*. Urbana: University of Illinois Press, 1949. Print.

Shapiro, James. *A Year in the Life of William Shakespeare: 1599*. London: Faber & Faber, 2005. Print.

Shaughnessy, Robert. "Immersive Shakespeare and the 'Emancipated Spectator.'" Shakespearean Performance Research Group, American Society for Theatre Research, November 2011. PDF file.

Shillingsburg, Peter. *From Gutenberg to Google: Electronic Representation of Literary Texts*. Cambridge University Press, 2006. Print.

Side by Sides: Romeo and Juliet. Clayton, DE: Prestwick House, 2004. Print.

Silent Shakespeare. Image Entertainment, 2000. DVD.

Sinfield, Alan. "When is a Character not a Character? Desdemona, Olivia, Lady Macbeth, and Subjectivity." *Faultlines: Cultural Materialism and the Politics of Dissent*. Berkeley: University of California Press, 1992. 52–79. Print.

Singer, Tania, and Susanne Leiberg. "Sharing the Emotions of Others: The Neural Bases of Empathy." *The Cognitive Neurosciences*. Gen. ed. Michael S. Gazzaniga. 4th edn. Cambridge, MA: MIT Press, 2009. 973–986. Print.

Sleep No More. Emursive and Punchdrunk Theatre. Dir. Felix Barrett and Maxine Doyle. Designed Gelix Barrett, Livi Vaughn, Meatrice Minns. Choreo. Maxine Doyle. McKittrick Hotel, New York. 18 March 2011. 31 March 2011. 5 May 2011. 5 September 2011. 28 August 2013. Performance.

"Sleep No More." Emursive and Punchdrunk Theatre. McKittrick Hotel, New York. 18 March 2011. Program.

"Sleep No More (2009 play)." Wikipedia. Web. Accessed 22 March 2011.

"'Sleep No More,' but Move Nonstop." New York Times 6 September 2011. Web. Accessed 29 September 2011.

Sleep No More NYC. Facebook. www.facebook.com/The McKittrickHotel. Web. Accessed 29 September 2011.

Smith, Abby. "Preservation." Schreibman, Siemens, and Unsworth, *Companion to Digital Humanities* 576–591.

Soloski, Alexis. "Verona Meets Verizon in The Kitchen's *Romeo & Juliet*." *Village Voice* 22 December 2009. Web. Accessed 7 October 2012.

Spolsky, Ellen. "Darwin and Derrida: Cognitive Literary Theory as a Species of Post-structuralism." Zunshine, *Introduction to Cognitive Cultural Studies*.

"Stage is Set. Ready for Your Part?" *Sunday New York Times* 20 March 2011: Arts and Leisure, 4. Print.

Stallybrass, Peter, Roger Chartier, J. Franklin Mowery, and Heather Wolfe. "Hamlet's Tables and the Technologies of Writing in Renaissance England." *Shakespeare Quarterly* 55 (2004): 379–419. Project MUSE. Web. Accessed 7 October 2012.

Stanislavski, Konstantin. *An Actor's Work: A Student's Diary*. Trans. and introduction Jean Benedetti. London: Routledge, 2008. Print.

Starr, G. Gabrielle. "Evolved Reading and the Science(s) of Literary Study: A Response to Jonathan Kramnick." *Critical Inquiry* 38 (Winter 2012): 418–425. JSTOR. Web. Accessed 7 October 2012.

States, Bert O. *Hamlet and the Concept of Character*. Baltimore, MD: Johns Hopkins University Press, 1992. Print.

Stern, Tiffany. *Documents in Performance in Early Modern England*. Cambridge University Press, 2009. Print.

Strauven, Wanda. "The Observer's Dilemma: To Touch or Not to Touch." Huhtamo and Parikka, *Media Archaeology*.

Sturgess, Kim C. *Shakespeare and the American Nation*. Cambridge University Press, 2004. Print.
Styan, J. L. *The Shakespeare Revolution: Criticism and Performance in the Twentieth Century*. Cambridge University Press, 1977. Print.
Svensson, Patrik. "Beyond the Big Tent." Gold, *Debates in the Digital Humanities* 36–49.
Taylor, Diana. *The Archive and the Repertoire: Performing Cultural Memory in the Americas*. Durham, NC: Duke University Press, 2003. Print.
Taylor, Gary. "General Introduction." *William Shakespeare: A Textual Companion*, by Stanley Wells and Gary Taylor, with John Jowett and William Montgomery. Oxford: Clarendon Press, 1987. 1–68. Print.
Reinventing Shakespeare: A Cultural History from the Restoration to the Present. Oxford University Press, 1989. Print.
Taylor, Mark C. *The Moment of Complexity: Emerging Network Culture*. University of Chicago Press, 2003. Print.
Theatre Finder. Web. Accessed 7 October 2012.
Thompson, Ayanna. *Passing Strange: Shakespeare, Race, and Contemporary America*. Oxford University Press, 2011. Print.
"Unmooring the Moor: Researching and Teaching on YouTube." *Shakespeare Quarterly* 61 (2010): 337–356. Print.
"Transcoding." Bay-Cheng et al., *Mapping Intermediality in Performance* 189.
Treasures in Full: Shakespeare in Quarto. British Library. Web. Accessed 7 October 2012.
Tribble, Evelyn B. *Cognition in the Globe: Attention and Memory in Shakespeare's Theatre*. Houndmills: Palgrave Macmillan, 2011. Print.
Turkle, Sherry. *Life on the Screen: Identity in the Age of the Internet*. New York: Touchstone, 1997. Print.
Twain, Mark. *Adventures of Huckleberry Finn*. Ed. Victor Fischer and Lin Salamo, with Harriet Elinor Smith and Walter Blair. Berkeley: University of California Press, 2010. Print.
User Reviews, New York Magazine. "*Sleep No More*." *New York Magazine*. 22 March 2011. Web. Accessed 7 October 2012.
Vaidhyanathan, Siva. *The Googlization of Everything (And Why We Should Worry)*. Berkeley: University of California Press, 2011. Kindle.
Vermeule, Blakey. *Why Do We Care about Literary Characters?* Baltimore, MD: Johns Hopkins University Press, 2010. Kindle.
Vermeule, Blakey, and Bruce McConachie. "Series Editors' Preface." Tribble, *Cognition in the Globe* ix–xi.
Vertigo. Dir. Alfred Hitchcock. 1958. Universal, 1998. DVD.
Visconsi, Elliott, and Katherine Rowe. *The Tempest* for iPad. Luminary Digital Media, 2012. iPad application.
Voice of the Shuttle. Web. Accessed 7 October 2012.
Walker, Elsie. "A 'Harsh World' of Soundbite Shakespeare: Michael Almereyda's *Hamlet* (2000)." *EnterText* 1.2 (June 2001): 317–341. Web. Accessed 7 October 2012.

Wallen, Emily. "It's All Within Site: Space, Performativity, and the Voyeur in Punchdrunk's *Sleep No More*." May 2011. PDF file.

Weaver, Warren. "Recent Contributions to the Mathematical Theory of Communication." Shannon and Weaver, *Mathematical Theory of Communication* 93–117.

Weber, Samuel. *Theatricality as Medium*. New York: Fordham University Press, 2004. Print.

Weimann, Robert. *Author's Pen and Actor's Voice: Playing and Writing in Shakespeare's Theatre*. Cambridge University Press, 2000. Print.

"Performance in Shakespeare's Theatre: Ministerial and/or Magisterial?" *Shakespearean International Yearbook* 10 (2010): 3–29. Print.

Weimann, Robert, and Douglas Bruster. *Shakespeare and the Power of Performance: Stage and Page in the Elizabethan Theatre*. Cambridge University Press, 2008. Print.

Wiens, Birgit. "Hamlet and the Virtual Stage: Herbert Fritsch's Project Hamlet_X." Chapple and Kattenbelt, *Intermediality* 223–236.

Wilmeth, Don B., and Jonathan Curley. "Timeline: Beginnings to 1870." Wilmeth and Bigsby *Cambridge History* 20–109.

Wilmeth, Don B., and Christopher Bigsby, eds. *The Cambridge History of American Theatre*. Volume 1, *Beginnings to 1870*. Cambridge University Press, 1998. Print.

Wilson, E. O. "Foreword from the Scientific Side." Gotschall and Wilson, *Literary Animal* vii–xi.

Wolfe, Cary. "Language." Mitchell and Hansen, *Critical Terms for Media Studies* 233–248.

Wooster Group. *Hamlet*. Public Theatre, New York. November 2007. Performance.

Worthen, W. B. "Disciplines of the Text/Sites of Performance." *TDR: The Drama Review – The Journal of Performance Studies* 39.1 (T-145, spring 1995): 13–28. Print.

Drama: Between Poetry and Performance. Oxford: Wiley-Blackwell, 2010. Print.

"Fond Records: Remembering Theatre in the Digital Age." *Shakespeare, Memory, and Performance*. Ed. Peter Holland. Cambridge University Press, 2007. 181–304. Print.

"Fond Records: Remembering Theatre in the Digital Age." Remembering Shakespeare Conference, University of Notre Dame. November 2004.

Modern Drama and the Rhetoric of Theater. Berkeley: University of California Press, 1992. Print.

"Performing Shakespeare in Digital Culture." *Cambridge Companion to Shakespeare and Popular Culture*. Ed Robert Shaughnessy. Cambridge University Press, 2007. 227–247. Print.

Print and the Poetics of Modern Drama. Cambridge University Press, 2005. Print.

Shakespeare and the Authority of Performance. Cambridge University Press, 1997. Print.

"Shakespeare Performance Studies." *Shakespearean International Yearbook* 10 (2010): 77–92. Print.

Yachnin, Paul, and Myna Wyatt Selkirk. "Metatheater and the Performance of Character in The Winter's Tale." Yachnin and Slights, *Shakespeare and Character* 139–157.

Yachnin, Paul, and Jessica Slights. "Introduction." Yachnin and Slights, *Shakespeare and Character* 1–18.

eds. *Shakespeare and Character: Theory, History, Performance, and Theatrical Persons*. Houndmills: Palgrave Macmillan, 2009. Print.

Young Company of the Classic Stage Company. "*Romeo and Juliet*: Study Guide." 20 January 2011. PDF file.

Zielinski, Siegfried. *Deep Time of the Media: Toward an Archaeology of Hearing and Seeing by Technical Means*. Trans. Gloria Custance. Cambridge, MA: MIT Press, 2008. Print.

Zunshine, Lisa, ed. *Introduction to Cognitive Cultural Studies*. Baltimore, MD: Johns Hopkins University Press, 2010. Kindle.

Index